LORDS OF ALBA

LORDS OF ALBA

THE MAKING OF SCOTLAND

IAN W. WALKER

SUTTON PUBLISHING

For Adam

Sutton Publishing Limited
Phoenix Mill · Thrupp · Stroud
Gloucestershire · GL5 2BU

First published 2006

British Library Cataloguing in Publication Data
A catalogue for this book is available from the British Library.

ISBN 0-7509-3492-1

Typeset in 11/15pt Sabon
Typesetting and origination by
Sutton Publishing Limited.
Printed and bound in England by
J.H. Haynes & Co. Ltd, Sparkford.

Contents

Black and white plates

between pages 78 and 79

List of Maps

Acknowledgements

The writing of this book proved more difficult than I anticipated. I originally planned to focus on the role of King Malcolm III and Queen Margaret in transforming Scotland. It quickly became clear, however, that the earlier period and, in particular, the reign of King Constantine II needed to be explored in order to place Malcolm more fully in context. The scope of the book therefore expanded as I wrote. The overall plan of the work consequently had to be revised to balance the original and the new material. This all meant that the writing took rather longer than intended. I am grateful to Christopher Feeney at Sutton Publishing for his patience during the extended writing period.

I would also like to thank the following people and organisations for their assistance in completing this book. The staffs of the National Library of Scotland and Edinburgh University Library, who provided invaluable assistance in locating many of the sources consulted. The numerous organisations and individuals, who assisted with the selection of illustrations and the associated permissions to reproduce them in this book. In particular, Kristina Watson and the staff at the Royal Commission for the Ancient and Historic Monuments of Scotland, Bryony Coombs at Historic Scotland and Helen Osmani at the National Museums of Scotland, all in Edinburgh. And last but not least Elizabeth Stone and Jane Entrican at Sutton Publishing for their assistance during the actual publication process.

Acknowledgements

I would also like to thank Douglas Ansdell for the chance to discuss some of the broader concepts featured in this book. I would finally like to thank my father and mother, who worked as unpaid proof-readers and saved me from making many errors. I am solely responsible for those errors that remain in the final work

Ian W Walker
Edinburgh
November 2005

Introduction

The early medieval history of the northern half of Britain, which subsequently developed into modern Scotland, has been somewhat neglected. The crucial years from 800 to 1125 seldom feature as more than a foreword to general accounts of medieval Scotland and have rarely been the subject of detailed study. In comparison, the early medieval history of southern Britain and of Ireland is much better served. The few works that do tackle early medieval Scotland often end or begin with the pivotal reign of Malcolm III, who is often known as Malcolm Canmore. They focus either on the period before this or on that which followed. This is strange since the reign of Malcolm III is arguably one of the most important periods in the history of what would later become Scotland.

The early medieval period witnessed the formation of a new political entity, the kingdom of Alba, to the north of the Forth–Clyde Isthmus. It was the product of a union between the Picts and the Scots of Dalriada under a single kingship. This infant kingdom was invaded several times by the Vikings, who transformed the political shape of the entire British Isles, and was almost snuffed out in the process. Instead, it survived the storm to emerge consolidated and confident, with the once mighty Vikings relegated to its outer fringes. The new kingdom, its people tempered in war, subsequently expanded southwards to conquer

1

new lands. It subdued and then absorbed the Britons of Strathclyde and the English of northern Northumbria to reach the Tweed and the Solway.

The latter part of this crucial period also witnessed a dramatic transformation in the cultural identity of the kingdom of Alba. In the eleventh century, under King Malcolm III, a gradual process of metamorphosis transformed the largely Gaelic society of Alba into the more mixed culture of medieval Scotland, with its strong English element. It was a change that represented the first major step on the road to the culture of modern Scotland. The subsequent impact of the Normans in the twelfth century, which undoubtedly accelerated the transformation of Gaelic Alba into Scotland, is much better documented and understood. This later change has been intensively studied almost to the exclusion of its eleventh-century beginnings.

These important events would be highly significant for the future of Scotland and northern Britain and deserve to make this crucial period the focus of major study. It was a time that witnessed the emergence in northern Britain of a large and powerful new kingdom of Scotland. It was a vibrant multicultural kingdom ruled by a single dynasty able to hold the allegiance of all its subjects. It controlled the richest agricultural lands in northern Britain and had managed to confine its enemies to the more marginal lands. It faced only one significant rival, the richer and more powerful kingdom of England to the south. In spite of tensions, the rulers of these realms managed to develop a workable modus vivendi. The existence of two major powers in Britain, which set the pattern for the future, was established in this important period.

A major reason for the lack of attention to the history of northern Britain in this period is undoubtedly the relative scarcity of sources, especially in comparison to those available for other parts of the British Isles. This is certainly a difficulty, but it should not dissuade us from at least attempting to discern some of the important processes at work at this time and to consider the relative importance of some key individuals. It must be confessed at the outset that a full history of this period simply cannot be written using local northern British sources alone. There are simply too few of them and they are often so brief, allusive and fragmentary that it is sometimes impossible to construct anything other than a skeletal framework. If these few scraps were indeed all that remained, then this period would be largely without a history.

The few local sources that do survive from northern Britain cast only a few, if bright, shafts of light on contemporary events. The narrative sources consist of a number of lists of kings, a single brief chronicle and a couple of saints' lives, including the important 'Life of Margaret'. This last is usually known as 'The Life of St Margaret', although it was not until later that the lady achieved sainthood, partly as a result of the persuasion of this work. The documentary sources include marginal notes in gospel books, some charters and related documents usually from the later part of the period. This is very little compared to the sources available for contemporary Irish or English history.

It is extremely fortunate that others were sufficiently interested in events in northern Britain to record some of what happened there in their own more plentiful and better preserved historical records. The main sources for northern Britain in this period are in fact Irish, English and Scandinavian.

The Irish sources are generally the most valuable in this context. They are often contemporary and reasonably well informed about events in northern Britain and sometimes offer a unique perspective. The Irish annals, particularly the 'Annals of Ulster', offer accurate and usually contemporary notices of many events in northern Britain that were of interest to their largely Irish audience. These notices are, however, often extremely brief and allusive in nature. They record the deaths of important secular or religious figures but seldom the circumstances of these deaths. They often relate the result of battles between northern peoples but seldom where they took place or what caused them. This can often make it difficult to interpret these otherwise important sources.

The wider Irish sources for this period, especially those dealing with society and social organisation, are so abundant that it is often tempting to draw on these to shed light on the relatively obscure society of contemporary Scotland. There is, however, an important reason to resist this temptation. Although the kingdom of Alba was Gaelic-speaking and an important part of the wider Irish Gaelic cultural world, it was not simply another Irish kingdom. It had originated from a synthesis of the Picts and the Scots and retained some distinct inheritances from this process. The official known as the *mormaer* or 'great steward', who is found throughout Alba, is not otherwise recorded in contemporary Ireland. It is therefore necessary to use such Irish sources with care and, generally speaking, only to do so where there is some confirmatory Scottish evidence.

In many ways the English sources are more difficult to use than the Irish ones. The English annalists, even when fairly contemporary, are not only as brief and allusive as their Irish cousins but they are often biased as well. They often seek to describe or interpret events in a way intended to enhance the status of English rulers. This results in a view of events that would not necessarily have been accepted by contemporary northerners. In addition, a number of more contrived accounts feature among the English sources, which are more distant in time from the events they describe. This means that they are more likely to have accrued errors, exaggerations and legendary material, which can all reduce their value as sources. The later English accounts should be used with great care and, wherever possible, in support of more reliable accounts rather than on their own.

The Scandinavian sources, which consist mainly of court poetry and sagas, are of much less value than the Irish or English ones. They were usually written down long after the events they purport to describe, sometimes 200 or 300 years afterwards. They should therefore only be used with a great deal of care and with the firm understanding that the information they offer may tell us more about Scandinavian society in the period of the saga writers than about the periods they describe. It is unfortunate that some historians attempt to extract specific details of contemporary events from some of these thirteenth- and fourteenth-century works. It is extremely unlikely that this degree of reliance can be placed on these sources, which clearly incorporate many legendary and folklore elements.

In addition to the relatively few contemporary sources, however, it is sometimes possible to make careful use of earlier or later sources to shed light on, for example, some aspects of society in this period. It is possible that evidence from earlier sources can allow us to assume that later society was capable of at least a similar level of sophistication. The tenth-century *Senchus fer nAlbann* or 'The History of the Men Of Alba', for example, records a sophisticated military recruitment system that existed in the seventh century and allows us to presume that the society of a later period could do likewise. In the same way later sources may sometimes preserve obsolete evidence that can shed light on earlier periods. Later charters sometimes refer to Gaelic officers and customs, which probably represent survivals from this earlier period. This kind of activity can be taken too far with unjustifiable results but, if used judiciously, can help to enhance our view of an otherwise dark period.

There are actually some advantages to this relative lack of sources. There are no official versions of northern history in this period seeking to persuade us of a particular view of events. There exists no equivalent for northern Britain to those English sources which consider that it was the manifest destiny of King Alfred and Wessex to unify the English peoples. This sort of problem is almost completely absent in early Scottish historiography. This does not mean that the scattered sources that exist are completely objective.

There is, however, in most cases no single guiding hand leading us towards a particular interpretation of events. The single exception to this general rule is The Life of St Margaret commissioned by Matilda, the daughter of St Margaret and the wife of Henry I of England. This work quite clearly sets out to portray Margaret, who was the wife of Malcolm III, as an ideal queen and actively selects its information to achieve this result. In the process, it offers a distorted picture of contemporary society.

The sparse and diffuse nature of the sources for northern British history in this period make it difficult to put together a coherent account of events. Indeed, the story of these centuries often seems to consist of little more than a grim, confusing and seemingly random succession of battles, killings and deaths. It is only after closer examination of these events and their potential connections that some underlying patterns begin to emerge. It is these that provide the key to the history of northern Britain at this time. They reveal the origins and subsequent development of the kingdom of Alba and its slow transformation into a new Scotland.

The chapters that follow focus on the period prior to the reign of King David I and the arrival of the Normans in Scotland, where others have already done a great deal of work. They review the changes that took place in the earlier period, including the formation of the kingdom of Alba, the southward expansion of this kingdom and the beginnings of a process of Anglicisation that would subsequently transform the kingdom. They consider the part played in these changes by the lords of Alba. They also consider the factors behind these changes and, in doing so, reassess the role of the English wife of Malcolm III, St Margaret. The Life of St Margaret has been instrumental in portraying her as the main driver behind the process of Anglicisation. The traditional view consists of three aspects. St Margaret used her personal influence over her husband to Anglicise the royal Court, as witnessed by the English names of their children. This transformation did not extend to wider

Scottish society, which remained largely Gaelic in speech and culture. It was not until the succession of David I in 1124 that the wider society of Scotland was transformed with the penetration of Normans and Anglo-Norman culture into Scotland.

This work will widen the scope of the investigation and explore alternative sources of English influence. It will also reconsider the respective roles of King Malcolm and his Queen, St Margaret, in sponsoring or exploiting these influences. The lords of Alba had been extending their influence southwards into English-speaking territories since the tenth century. In the period between 954 and 1016, they gradually brought an increasing proportion of English territory under their control. In the mid-eleventh century, King Malcolm III spent some fifteen years of his youth in exile in England. He subsequently moved the main focus of the kingdom southwards into former English territory. The period after the Norman Conquest of England in 1066 witnessed an influx of English refugees into southern Scotland. These events all probably contributed to the increase in English influence in Scotland at this time. The relative importance of these various elements in the transformation from Alba into Scotland will be reassessed.

1

The Viking Onslaught

At the end of the eighth century the political map of the British Isles consisted of a mosaic of large and small kingdoms. These kingdoms were engaged in a constant competition for control of land and wealth. This competition took the form of almost incessant warfare, ranging from small-scale raiding to major campaigns aimed at securing tribute or control. In this struggle individual kingdoms sought to secure supremacy over their neighbours, whether temporarily or over a longer time frame. A number of the more consistently successful kingdoms were slowly beginning to emerge as nascent superpowers. They included the Ui Neill kingdoms in Ireland, the Mercian imperium in southern Britain and, in the north, a new union of the two previously independent kingdoms of the Picts and the Scots. The last of these would subsequently develop into the medieval kingdom of Scotland.

The traditional account of the origins of the united kingdom of the Picts and the Scots centres on the dramatic story of a brutal massacre carried out by a ruthless warlord. This is the story of Kenneth MacAlpin and his massacre of the Picts at Scone in 849. The fullest version of the legend can be found in the twelfth-century account of Gerald of Wales, which may itself be based on an earlier Irish tale, now lost, called *Braflang Scoine* or 'The Treachery of Scone'. It runs as follows:

. . . [The Scots] brought together as to a banquet all the nobles of
the Picts, and taking advantage of their excessive drunkenness and
gluttony, they noted their opportunity and drew out the bolts
which held up the boards; and the Picts fell into the hollows of the
benches on which they were sitting, caught in a strange trap up to
the knees, so that they could not get up; and the Scots
immediately slaughtered them all.[1]

It is still widely believed that it was as a direct result of this
episode that Kenneth was able to eliminate the Picts and establish a
Gaelic-speaking Scottish kingdom in their place. He is widely
credited with transforming forever the political shape of northern
Britain through this violent act. In fact, the origins of the medieval
Scottish kingdom are much more complex than this would suggest.
They were not the result of a sudden revolution. Instead, they were
the result of an evolutionary process whereby relations between a
number of neighbouring peoples developed over a period of
centuries. The first of these peoples to come together and form the
core around which the later Scottish kingdom formed were the Picts
and Scots.

The neighbouring Picts and Scots had, in fact, been drawing
together over a long period of time. This was a process fostered by
increasingly close political ties – including dynastic intermarriage,
some commonality of religious traditions, the settlement of Gaelic-
speakers in Pictish territory and cultural assimilation. It was also a
process promoted by the arrival on the scene of a common enemy in
the form of the heathen Vikings from Scandinavia. The latter came
from a rather different cultural tradition with no access to
Christianity, few close contacts with the British Isles and a Germanic
language and culture.

Kenneth MacAlpin did not establish the medieval Scottish
kingdom by a massacre of the Picts. He was not even the first man
to rule both Picts and Scots. This feat had already been achieved

during the preceding century, most notably by Oengus, son of Fergus, King of the Picts (729–61), who also ruled the Scots of Dalriada between 741 and 750. He had managed to secure at least temporary supremacy over both peoples. The success achieved by such powerful men often consisted of some form of overlordship rather than direct rule and was usually brief. It nevertheless introduced the concept of a united rule of these two peoples.

There was much more than such temporary episodes of common rule working in favour of integration of these two peoples. There was clearly a great deal of intermarriage among the ruling elites as witnessed by the increasing appearance of Gaelic names among the Pictish kings. The appearance of St Columba and other saints from Gaelic Ireland among the Picts from the 590s had introduced a major Gaelic cultural influence. This brought the Picts within the Gaelic cultural sphere for the next 200 years and produced a Christian society heavily influenced by Gaelic models. In 697 at the synod of Birr in Ireland, Adomnan Abbot of Iona, promulgated his *Cain Adomnan* or The Law of the Innocents, which was designed to protect non-combatants – the elderly, women, children and the clergy – from the effects of warfare. It was endorsed by no less than 40 leading churchmen and 51 kings, all of them Gaelic with the exception of Bruide, son of Derile, King of the Picts, who was nevertheless clearly considered a ruler from the Gaelic cultural world. In addition to this cultural influence Gaelic colonisers had also begun to infiltrate Pictish territory from the kingdom of Dalriada on the west coast. This seems to be confirmed by the appearance of the name 'Atholl' for one of the Pictish provinces, which probably originated as the Gaelic *ath Fhodla* or 'New Ireland'. In all these ways Gaelic influence was gradually transforming the kingdom of the Picts.

The honour of being the first ruler of a properly united kingdom of Picts and Scots also belongs not to Kenneth MacAlpin but to a man called Constantine, son of Fergus. In 789, he succeeded in seizing the Pictish throne through a military victory over Conall, son of Tadg, King of the Picts, who was driven into exile in Strathclyde or, possibly, in Ireland. The origins of this individual are unclear but the name of his father suggests perhaps a Gaelic or Gaelic-influenced background. The name of Constantine that he himself bore suggests a strongly Christian background and perhaps even a hint of wide ambition. He was almost certainly named after Constantine the Great, the Roman emperor who had secured Christianity as the official religion of the empire. In 792 the Annals of Ulster record the death of Donn Corci, King of the Gaelic Scots of Dalriada, and Constantine, King of the Picts, appears to have succeeded him as the direct ruler of Dalriada rather than simply as an overlord, like Oengus mac Fergus thirty years before. The later king-lists seem to confirm this, although it is possible that these have been adjusted to reflect subsequent political realities. The new united kingdom appears to have been known as the kingdom of Fortriu after its central province, but its rulers were still sometimes referred to as kings of the Picts.

King Constantine, son of Fergus, was now joint ruler over the Picts and the Scots and, while the written sources for his rule are meagre, a unique monumental record of his reign survives. The Dupplin Cross, which once stood on a hillside overlooking the site of a royal palace at Forteviot in Perthshire, can now be found inside the later church at Dunning nearby. It bears a badly weathered inscription in a panel on its west face. It has been interpreted to read *Custantin filius Fircus rex* . . . or 'Constantine son of Fergus, King . . .' with the rest now tantalisingly illegible. The king himself is portrayed on the opposite face of the cross as a mounted warrior above four foot soldiers who probably represent his army. The iconography of the biblical King David on other panels confirms Constantine's status as a Christian ruler in the Old Testament mould. This cross is clearly a major monument created for an important and powerful Christian warrior king.

King Constantine was certainly a powerful enough figure to take an interest in the internal affairs of the neighbouring kingdom of Northumbria to the south. In 796 he offered refuge to Osbald, who had been King of Northumbria for only 27 days in the spring of that year. An aristocratic faction led by *Ealdorman* Wada had killed King Aethelred at Corbridge on the Tyne on 18 April 796 and Osbald, one of their number, was raised to the kingship. He was however quickly put to flight and driven from the kingdom by the supporters of Aethelred and arrived by ship, presumably in the Tay. He lived in exile as Constantine's guest until his death in 799, and he was replaced in Northumbria by a man called Eardwulf, who defeated *Ealdorman* Wada. In 807, the exiled Conall, son of Tadg, formerly king of the Picts, was killed in Kintyre by another Conall, the son of Aedacan, who was perhaps the local ruler. This exile may have been attempting to restore his fortunes but, if so, the location of his death, on the far fringes of Constantine's rule, suggests that he was not very successful.

King Constantine was also one of the first rulers in the British Isles to face an unexpected threat from across the North Sea. It was in 794, during the early years of his reign, that the first raiders from Scandinavia devastated the islands of Britain. In the following year, they pillaged and devastated Iona and Skye on the west coast of his newly expanded kingdom. In 798, they made further incursions in Scotland and the Hebrides, although the extent of these is unrecorded. This pattern will be familiar to students of the Vikings elsewhere in Western Europe. It marked the initial phase of Viking activity, when small groups of raiders launched seasonal hit-and-run attacks against wealthy coastal sites. In Constantine's kingdom the prime focus for such raids was, of course, the wealthy head monastery of the church of St Columba on the island of Iona. It was attacked in 795, the monastic buildings were burned in 802 and worse was to come in 806. In 801 Bresal, son of Segene, who had been Abbot of Iona since 770, died, a circumstance possibly hastened by his experiences at the hands of the Vikings in 795. In

806, however, no less than 68 monks of the community were killed and the monastic buildings were burned for a second time. This terrible massacre seems to have prompted Abbot Cellach, who apparently survived it – perhaps he was taken captive and subsequently ransomed – to flee to relative safety in Ireland and commence the construction of a new monastery at Kells.

In the next century or so these Viking raiders would transform the politics of the British Isles. The intervention of increasing numbers of these outsiders effectively subverted the existing political system. Many long-standing kingdoms were overwhelmed or undermined while others managed to weather the initial assault before recovering and striking back. The political map of the British Isles would be transformed by the intervention of the Vikings and an entirely new system would emerge. In Ireland the Ua Briain kings of Munster would rise to challenge the Ui Neill. In southern Britain Wessex would unite with its old rival Mercia to strike back at their Viking tormentors and ultimately form a united kingdom of England. The consequences of Viking activity for northern Britain have been the subject of far fewer accounts. In essence the experience of northern Britain was very similar to that of the rest of the British Isles but it deserves more consideration than it has previously received.

The initial phase of Viking raids, in common with elsewhere in Europe, appears to have died down during the 810s. This is reflected perhaps in the fact that, when Abbot Cellach resigned his abbacy in 814, he retired to Iona to reside there until his death the following year. This suggests that the monastery had at least recovered sufficiently to provide a suitable place for Cellach, who had fled from there eight years previously, to spend his final years there in peace. He was subsequently buried on the island, presumably with appropriate funeral rites. In 818, Cellach's successor, Abbot Diarmait was able to journey between Kells and northern Britain in apparent safety from Viking attack.

In 820 Constantine, son of Fergus, King of Fortriu, died peacefully after a reign of some thirty years. This was a long reign for this early period when the rule of kings tended to be short and to end in violence. There was, however, something even more remarkable about the rule of Constantine. In contrast to previous rulers Constantine successfully managed to pass on his joint rule over Picts and Scots to his brother and successor, Oengus II, son of Fergus. This happened almost thirty years before Kenneth MacAlpin is supposed to have eliminated the Picts.

It was during the reign of Constantine's brother, Oengus II, son of Fergus, that the Viking assaults resumed. They now entered a new phase with larger raiding parties making more intense attacks on the richest targets. Inevitably, Iona was chief among these and, on 24 July 825, it suffered its worst experience to date at the hands of the Vikings. The Annals of Ulster simply record 'the martyrdom of Blathmac at the hands of the heathens on Iona'. A more elaborate account of events is provided by Walafrid Strabo, a German monk, in his poem on the martyrdom of Blathmac. He recorded:

The violent accursed host came rushing through the open
buildings, threatening cruel perils to the blessed men; and after
slaying with mad savagery the rest of the company, they
approached the holy father [Blathmac] to compel him to give up
the precious metals wherein lie the holy bones of St Columba; but
[they] had lifted the shrine from its pediments and had placed it in
the earth, in a hollowed barrow, under a thick layer of turf,
because they knew of the wicked destruction to come. This booty
the Danes [sic] desired; but the saint remained with unarmed
hand, and with unshaken purpose of mind; [he had been] trained
to stand against the foe, and to arouse the fight, and [was] unused
to yield.
    There he spoke to thee, barbarian, in words such as these:–
'I know nothing at all of the gold you seek, where it is placed in

the ground or in what hiding-place it is concealed. And if by
Christ's permission it were granted me to know it, never would
our lips relate it to thy ears. Barbarian, draw thy sword, grasp the
hilt, and slay; gracious God, to thy aid commend me humbly.'

Therefore the pious sacrifice was torn limb from limb. And
what the fierce soldier could not purchase by gifts, he began to
seek by wounds in the cold bowels of the earth.[2]

This raid reinforces the impression that the monastery had
recovered from previous attacks. It had a significant number of
buildings, large numbers of monks and rich treasures worth stealing.
Indeed, otherwise it would have provided a poor return for the
raiders.

In the following decades, the Viking raids on the British Isles
gradually increased in scale, ferocity and intensity. They were also
more frequent in northern Britain, although they may still have been
seasonal and did not occur in every year. In this region, however,
few records survive to illuminate the Vikings' activities and their
impact on the local population. Instead we are left with little more
than speculation. The local populations of the Hebridean islands
and the west coasts probably withdrew as the heathen incomers
commenced the settlement of these outlying areas of the Picto-
Scottish kingdom. The Vikings appear to have been less prevalent on
the east coast of northern Britain although this may be a quirk of
the surviving sources. They failed, however, to sever entirely the sea
lanes between northern Britain and Ireland, which continued to
offer safe, if possibly irregular, passage for members of the
Columban church at Iona. Thus Abbott Diarmait crossed safely to
Scotland with the relics of St Columba in 829 and returned with
them in equal comfort two years later.

In 834, Constantine's brother and successor, Oengus II, son of
Fergus, King of Fortriu died. He was succeeded by his son Eoganan,
who would face the first major crisis of this second Viking

onslaught. In 839 the Viking attacks reached a climax when a major Viking force invaded the heartland of the Picto-Scottish kingdom. The Annals of Ulster record that 'The heathens won a battle against the men of Fortriu and Eoganan son of Oengus, Bran son of Oengus, Aed son of Boanta and others almost without number fell there'. This major defeat was a disaster of huge proportions for the newly combined kingdom. It not only lost two adult members of its ruling dynasty, it lost other important senior figures, like Aed, and many of its best warriors. It was the sort of calamity that could result in the downfall of the kingdom. In 839 it must have seemed to many that the kingdom of Fortriu was on the verge of becoming the first kingdom in the British Isles to fall to the Vikings. Indeed, the English kingdoms of Northumbria and East Anglia would fall to Viking assault in precisely this way in the 860s and 870s.

The kingdom did not fall, however, in spite of a period of internal crisis that followed this defeat and which witnessed five different rulers in the short space of ten years. Why were the Vikings who defeated Eoganan and his army apparently unable to subjugate his kingdom? There may be a number of explanations for this. The relatively small Viking armies of this early period were independent forces with no central control or direction. They appear to have consisted of units of thirty or so ships under leaders of local status. They might combine when an opportunity presented itself but such alliances were usually short-term and quickly dissolved. The force that defeated Eoganan in 839 may have been such a temporary alliance. It may have broken up in the immediate aftermath of its victory and its component parts were thereafter perhaps too small to conquer the entire kingdom. Its unknown leaders may have quarrelled about the spoils or been killed in the fighting. It seems likely that a combined Viking force gained the initial victory but thereafter dissolved and was therefore unable to exploit it fully.

It is possibly significant in this context that the years immediately following witnessed a significant increase in Viking activity in neighbouring Ireland with widespread raiding around Lough Neagh and the construction of the first fortified camps at Dublin and Annagassan in Louth. It seems possible that the Viking force which had defeated Eoganan was attracted to participate in this new assault on Ireland. This provided them with rich pickings – possibly richer than in northern Britain – for the next few years, with raids across Ulster and Leinster and on wealthy targets like Armagh, Clonmacnoise and others. In subsequent years, the Vikings encountered stiffer resistance in Ireland and endured a series of heavy defeats which must have depleted their resources and prevented them from resuming their activities in northern Britain. In 848, in particular, the Annals of Ulster record the deaths of hundreds of Vikings in a series of battles with the Irish, including that of a *Jarl* Tomrair, who is described as 'tanist' of the King of Norway.

In 849 the Vikings finally received reinforcements from Norway, but these arrived at a price. The Annals of Ulster make it clear that the intention of these men was to impose political control over their predecessors and fellow countrymen already in Ireland. They were clearly keen to obtain direct control over the rich flow of treasure and slaves at its source. They were almost certainly led by a man called Olaf, although he is not actually named until 853. He is described as the son of the King of Norway and he may have been related in some way to the Tomrair killed in 848. He was precisely the sort of significant political figure who might be expected to lead such a campaign to impose hegemony on the early raiders. It would naturally take Olaf some time to rally or subdue the many existing and formerly independent Viking bands to his authority. While many were possibly docile or weak enough to accept or even welcome his overlordship, others must have been reluctant to surrender their independent status as easily.

The position was further complicated by the arrival of the first Danish Vikings in Ireland in 851, led, according to a later source, by a man named Orm. They had been raiding south-western England and after rounding Cornwall had entered the Bristol Channel. They had suffered defeats in Dorset and Devon and now sought to muscle in on the lucrative Irish raiding scene. The result was conflict between the newly arrived 'dark gentiles' or Danes and the existing 'fair gentiles' or Norwegians already in control. This short but ferocious conflict over a lucrative prize blazed for two years until Olaf eventually emerged victorious over the Danes in 853. The Annals of Ulster report that 'Olaf, son of the King of Norway came to Ireland and the foreigners of Ireland submitted to him . . .' In the period after this the defeated Danes under Orm appear to have become restive, probably under pressure from a victorious Olaf. They seem to have attempted to leave Ireland and try their luck elsewhere. In 856 the Welsh Annals record that the Danes raided Anglesey. In the following year the Annals of Ulster report that the Welsh prince Rhodri, son of Merfyn defeated and killed Orm, the leader of the Danes in north Wales.

It seems likely that this defeat of the Danes ensured the consolidation of Olaf's authority over all or most of the independent Viking groups. A brief period of recovery and reorganisation probably followed this since the Irish sources record no further significant Viking activity until 856. In that year the Irish High-king Mael Sechnaill attacked them with the support of a mixed Norse–Irish force under a man called Ketill. Olaf and Ivar subsequently defeated Ketill and his force in Munster in the following year, 857. This further period of internal warfare appears to have drawn Olaf and his men into Irish internal politics for the next few years and effectively protected distant northern Britain from their attentions.

In northern Britain, meanwhile, in spite of the absence of Viking attacks, the period following the defeat of Eoganan in 839 was clearly one of crisis for the brand-new Picto-Scottish kingdom. The later king-lists record a number of rulers with very short reigns and give little indication of the extent or security of their rule. There was undoubtedly some form of power vacuum which a series of local warlords sought to fill, only to be ousted by their rivals. This ushered in a decade which featured a confused succession of short reigns: Ferat, Bruide, Kenneth MacAlpin, Bruide, Drust, Kenneth MacAlpin again until after 848. The breathing space from outside attack provided by the Viking preoccupation with Ireland, allowed Kenneth I MacAlpin or *Cinaed mac Alpin* to emerge from this confusion and establish and secure his position as ruler of the Picto-Scottish kingdom in the decade from 848 to 858.

It is surprising just how little is known about this pivotal figure in Scottish history. He is generally identified as the son of a man called Alpin, who is recorded in later sources as an apparently independent king of Dalriada from 839–41. It is assumed that Kenneth succeeded his father as ruler of Dalriada, although there is only late evidence for this. He is said to have launched a series of attacks against the Picts during their period of decline after 839. He then assumed direct rule over them, probably following the death of Drust, the last of Ferat's short-lived dynasty in 848. It is usually at this point that he is supposed in later legend to have destroyed the Picts, as related at the opening of this chapter. He almost certainly defeated or subdued any Pictish opposition, including any supporters of rival claimants such as Ferat, Bruide and Drust.

In around 849, according to some of the first entries in the native Scottish Chronicle, he installed the relics of St Columba in a new church he had built at Dunkeld. In 849 the Ulster annals record the arrival in Ireland of Indrechtach, Abbot of Iona, who brought the relics of St Columba to Ireland, perhaps after leaving some with King Kenneth at Dunkeld. What does this signify? It seems that King Constantine, son of Fergus had already built a church here, so it was not a new foundation. This act by King Kenneth I was rather an important sign of the consolidation of the new united realm of the Picts and Scots. He placed the relics of St Columba, who was an important saint to both peoples but especially to the Scots, at the heart of the new united kingdom. He thus transformed Dunkeld into the head church of the new kingdom and irrevocably positioned the primary focus of Scottish religious devotion squarely within it. He had cut the umbilical cord that connected them to Iona and the west coastlands. In 865 the Annals of Ulster report the death of Tuathal, son of Artgus, chief Bishop of Fortriu and Abbot of Dunkeld, which confirms this transformation.

The Vikings appear to have remained largely quiescent for much of Kenneth's reign. They were probably preoccupied with their activities in Ireland. It is true that the Scottish Chronicle includes mention of a single Viking raid on his kingdom, but it is not easy to place this event in the chronology of the period. The Chronicle lists a whole series of events which supposedly occurred after the seventh year of his reign, or 849, but with no further indication of their dates. The events include no less than six invasions of England by Kenneth, encompassing the burning of Dunbar and Melrose, the burning of Dunblane by the Britons of Strathclyde and the wasting of the 'land of the Picts' as far as Clunie and Dunkeld by 'Danes' who were almost certainly Norwegians Vikings from Ireland. There is no way of telling exactly when any of this occurred and no independent confirmation that it occurred at all.

It is an outside possibility that the Scottish Chronicle means that all these events took place in Kenneth's seventh year of 849. If so – and this is a big assumption – it may be that Olaf of Norway's first foray into British politics was not his intervention in Ireland but an attack on the Picto-Scottish kingdom. It is in this year that the Annals of Ulster first record the appearance of a northern fleet intent on subjugating the Vikings in Ireland and Britain, although it is only later that they record Olaf as its leader. This new force is just the sort of group that would be powerful enough to challenge Kenneth on its way to Ireland. If this was the case it might provide the context for a subsequently noticed marriage between Olaf and a daughter of Kenneth. This marriage admittedly appears only in later Irish sources with some legendary accretions. It might, however, provide an explanation for the relative lack of Viking intervention in Kenneth's kingdom.

The record, such as it is, appears to confirm Kenneth's reputation as a significant warlord of the period. He had made good use of Viking preoccupation with Ireland to establish his authority across the Picto-Scottish kingdom. He established a new religious focus for the kingdom at Dunkeld and turned it into the head church of the chief bishop of Fortriu. He finally died peacefully on 13 February 858 in his palace of Forteviot in Strathearn as the acknowledged King of Picts and Scots. The later 'Fragmentary Annals of Ireland' preserve a praise poem about him:

> Because Kenneth with many troops lives no longer
> There is weeping in every house;
> There is no king of his worth under heaven
> As far as the borders of Rome.[3]

In the best demonstration of his transformation of the chaotic situation since 839, Kenneth was succeeded peacefully by his brother, King Donald I or *Domnall mac Alpin*, as ruler of the same combined kingdom of Fortriu. King Donald was also fortunate in that Viking attention remained focused on Ireland during his brief and relatively uneventful reign of four years. The Scottish Chronicle records that Donald 'made the rights and laws of the kingship of Aed son of Eochaid' at Forteviot. It is not clear what this signifies, but it may mean that Donald imposed the Gaelic succession system on the Picts or that he introduced Gaelic laws more generally. This was almost certainly an important stage in their absorption into the increasingly Gaelic culture of the new kingdom. Donald died peacefully in the palace of *Cinnbelathoir* at *Rathinveralmond,* which is unknown but may be the modern Scone, in 862.

It would be during the reign of Donald's nephew and successor, King Constantine I, son of Kenneth or *Castantin mac Cineada*, that the Vikings would once again resume their activities in Scottish territory. They did so in a new and more deadly form than ever before. The Viking forces were now larger and more united and led by senior political figures. The new Viking leaders had an agenda, which might easily extend beyond mere pillage. In 866, according to the reliable Annals of Ulster, 'Olaf and Audgisl went into Fortriu with the foreigners of Ireland and Scotland and they raided all the land of the Picts and took hostages from them.' This event is also mentioned in the Scottish Chronicle, misdated to 865, which adds that the Vikings spent a period of almost eleven weeks from 1 January to 17 March 866 plundering the Picto-Scottish kingdom. The later Fragmentary Annals also record this event: 'The Norwegians laid waste and plundered Fortriu and they took many hostages with them as pledges for tribute; for a long time afterwards they continued to pay them tribute.'

It may be significant that this major Viking assault on northern Britain by Olaf and Audgisl took place in exactly the same year of 866 as the major assault on East Anglia. The 'great army' that descended on East Anglia was apparently commanded by three men, Halfdan, Ubbe and Ivar, the last a colleague of Olaf in Ireland during the 850s and 860s. This great army subsequently destroyed the East Anglian and Northumbrian kingdoms and severely battered Mercia and Wessex. If Olaf had achieved the same in northern Britain and destroyed the new realm of the Picts and Scots, it would have placed the Vikings in control of much of Britain. It is surely not beyond the realms of possibility that they could have organised such a strategy. It was certainly an ambitious scheme but it actually came very close to success.

In 867 the Viking leaders appear to have fallen out, since the Annals of Ulster announce that 'Audgisl, one of three kings of the heathens was killed by his kinsmen in guile and parricide.' The common description of Viking leaders as 'kinsmen' should not necessarily be taken as a reference to a genetic relationship in every case. It may have been used by the Irish to describe a relationship that was perhaps closer to that of 'sworn-brothers' or partners in a raiding enterprise. The conflict of 867 was therefore probably more of a dispute between partners. They may have fallen out over the spoils of their recent raid or about strategy. They may have disagreed about whether to concentrate on their Irish base or to extend their activities more widely across Britain. The Fragmentary Annals, which often seek to find good motivation for events whether real or not, attribute the murder of Audgisl by Olaf to jealousy about military prowess and to rivalry over a woman. This woman was, of course, no less a person than Kenneth MacAlpin's daughter and Olaf's wife. If there is any truth in this, it may suggest perhaps that the dispute centred on whether to settle for tribute from Constantine or to depose him and conquer his kingdom. Whatever the case, this internal dispute, combined with Irish successes, including the conquest of Clondalkin near Dublin in 867, probably prevented further raids on Scottish targets. On this occasion the Vikings settled for tribute or taxes from King Constantine I and there was no Viking conquest. It may even have been now that Olaf actually married the daughter of Kenneth MacAlpin and sister of Constantine as part of the treaty arrangements.

In 870 the Viking attacks on northern Britain resumed with a spectacular combined raid against the Britons of Strathclyde at Dumbarton. This expedition involved a large combined force led by the partners Olaf and Ivar, who were once again working together. Ivar had probably travelled north from York with his followers and spoils, including prisoners, leaving his colleague Halfdan in charge of the rest of Viking army based there. This would certainly account for the presence of Englishmen among the Viking prisoners mentioned in the following year. It also raises the interesting possibility that the attack on Dumbarton consisted of a two-pronged assault from east and west. In any case the two Viking leaders and their forces combined to besiege the capital of Strathclyde at Dumbarton. The Fragmentary Annals report that 'The Norwegian kings besieged Strathclyde of the Britons, camping against them for 4 months; finally, having subdued the people inside by hunger and thirst – the well that they had inside having dried up in a remarkable way – they attacked them. First they took all the goods that were inside. A great host was taken out into captivity'. This marked a defining moment in the history of the kingdom of Strathclyde. It would no longer be a significant player in the politics of northern Britain. It is also possible that the Vikings retained control of Strathclyde in the aftermath of this invasion, perhaps through a puppet king, possibly Arthgal, on the model of Northumbria or East Anglia.

The two Viking leaders appear to have followed up this major victory, probably using their newly acquired base at Dumbarton on the Clyde, with an invasion of the kingdom of Fortriu in 870 or 871. This is nowhere recorded in our surviving sources but it is implied. In 871 the Annals of Ulster record that 'Olaf and Ivar returned to Dublin from Alba with 200 ships bringing away with them in captivity to Ireland a great prey of English and Britons and Picts.' The British prisoners may have included Arthgal, King of Strathclyde. The Britons were taken at Dumbarton; the English were presumably brought from York or captured en route by Ivar; where the 'Picts' came from is unrecorded but it can only have been from a new attack on the kingdom of Fortriu.

In 872, according to the Ulster annals, 'Arthgal King of the Britons was killed at the instigation of Constantine, son of Kenneth'. It has been suggested that Arthgal was a prisoner and that this refers to a failure by Constantine to deliver a ransom for his release. This might imply that Arthgal was a sub-king who had acknowledged the hegemony of Constantine and that the latter therefore had an obligation to assist him. This is certainly a possibility but it does not appear to be supported by any contemporary sources. The annals might equally be implying that Constantine reached an arrangement with the Vikings to dispose of this rival or that Arthgal was a Viking puppet whom Constantine deposed. This would fit with the suggestion above that the Vikings had set up a puppet regime. If this was the case, Constantine would naturally have wished to support his own candidate to rule the Britons of Strathclyde. Rhun, the son of Arthgal, would later be, or perhaps already was, Constantine's son-in-law. Constantine perhaps intended him to become a sub-king, acknowledging his overlordship on the model created by King Offa in other English kingdoms in the 790s.

In 873, the Viking leader Ivar died, acknowledged by the Irish annals as 'King of the Norsemen of all Ireland and Britain'. It would seem from this that his partner Olaf may have predeceased him although, if so, there is no similar report of Olaf's death. He is last mentioned in 871 on his return with Ivar to Dublin from their successful joint raid on northern Britain. The Scottish Chronicle claims that King Constantine I killed a man called Olaf 'while taking tribute' in the thirteenth year of his reign, i.e. 874 or 875. It seems unlikely, at first, that this could refer to the Irish-based Olaf who died before 873. This source is, however, a little imprecise and even inaccurate in its dating of events. It is difficult to resolve these apparently contradictory sources. It may simply be the case that Ivar predeceased Olaf but was endowed with an over-inflated or flattering title by the Irish annalist. This would allow Olaf to survive him and be killed by Constantine during a tribute-taking expedition in 874 or 875. If this is the case, Constantine was perhaps seeking to exploit the recent death of Ivar to strike at the weakened Vikings.

In 875 'The Anglo-Saxon Chronicle' records that the Viking leader Halfdan, who had left the great army at Repton in Mercia a year earlier and had led his forces north into Northumbria, emerged from his winter quarters on the Tyne. He had temporarily subdued the rest of Northumbria but now led raids north into Strathclyde and the lands of the Picts. He may have hoped to secure control of the tribute from these regions lost following the death of Olaf. It was presumably during this raid that King Constantine fought the battle at Dollar against Halfdan, which is recorded in the Scottish Chronicle. The king had perhaps hoped to repeat his earlier success in killing Olaf but instead he was defeated with 'great slaughter' and subsequently withdrew into Atholl to escape the Viking pursuit. The victorious Halfdan is then reported to have occupied the kingdom, or at least the lowland parts of it, for a whole year after this. It appeared that Fortriu had followed Northumbria, East Anglia, Strathclyde and a significant part of Mercia into Viking control.

In the same year, Halfdan may have followed up this success in northern Britain by crossing to Ireland in pursuit of control over the Vikings there. In the Annals of Ulster, it is recorded that a man called Halfdan was reported to have deceitfully killed Haesten, son of Olaf, in 875. It seems that Halfdan had temporarily achieved his ambition to control the entire Viking forces in northern Britain and Ireland and that he also dominated the kingdom of Fortriu. In 876 he returned to northern England and 'shared out the land of the Northumbrians' among his victorious but exhausted army which settled in the area around York. The Vikings proceeded, in the words of the chronicler, 'to plough and support themselves' although it is likely that their English slaves performed such menial tasks for them. Halfdan, however, would not enjoy this extensive hegemony for long and in 877 the Annals of Ulster report that Halfdan was killed in a skirmish with other Vikings at Loch Cuan in Ireland. The withdrawal of Halfdan to York in 876 and his death the following year must have released Constantine and his kingdom from Viking subjection.

In 876 the unlucky Constantine I, died as 'King of the Picts', according to the Annals of Ulster. The later Scottish king-lists imply that Constantine was killed by Vikings at Inverdovat but the Ulster annalist appears to believe he died of natural causes. He had had a rather undistinguished reign which featured a series of defeats at the hands of the Vikings. In spite of this, he had managed, like King Alfred, to survive and, in so doing, to preserve his kingdom in some shape or form. This was more than the rulers of Strathclyde, East Anglia, Mercia or Northumbria had managed. Constantine was succeeded as 'King of the Picts' by his brother Aed, son of Kenneth or *Aed mac Cineada.*

In 878, the Irish annals report that 'the shrine of Columba and his other relics arrived in Ireland having been taken in flight to escape the foreigners.' Unfortunately, there is no further explanation of the circumstances of this crisis. It seems too late to be connected with the disastrous events of Halfdan's conquest and it may simply have been an internal Viking dispute in the Western Isles. In this same year, King Aed fell victim to dynastic rivals after a reign of little more than a year. According to surviving sources, King Aed was killed at the monastery of Rossie in Strathallan by his 'own associates'. Later sources name these associates and declare that Aed was killed by his cousin Giric, son of Donald. The exact meaning of the surviving accounts is unclear but there is at least a hint of treachery.

The precise details of the succession to King Aed are complex. The sources report two rulers of the kingdom after Aed: Giric son of Donald I or *Giric mac Domnaill,* who had killed him and came from the royal lineage, and Eochaid, son of Rhun of Strathclyde and a daughter of Kenneth MacAlpin, who was Giric's nephew but possibly also the contemporary ruler of Strathclyde or his son. This arrangement, involving two co-rulers, if such indeed it is, appears to be unique in the history of the kingdom and it may mean that Giric was too weak to rule on his own and relied on support from the remnants of Strathclyde. Alternatively, it may be intended to indicate that Strathclyde had escaped from its recent dependence on its larger northern neighbour. The lack of reliable evidence makes it impossible to be certain about any of this. It was King Giric, according to the Scottish king-lists, who was 'the first to free the Scottish church which was in servitude up to that time after the custom and fashion of the Picts.' It is not at all clear what this means but it may have involved exempting the Church from certain customary tributes. If this is the case, it may reflect an insecure monarch seeking to secure the support of the Church by making concessions.

In 889 King Giric died at Dundurn and, presumably as a consequence of this, his associate Eochaid, son of Rhun was expelled from the kingdom, although whether the kingdom of Fortriu or Strathclyde is meant is unclear. The man who expelled Eochaid was Donald II, son of Constantine or *Domnall mac Castantin*, who ruled quietly for some eleven years. In this period the Danes, who had settled around York under Halfdan and others, participated in a number of raids launched by other Vikings, who had arrived from the Continent in 891. The raids were directed principally against Mercia and Wessex until the combined Viking forces were defeated at Buttington in 893 and withdrew to Northumbria in 896. This failure in the south perhaps encouraged the Danes to turn their attentions to the north again. The Scottish Chronicle reports that Northmen, presumably from York, ravaged the kingdom of Fortriu during Donald's reign although it fails to date this event.

In 900 the Annals of Ulster report the death of Donald, son of Constantine, who is for the first time styled *ri Albann* or 'King of Alba'. This is the first mention of this new name for the united kingdom of the Picts and Scots and serves, perhaps, to mark its coming of age. The kings had previously borne the title *ri Fortrenn* or 'King of Fortriu' in Gaelic texts and *rex Pictorum* or 'King of the Picts' in Latin texts. The kingdom, first brought together by Constantine, son of Fergus, in 792 and subsequently reinvented by Kenneth MacAlpin in the 850s, had been forged as a result of its rough handling by the Vikings into a single, unified kingdom, recognised by its new name of 'Alba'. The name had originally signified Britain as a whole but would from now on be employed for that northern part of Britain controlled by Gaelic speakers. The union between the Picts and Scots, whether originally enforced or not, had brought to an end the warfare between these peoples and produced a new and stronger kingdom. Its inhabitants were no longer Picts or Scots but *fir Albann* or 'men of Alba' and its kings were no longer rulers of Picts or Scots but bore the title *ri Albann* or 'King of Alba'. This larger and more powerful kingdom of Alba had the potential to become more than the sum of its parts. It was free from the constraints of earlier disputes and might therefore play a much larger role in the politics of northern Britain than either of its predecessors. Whether it would ever fulfil this potential would depend very much on its rulers and their abilities.

The new kingdom was not entirely free from internal dissent from those unreconciled to the new polity, especially given its custom of alternating the succession to the kingship between contending lines of descent. The existence of rival candidates for the throne provided plenty of opportunities for malcontents to exploit. This meant that few of its rulers went unchallenged at some point during their reign and many ruled too briefly to make any impact at all. The new kingdom still faced serious danger of encirclement and perhaps even elimination. The threat came mainly from a series of fluid but threatening coalitions of Viking powers, which might unite against it at any time. In the north was the earldom of Orkney with its satellite settlements stretching southwards on the mainland as far as the Cromarty Firth. In the west was an at times fragmented but potentially powerful kingdom in the Isles, which included most of the Western Isles and sometimes the Isle of Man. In the south was the Viking kingdom of York, which included a large part of northern England. The situation was not entirely bleak, however. The new kingdom was also presented with opportunities in the shape of a couple of small states to the south, which had been even more severely damaged by the Vikings: the weakened British kingdom of Strathclyde, which stretched from the Clyde Valley southwards into north-west England; and the truncated remnant of English Northumbria, which extended from the Firth of Forth to the northern borders of the later Yorkshire. In these circumstances, the various individual kings of Alba faced tremendous challenges, which only a few were able to master sufficiently to make a difference.

2

The Kingdom of Alba

In the year 900 the kingdom of Alba was a brand new creation. It was an entirely new polity first mentioned in the Annals of Ulster on the death of King Donald II, son of Constantine, under the year 900. It had been created from the fusion of the earlier independent kingdoms of the Picts and Scots. It had first appeared in this form at the end of the eighth century under Constantine, son of Fergus, and received its future dynasty during the middle of the ninth century under Kenneth MacAlpin. The new kingdom had far deeper roots than this, however. The Picts, who probably spoke a Celtic language closely related to Welsh, had been present in northern Britain since pre-Roman times and were still there when the Romans left in the fourth century. The Gaelic-speaking Scots had arrived on the western shores of Scotland from Ireland some time before their first appearance in historical records in the late Roman period. These two peoples had therefore been close neighbours for at least five centuries before their union under a single kingship. They probably also shared to some extent a common Celtic cultural background. They had exchanged gifts and trade goods and intermarried since the earliest times.

In the sixth century, the completion of the conversion to Christianity of the Picts provided the two peoples with a common faith. This increased intellectual contacts and reinforced existing cultural affinities. The associated introduction of the Latin language provided a new common channel of communication and removed the need for translation. The flourishing artistic tradition of northern Britain in the period between the sixth and the eighth centuries bears witness to this rich fusion of cultures. The comparison of Pictish sculpture with illuminated Gaelic manuscripts and of decorated metalwork from Ireland and northern Britain reveals the common cultural heritage of the two peoples.

In the eighth and early ninth centuries the political, social and cultural contacts between the Picts and the Scots increased and intensified. In this period Scots began to migrate eastwards across the mountains into Pictish territory. In the same period Pictish and Scottish kings contested for control of northern Britain and this process occasionally but increasingly succeeded in uniting the two polities under a single rule. The intermarriage of the respective royal families of these peoples increasingly blurred the distinctions between them and made the rival kings more acceptable to both peoples. This intermittent joint rule became more or less continuous from around 790 onwards under a dynasty which although usually identified as Pictish, appears in effect to have been of mixed race. This process reinforced the common aspects of the cultural identity of Picts and Scots over a long period of time. It finally resulted in a Picto-Scottish kingdom under a Picto-Scottish king.

In the middle of the ninth century, when Kenneth I, son of Alpin, stepped onto this stage as King of the Picts and the Scots, he was completing a gradual process of the merging of two cultures which had begun centuries before. As mentioned in the previous chapter, he did not massacre the Picts en masse to replace them with Scots. There was no ethnic cleansing in northern Britain but rather a slow fusion of two cultural groups over a long period of time. It should be noted, however, that the new kingdom of Alba itself does not appear to be associated with Kenneth MacAlpin himself. In the Irish annals Kenneth and his immediate successors, Donald I, Constantine I, Aed and Giric, still appear as *rex Pictorum* or 'King of the Picts'. It is not until the turn of the century, in 900, that

Donald II, son of Constantine appears as the first *ri Albann* or 'King of Alba'. What happened to bring about this significant change?

The name 'Alba' had previously been used to represent the island of Britain itself, rather than any particular political entity. The new use of this name in 900 was clearly meant to indicate a wider hegemony than could be represented by existing terminology. The Picts and the Scots were now so intermingled that old ethnic titles like 'King of the Picts' or 'King of the Scots' were no longer adequate. In addition, this same period probably witnessed the subjection of the last independent kings of Strathclyde, either in 872 or perhaps in 889. The new kings exercised hegemony over every non-English Christian people in the north of Britain. This was the context for the introduction of the new title, 'King of Alba'. It signified the fact that the new kingdom encompassed the entire non-English Christian sphere of northern Britain. The kingdom of Alba was now to all intents and purposes the equivalent of 'Britain' as far as the wider Gaelic-speaking world in Ireland was concerned.

The new kingdom of Alba was therefore the product of a complex process of long-term cultural assimilation and more recent political creation. What was it like? It was undoubtedly a 'Celtic' kingdom, despite this term becoming increasingly unfashionable among historians. Its people spoke a Celtic language and had a largely Celtic culture. They were probably already increasingly Gaelic in speech and more and more representative of the culture common to Gaelic Ireland and its colonies in northern Britain, although residual Pictish elements still remained. It is usually fairly easy to trace the Gaelic elements in the society of Alba through comparisons with contemporary society in neighbouring Gaelic Ireland. It is not possible, however, simply to adopt Irish models in their entirety since there are important differences in Alba, which derive from its Pictish element. On the other hand, it is impossible to establish the Pictish elements, in this way, since there are simply so few records of any kind of Pictish society. The best that can be done is to identify aspects of the society of Alba which have no close comparisons in contemporary Ireland. It can then be assumed – although this can only be an assumption – that these aspects are likely to be Pictish.

In the new kingdom, the rulers bore the Gaelic title *ri Albann* or 'King of Alba'. They also had predominantly Gaelic names and this appears to have provided their primary cultural roots. They certainly boasted genealogies that traced their ancestry back to the kings of Dalriada, however dubiously, rather than to those of the Picts. They were most probably actual descendants of Gaelic families but they clearly also wished to associate themselves with the increasingly predominant Gaelic culture in the new kingdom. In light of this, it is therefore quite natural to assume that they were identical in other respects to kings in Gaelic Ireland. It is dangerous, however, to rely on this assumption entirely. They were after all rulers of an entirely new and composite political entity formed on the basis of Pictish and Gaelic traditions. The origins of their new office might therefore contain elements drawn from either or both traditions.

If, for example, the names of the kings of Alba are considered in more detail, a few exceptions to the Gaelic predominance noted above will be found. The most obvious is the name 'Constantine', which was carried by no less than three kings of Alba. This name appears nowhere else in Gaelic tradition. Its use appears to have been inspired by the great Constantine, son of Fergus, who ruled jointly over the Scots and Picts from 789 to 820 before the succession of the dynasty of Kenneth MacAlpin. In spite of this man's own possible Gaelic origins, 'Constantine' is not a name found among the dynasty of Dalriada. Indeed, in the period before 789 the name Constantine is only found in Britain among the British kingdoms, i.e. St Constantine and Constantine of Dumnonia. It was derived in British tradition from the Christian Roman Emperor, Constantine the Great. It seems to have arrived in Pictland either directly from Roman Imperial and Christian traditions or indirectly from the British kingdoms, possibly neighbouring Strathclyde.

The succession system followed by the kings of Alba also appears to be derived directly from Irish tradition. There was no primogeniture at this time when it was crucial that kingdoms were ruled by able-bodied adult males who could command military forces in person. In place of primogeniture, the kingdom of Alba followed a system largely based on the Gaelic *derbfine* or 'certain kin', which identified those male relations of a ruling king from which the *rigdamnai* or 'royal heirs' might be selected. This *derbfine* included all those males whose great-grandfather had been a king and who were therefore theoretically eligible for the kingship. It must be admitted that contemporary Pictish succession practices are highly obscure, at least in our scarce sources. The little that can be glimpsed, however, does not suggest any close resemblances to the system used in Alba. It is only at the very end of the independent Pictish kingdom under the united kingship established by Constantine son of Fergus and his successors that any sign of Gaelic succession patterns appears. This is a time when the kingdom was clearly falling under Gaelic influence and it might therefore be expected.

This succession system meant that the kingship could be claimed by any fit adult male descendant of a previous king. It effectively ensured that a suitable adult male was always available to rule the country and lead its armies and avoided the potential dangers of minority rule. It usually meant a predominance of succession by brothers and cousins across the same generation with the succession of their sons in the next generation effectively postponed until after their deaths. It almost never witnessed the succession of a father by his own son. The system had a tendency, however, to encourage competition between different lineages over time as brothers with close ties were replaced by cousins who were only distantly related. This resulted in a great deal of factional unrest within the later kingdom, which produced much bloodletting and eventually civil war.

The main function of the king of Alba was to lead the *fir Albann* or 'men of Alba' in war. It is this vital function that is also best recorded in our few surviving sources. Unfortunately, the precise nature of the powers of the king in this area is now obscure and probably lost to us. It may, however, be possible to recover some of them from later sources, provided caution is used. What appears to be an ancient power features as 'common army' or 'Scottish army' in twelfth-century charters, presumably to distinguish it from later knight service. It must therefore reach back at least to pre-feudal times in the eleventh century and probably much further than that. Unfortunately, the references to this military service in the charters provide no detail since it is assumed that everyone knows exactly what is involved. This common army was undoubtedly based on some form of local assessment system. The tenth-century text known as *Senchus fer nAlban* or 'The History of the Men of Alba', records a sophisticated system of assessment employed in early Dalriada to recruit armies and navies. The existence of this text establishes beyond reasonable doubt that the later kingdom of Alba had a similarly sophisticated system, even if its details are no longer recoverable.

The kings used this military power in the first place to defend their kingdom and their subjects against external foes. Constantine I fought to defend his kingdom and his faith against the heathen Vikings with variable results and Constantine II fought against the same opponents with much more success in Strathearn in 904. They also used military power to control their own kingdom by crushing internal opposition or rebellion. Malcolm I and Malcolm III struck against the recalcitrant *mormaers* of Moray in 943 and 1077 respectively. They used the same power frequently to launch campaigns of raiding or conquest against neighbouring kingdoms. Malcolm I, Malcolm II and Malcolm III all launched raids into England to secure cattle and slaves but also perhaps to seize territory in 950 and 952, in 1006, and in 1070 and 1093 respectively. Constantine II also launched more far-reaching campaigns in league with allies and fought major battles at Corbridge in 918 and *Brunanburh* in 937.

In contrast, there are few written records which provide us with information on the actual armies led into battle by the kings. It is fortunate therefore that surviving examples of monumental stone sculpture offer a unique pictorial representation of these armies. The Dupplin Cross in Perthshire, which commemorates King Constantine, son of Fergus, shows the king as a mounted warrior in a panel on its east face. Immediately below, another panel portrays the royal army as close ranks of well disciplined infantry, equipped with spears and shields. Sueno's Stone near Forres, which commemorates a famous but so far unidentified battle of this era, also offers a sophisticated portrait of a contemporary army. It consists of organised units of both cavalry and infantry, fully equipped with swords, spears and shields. This builds on the picture of military sophistication already displayed on earlier Pictish stones including that at Aberlemno, which is thought to commemorate the Battle of Dunnichen in 685. The men of Alba were not a rabble of painted savages but a sophisticated and well organised military machine broadly comparable to those of their English and Viking opponents.

The king of Alba also appears to have had a role in the administration and delivery of justice in the kingdom. The contemporary Scottish Chronicle records a number of examples of legislative pronouncements by the kings. The establishment of 'the rights and laws of the kingship of Aed, son of Eochaid' was announced by Donald I around 860. In 906, Constantine II and Bishop Cellach 'covenanted to guard the laws and disciplines of the faith and also the rights of the churches and gospels'. The precise meaning of these announcements is no longer clear but they do appear to relate to the introduction of new laws or the proclamation of existing laws. The Life of St Margaret confirms the royal legislative role, when it declares, 'by her [Margaret's] counsel the laws of the kingdom were put in order', although it seems more likely that the king actually fulfilled this role. The Life of St Margaret also mentions 'the tumult of lawsuits' as a feature of the royal Court, which suggests a judicial role in addition to the legislative one. In earlier times their Pictish and Dalriadic predecessors had fulfilled a similar function. In 697, Bruide, son of Derile, King of the Picts, and Eochaid, son of Domangart, King of Dalriada, were among those who endorsed Adomnan's 'Law of the Innocents', which offered protection to non-combatants.

The king of Alba also controlled significant personal resources in terms of the ownership of lands and estates and of payments, usually in kind, due from the lands of the entire kingdom. The lands originally controlled directly by the kings are generally believed to be indicated by the later existence of units of land subsequently known as 'thanages'. If the sites of these thanages, as recorded in twelfth-century or later records, are plotted on a map they reveal a concentration in the eastern lowlands of the kingdom. They are sited mainly in the eastern plains between Moray and Fife with relatively few outliers in the upland areas. This represents the heartlands of the kingdom of Alba and of its predecessor, the Pictish realm. This area might perhaps be expected to contain the bulk of royal lands since it also provided the richest agricultural lands. It would be natural for the kings to retain this wealth in their own hands to provide a secure basis for their power. The thanages also include a significant number of royal centres, including Forteviot and Scone.

The royal lands in these thanages were supervised by officials later known as 'thanes' but probably at this time still identified by the Gaelic title of *toiseach* or 'leader'. The Book of Deer mentions a number of these officials whose role was to run an estate or estates on behalf of the king and to ensure that its surplus was available for royal consumption. This consumption would occur either when the king visited the estate in person or when the surplus was delivered by the *toiseach* to wherever the king currently resided. In order to minimise the need for transportation, important royal residences were often located at or near royal estates, such as the palaces recorded at Forteviot and Scone. It was at these residences that the thanes would collect the food and other resources collected from surrounding royal estates. At this time, kings did not have single capitals but toured the country visiting a number of different residences during the year. This allowed them to consume local resources evenly across the kingdom without depleting those of a particular area. In this period before fast transport and refrigeration, food needed to be stored and consumed as close as possible to where it was produced.

In addition to the produce from their own royal estates the kings of Alba had access to dues drawn from lands across from the whole kingdom. There were two principal items which fell due to the kings by right of their position of lordship over the kingdom. The first of these was *cain* or 'tax', which was a tribute due from all the king's subjects in respect of his royal lordship. It was normally paid in kind during this period and only much later converted into a monetary payment. There are mentions in the charters of *cain* in the form of corn, malt, cattle, sheep, swine, cheese, hides and foals and it could also be collected on trade goods. This is the most prominent royal resource in later charters and was undoubtedly the most substantial source of royal wealth in this early period. The second royal resource was *coinmed*, 'conveth' or 'hospitality', which represented the hospitality due from a subject to his lord, the king. It was obtained from all royal subjects from a *mormaer* or ear downwards and consisted of a duty to accommodate and supply the royal Court as it toured the country. This had over time been transformed into an equivalent payment in kind. The royal dues of *cain* and *coinmed* were collected by the *toiseach* or thane from across the kingdom and brought to central points at particular thanages and royal residencies.

The king of Alba appears to have maintained himself using the resources of his own royal lands and the dues and hospitality collected from his subjects, along with whatever additional resources could be secured by pillage. There are no indications in this early period of attempts to introduce new forms of revenue. The distribution of these resources to the king and his family and wider household or to particular subjects was organised by a royal official. He is not noticed by contemporary sources but twelfth-century charters record the existence of a man called the *rainnaire* or 'distributor'. The function of this man was clearly to allocate or redistribute the resources collected at royal residences or estates by the *toiseach* or thane. He appears to have done so regardless of whether the resources derived from the royal estates themselves or had been received as dues from royal subjects. He was obviously a key official of the royal household or Court who fulfilled the duties of the later stewards, but there must also have been others.

Unfortunately, the royal household or Court of Alba at this time is nowhere described in detail in contemporary sources. It can only be reconstructed from occasional hints, since it is unwise to depend on Irish comparisons, and it is impossible to be certain about its precise composition. It centred on the king, his wife and their children and perhaps a wider family group, including foster-children. It is unlikely, however, that it ever extended to the entire *derbfine*. This inner family circle would have been accompanied by a body of servants of various ranks and slaves, who would attend to all their bodily needs. The Life of St Margaret mentions men and women, including stewards, in the service of the royal couple, many of whom were themselves of noble origin. It would also have included a military retinue or bodyguard to provide immediate protection for the family, its household and its transportable wealth. It would have included the *rainnaire* and various subordinate stewards. On the basis of Irish comparisons and later evidence, it is likely that it also included at least one *bard* or 'poet' to provide praise poems for the king, satires about his enemies and other entertainment and a *sennchaid* or 'historian' to record the genealogy and deeds of the king. It must also have included a number of clerics, who provided not only spiritual services but also, as almost certainly the only literate individuals available, administrative ones. The Life of St Margaret states that King Malcolm III was illiterate and it seems likely that most other rulers in this period were the same.

In addition to these constituent parts of the royal household or Court there would have been a variety of other figures who either followed the Court as it toured around the kingdom or who visited it while it was in the local area. This might include secular individuals, including *mormaers*, thanes and other landowners, clerics including bishops, abbots and priests, as well as sundry merchants, poets or warriors. Whether secular or clerical, the individuals who accompanied the Court on these occasions were probably either seeking royal favour and rewards or offering advice and counsel. The material rewards of patronage that the king could bestow were potentially immense. They could involve a wide range of things from resources of food, drink or goods in kind, livestock, rich treasure items, secular and religious offices and lands. The sort of advice or counsel that they offered the king could similarly relate to a wide range of subjects including royal marriages, foreign policy and warfare, internal politics and religious policy.

In the hierarchy immediately below the king stood a cadre of regional rulers, who appear to be unique to the kingdom of Alba and who probably therefore derive ultimately from Pictish origins. They were known by the Gaelic title of *mormaer* or 'great steward' and later by the English title of 'earl'. The precise origins of this office are now lost to history but the inclusion in their title of the term 'steward' clearly implies a relationship of service to the king on the model of the equivalent English office of *ealdorman* or 'earl'. It seems likely that this office originated and evolved in a similar way. The English title *ealdorman* originally referred to either previously independent subordinate kings, who were reduced in status to subordinate officials, or to royal officials appointed to rule conquered areas under the authority of the king. They were usually men with strong local power bases built around local landholdings whose service to the king ensured the loyalty of their locality. They represented the king in areas where he was perhaps seldom seen in person and in turn represented their local areas before the king. They allowed the king to extend his personal sphere of influence far beyond the core area of his kingdom where his own lands were situated.

This situation is reflected in the locations, as recorded in the thirteenth century, of the provinces ruled by men who had previously been *mormaers* but were then known as earls. There is a need for caution here since it is not entirely certain that all the later earldoms existed in the early kingdom. If the earldoms of Dunbar, created in the 1070s, and Carrick, created in the 1150s, are ignored, the nine other earldoms are all located within or on the edge of the former Pictish kingdom. There are no records of any *mormaers* or earls based in the former Dalriada. This seems to confirm the likelihood that they have Pictish origins. The nine earldoms appear to form a defensive shield around the heartlands of the Pictish kingdom and its successor the kingdom of Alba. They run in an arc from north to south along the western fringes of the eastern lowland heart of the kingdom. They range from Moray and Buchan in the far north on the borders of Viking-occupied territory, through Mar, Atholl, and Strathearn on the edge of the Highlands to the west of the central core of the kingdom, ending with Mentieth and Lennox in the south on the borders of the British kingdom of Strathclyde. The exception to this pattern is represented by Fife and Angus which are located within the old heartlands. It is almost certain, however, that Fife is a later creation set up, perhaps during the eleventh century, to accommodate an ousted royal line. This leaves Angus as the odd man out positioned in the heart of the kingdom of Alba. Its *mormaers* feature prominently in the Scottish Chronicle – perhaps a reflection of their importance or their central location.

In the context of a cautious approach, it is true that only four of the nine future earldoms (excluding Dunbar and Carrick) can with certainty be established to have existed before the eleventh century. They are Angus, Atholl, Mar and Moray. There seems, however, no good reason to discount the existence of the others. The Book of Deer preserves the memory of a *mormaer* of Buchan from early times. The locations of the earldoms suggest that their most important function was to protect the heart of the kingdom where the bulk of royal lands and wealth were located, as signified by the location of the thanages (see Map 3). An enemy invading the kingdom of Alba from the north, west or south-west would need to penetrate one or more of these provinces before they could reach the heart of the kingdom. This effectively meant that the *mormaers*, who had a vested interest in protecting their own lands, were also protecting the entire kingdom. The king effectively had a first line of defence for his own lands against his external enemies.

The *mormaers* who ruled these important border provinces were clearly important figures in the kingdom. The fact that the contemporary Scottish Chronicle and the Irish annals record the deaths of some of them in their extremely brief entries is enough to show this. The office of *mormaer*, whatever its origins and its relationship to the kings, appears to have become hereditary by the tenth and eleventh centuries. This occurred not only in the distant and semi-independent province of Moray, which might have been beyond royal control, but also in the central province of Angus. Thus Maelbrigte succeeded his father Dubucan as *mormaer* of Angus, and a number of individual *mormaers* of Moray were from the same family. If Moray can be considered typical of other provinces – and there are reasons to think that this may not be the case – then they also appear to have adopted a similar succession system to that of the kings themselves. They appear to have recognised a *derbfine* or 'certain kin' in their own province which offered suitable candidates for *mormaer*. There is, however, not enough evidence to reach any similar conclusions about the other provinces.

The *mormaers* were important supporters of the king but if he did not foster them, they could also pose a threat. A number of *mormaers* were caught up in the struggles for the kingship between rival lineages, including Dubduin, *Mormaer* of Atholl who was killed in battle at Duncrub in 965 during the struggle between Dub and Culen. Others were more directly implicated in the deaths of kings. In 995 Cunthar, *Mormaer* of Angus killed King Kenneth II at the thanage of Fettercairn. The men of the Mearns were accused of killing two kings, Malcolm I at Fetteresso in 954 and Duncan II at Mondynes in 1094. On the second occasion, the men of the Mearns were commanded by Maelpetair, son of Malcolm, *Mormaer* of Angus, and this was probably also the case in 954, when Maelbrigte, son of Dubucan was *Mormaer* of Angus. In the ultimate betrayal, one of these men, Macbeth, *Mormaer* of Moray, who had probably been installed with help from King Malcolm II, killed King Duncan I and seized the kingship itself.

The powers of these provincial rulers seem to represent a reduced or subordinate form of royal powers. They appear to have commanded the military forces of their provinces either in local defence or as an element of the larger royal army. This is clear from contemporary sources which record the presence of *mormaers* in a number of battles. The report on the Battle of Corbridge in 918 in the Annals of Ulster mentions that 'none of their [the Scots] kings or *mormaers* were killed.' The military responsibility of *mormaers* is also indicated by twelfth-century and later charters which record the duty of the earls to lead the 'common army' of their earldom.

The *mormaers* also appear to have had subordinate judicial functions, like Constantine, *Mormaer* of Fife, who features as a *judex* or 'judge' in twelfth-century charters. They were also able to collect *cain* and *coinmed* from their own lands and others on a lower scale to that collected for the king. This was their share of the surplus produced by farming. It supported their office in the same way that it supported the king himself, but on a smaller scale. They could also grant lands and a share of the dues that fell to them to secular individuals and to churches. This allowed them to build up personal support in their provinces by winning over other local men and local churches with gifts of lands and dues. The Book of Deer records grants of land by Maelsnechtai, son of Lulach, *Mormaer* of Moray and Muiredach, son of Morgann, another *mormaer,* possibly of Buchan. They also record the grant of dues by a *mormaer* called Matain, son of Cairell, whose province is unknown but could have been Mar or Buchan. The Book of Deer also reveals that *mormaers* also had the power to 'quench' the collection of *cain* and *coinmed*. This freed churches from the need to collect and deliver these dues and to use them themselves instead. It was another way to secure support and one used by Colban, *Mormaer* of Buchan.

In the social hierarchy immediately below the *mormaers* were the men known by the Gaelic title of *toiseach* or 'leader', who feature in Gaelic grants inserted into The Book of Deer. They would later be known by the imported English term 'thane' from the Anglo-Saxon *thegn* or 'servant'. They also may have Pictish origins, if we can rely on the locations of the royal thanages which are located in the heart of the old Pictish kingdom. As mentioned above, these men were initially royal servants, who administered the royal estates or thanages later associated with them, but the term was probably later extended to all noble landowners of a certain rank. The *toiseachs* or thanes managed individual estates or thanages across the kingdom and provided support and services to the king. They provided the key link between the *mormaers* at provincial level and the local communities on individual estates in the same way as the *mormaers* themselves mediated between the provincial communities and the kings.

They were also, as their Gaelic title *toiseach* or 'leader' suggests, the leaders of local groups which are described in The Book of Deer as 'clans' or 'kindreds', which appear to have claimed descent from a common ancestor. Comgell, son of Cainnech was *toiseach* of Clann Channann and Donnchad, son of Sithech was *toiseach* of Clann Morgainn. The *toiseach* was probably responsible for the collection of dues from this clan and its lands and offered them his protection in exchange. He also led the military forces of this clan in the common army of the *mormaer* or king. He also had some role in judicial proceedings and was able to grant lands or dues to the Church and others. The extensive grants made by Cathal, son of Morgann, *toiseach* and probably brother of Muiredach the *Mormaer,* and recorded in The Book of Deer are described below. Other *toiseachs* also made grants, including Cu Li, son of Baithen.

The Life of St Cadroe of Metz, which was composed around 980, provides a flavour of the life of a noble who was probably of the rank of *toiseach*. Cadroe was the only son and heir of a rich and noble couple called Fochertach and Bania, who owned an estate that included a stable and horses. He was weaned and fostered by another noble family, according to the Gaelic custom of the land. Once he had reached maturity, he returned to his own family to be educated in secular matters, presumably including the arts of war, by his father Fochertach. It was at this point that Fochertach was approached by a cousin, who wanted the boy to train as a priest. Fochertach rejected this request since Cadroe was his only son and would be expected to inherit the family lands. He was expected to defend not only his own family property but also that of his foster-family. The latter were robbed by thieves and Cadroe was preparing to pursue them and recover the stolen goods by force. It was then that he received the call to religion fortuitously when he also had a new brother to inherit the family land.

The Christian Church played a central role in the society of Britain in the early medieval period. What do we know about the

Christian Church in the kingdom of Alba? The answer to this question is: surprisingly little in view of the fact that the Church in Alba was presumably, as elsewhere in Europe, the main repository of literacy and learning. In fact, there is remarkably little surviving evidence for this undoubtedly important institution. The subsequent erosion and eventual demise of the Gaelic language in eastern Scotland presumably contributed to this circumstance. It meant that any records or documents in the Gaelic language lost their usefulness and were thereafter lost or destroyed. This cannot, however, explain the scarcity of Latin documents from this period which obviously did not suffer any loss of intelligibility. If, however, the Church in the kingdom of Alba reflected the practice of its Irish neighbours, then a large portion of its records were presumably in Gaelic and were therefore lost. In addition, the introduction of new clergy and new practices from England and the Continent from the twelfth century onwards probably hastened the replacement of old records.

The origins of Christianity in what became the kingdom of Alba are extremely complex. They incorporate a wide range of influences, which produced a Church that has points in common with several neighbouring churches but which nevertheless remains distinct. The Irish influence, as in the sphere of secular society, is, however, almost certainly the strongest one. The Irish tradition was based around the expansion of a single monastic church dedicated to a particular saint, through the foundation of daughter churches. The result was a *familia* or family of such daughter houses spread over a wide area, including into other kingdoms. The most famous of these churches in Alba was of course St Columba's monastery on Iona, whose daughter houses were spread across Alba and throughout Ireland too. In Alba this pattern was followed by other important churches, including the bishoprics of Brechin, Dunkeld and St Andrews, and the earliest diocesan structures revealed in the twelfth century preserve evidence of such origins. They consist of a pattern of scattered dependent churches spread across the kingdom under the authority of a head church. The diocese of Dunkeld, for example, has a central block of territory in Atholl but outliers scattered throughout Angus, Fife and Lothian (see Map 4). The diocese of St Andrews stretches along the east coast from Aberdeen in the north to the English border in the south but is interspersed with small areas belonging to Brechin and Dunkeld. In contemporary England, by contrast, bishoprics were made up of compact uniform territorial units. In Ireland these families of churches were often supervised by the abbot of the original or head monastery.

The Church in Alba also included British and Northumbrian influences as a result of British missionaries like St Ninian and the introduction of Northumbrian traditions under Nechtan, King of the Picts, from 711 onwards. The main impact of these other traditions appears to have been the greater prominence of bishops in Alba than in Ireland. In Alba each *familia* or family of churches appears to have been supervised not by an abbot but by a bishop, although one individual might hold both titles. This complex background resulted in a number of dioceses, although we only have secure contemporary evidence for one or two. They each consisted of a head church, which controlled a group of widely scattered individual churches. The head church provided the residence for the bishop who supervised the other churches, including the monasteries under their individual abbots. The existence of an individual, variously known as *ardescop* or *prim-escop*, i.e. 'senior Bishop', or simply as 'the Bishop of Alba' suggests the existence of a recognised head of the Church. This appears to be the case in spite of the lack of any officially recognised metropolitan archbishop in the kingdom at this time. It also supports the existence of other bishops who presumably owed him obedience

This senior bishop or bishop of Alba was based in the most important head church in Alba. In 865 the Annals of Ulster report the death of Tuathal, son of Artgus, senior Bishop of Alba and

Abbot of Dunkeld. In around 849 the Scottish Chronicle had reported the transfer of the relics of St Columba to Dunkeld by Kenneth I. This act transformed the church at Dunkeld into the most important church in Alba and naturally into its head church and the residence of the senior bishop. In the next fifty years the situation changed as St Andrews became increasingly important and gradually usurped the position of head church. It was St Columba's crozier that was still carried before the Scottish army in 904 and 918, but it was Bishop Cellach of St Andrews who dealt with Constantine II at Scone in 906. In 943 Constantine II chose to retire to the monastery at St Andrews rather than Dunkeld. In the 950s King Idulf exiled Fothad, Bishop of St Andrews and not Dunkeld to the Isles. Thereafter there are a number of references to a senior bishop or bishop of Alba and all associated with St Andrews. It appears that St Andrews had replaced Dunkeld as the head church of Alba towards the end of the ninth century and, from then on, the senior bishop or bishop of Alba would be identical to the bishop of St Andrews. In the eleventh century, Maelduin and Fothad, two senior bishops of Alba mentioned in Irish annals, are firmly associated with St Andrews.

In the Church hierarchy, immediately below the bishops were the abbots or heads of individual monasteries. A number of abbots feature in the scarce records that survive about the kingdom of Alba. In the early ninth century, an unbroken succession of abbots of Iona were among the most important clerics in the Gaelic world. The Viking assaults hit Iona hard and led Abbot Cellach to build a refuge at Kells in Ireland in 814. Thereafter the abbots of Iona who feature in the annals were probably infrequent visitors to that island. They were probably resident in Ireland although they still attempted to travel around their extensive *familia* of churches across Ireland and northern Britain. They visited the kingdom of Alba in 818, 829, 849 and 865 but although abbots of Iona are mentioned in 880 and 891 it seems unlikely that these last men visited Alba, let alone Iona itself. There are also references from 865, 873, 965 and 1045 to abbots of Dunkeld. The Life of St Cadroe of Metz also features Abbot Maelrodair, probably of the monastery of St Brigit at Abernethy, who was an adviser to Constantine II. There were other monasteries, including Deer and Loch Leven, which were the recipients of grants of lands and dues. Unfortunately, few of these monasteries are more than names and no information has survived about their abbots.

If there is little information about the abbots, there is almost none about the ordinary priests who formed the backbone of the Church at this time. The priest Bean who sponsored St Cadroe was described as vigilant in prayers and devoted to works of charity, but this description is largely conventional and hardly informative. It is far more interesting that Cadroe himself was educated in the Irish schools of Armagh, although it is made clear that few priests were so well educated at the time. Cadroe's studies apparently included Plato, philosophy, poetry and astronomy and on his return he taught others. This high standard of education is enough to explain his later welcome at Metz.

The monasteries and churches of Alba were maintained through grants of land and donations of goods and wealth, often in kind. The Register of St Andrews Priory preserves in Latin translation some eleventh-century *notitiae* or 'notes' of grants made to St Serf's monastery at Loch Leven in Fife. They were copied into the register from 'an old volume written in the ancient idiom of the Scots', i.e. Gaelic, which arrived at St Andrews when the latter assumed control of Loch Leven in the twelfth century. They include a series of records of grants of land and churches and confirmations of these by three bishops of St Andrews and four kings, including Macbeth and his wife Gruoch and Malcolm III and his wife Margaret. The Book of Deer preserves some original Gaelic *notitiae* from this same period. They record the donations made to St Drostan of Deer by a wide range of people including King Malcolm II, Maelsnechtai,

Mormaer of Moray and Muiredach, son of Morgann, who was possibly *Mormaer* of Buchan. It is perhaps worth considering the generous donations of a single individual Cathal, son of Morgann, perhaps a brother of the *mormaer*:

> Cathal son of Morgann gave *Achad na Cleirich* or 'The Field of the Clerics' to Drostan . . . Cathal 'quenched' his *toiseach*'s dues on the same terms [in return for giving him his goodwill], and gave a banquet for a hundred every Christmas and every Easter to God and to Drostan. Cainneach son of MacDobarchon and Cathal gave Altrie from the cliff of the birch of the river bend as far as the birch between the two Altries. Domnall and Cathal gave Ednie to God and to Drostan. Cainneach and Domnall and Cathal 'quenched' all the grants in favour of God and Drostan from beginning to end free from *mormaer* and *toiseach* till Doomsday and the blessing of the Lord on every *mormaer* and on every *toiseach* who shall comply with it and to their descendants after them.[4]

It was this wealth that enabled the churches to maintain their ability to serve the wider community and to meet their many needs for spiritual and other services.

The relationship between the kings and the Church was considered vital to the well-being of the wider kingdom. The majority of the kings were therefore keen to associate themselves with the Church. In 849 Kenneth I brought the relics of St Columba to Dunkeld in order to associate this key saint with this church and the new kingdom of the Picts and Scots. In 904 and 918 Constantine II carried St Columba's crozier before his army into crucial battles against the heathen Vikings. In 906 Constantine II cemented relations with the Church with a covenant agreed on the Hill of Faith at Scone. In the early 970s Kenneth II founded or expanded a monastery at Brechin. The strong Christian iconography featured on contemporary sculpture is an important reflection of this. The

Dupplin Cross which was erected to commemorate Constantine, son of Fergus proclaims the Christianity of the king and is accompanied by pictures of King David, the biblical king par excellence. The unknown but clearly significant figure who commissioned Sueno's Stone to commemorate an important military victory, was also eager to proclaim his Christianity, and a huge cross covers almost the whole of the opposite face. The relationship between the kings and the Church was therefore close throughout this period. This does not mean, however, that the relationship was entirely uncritical. There were also disputes between the secular and religious authorities. King Idulf had Bishop Fothad exiled to the Isles in the 950s for most of his reign.

The Church played an important role in the society of Alba at this time. It offered an explanation for the state of things in what was a very confusing and frightening world. It provided spiritual solace and uplift through prayer and eventually secured passage into a better world after death. The popularity of Christianity and the cults of its saints appears amply demonstrated by the number of personal names containing the Gaelic elements *Mael* or *Gille* meaning 'servant' combined with the name of Christ or one of his saints. The saints include Brigit, Columba, Michael, Peter and the Virgin Mary. The role of the clergy in this period was to offer prayers for the souls of the dead and for the health and welfare of the living. The significance of the salvation of souls is clear from the frequent references to this. The earliest Scottish charters to Durham include provision for prayers for the souls of dead relatives and for the bodies and souls of the living. The personal gospel owned by Queen Margaret includes a poem about how the book was lost and found again which ends with a blessing:

May the king be saved forever, and his holy queen,
Whose book from out of the river was rescued only now
and great glory be to God, the saviour of this self-same book.[5]

The *notitiae* in The Book of Deer request the blessing of the Lord not only for its benefactors but also for all those who comply with their donations. The scribe of the gospel text itself ends with a request to 'everyone who uses this splendid little book, that they say a blessing for the soul of the wretch who wrote it'.

In relation to the world of the living, The Life of St Cadroe reports that Fochertach and his wife prayed at the shrine of St Columba in Dunkeld for a son and were subsequently blessed with two, including the saint himself. The Book of Deer attributes the foundation of the monastery to the miraculous healing of the son of the local *mormaer,* and the gospels themselves were probably used as a holy relic to heal the sick since they incorporate a Latin mass for the sick: 'The body with the blood of our Lord Jesus Christ be health to you for perpetual life and salvation.' They almost certainly also had an important role in almost every rite of passage in the life of every individual and community, baptism, marriage and death. The *notitiae* in The Book of Deer, quoted above, mention that Cathal provided feasts for 100 people at Christmas and Easter which had a charitable purpose. The Life of St Margaret sets out elaborate rituals for these important festivals, including the feeding of 300 paupers at the royal Court, a larger scale of generosity appropriate to the king.

The Church offered intercession with important saints whose holiness placed them close to Christ and to God himself. They could therefore form a conduit for prayers and admonitions for all sorts of reasons. There were several categories of saints, headed by Columba and Andrew who competed for seniority during this period. The start of the period shows Columba in highest favour with the early kings, including Kenneth I, who brought his relics to Dunkeld. The name Malcolm or *Mael Coluim,* which means 'servant of Columba', was held by several kings. In 865 the Bishop of Alba was also Abbot of Dunkeld. In 904 Constantine II called on Columba's aid in his contest with the heathen Vikings. In the later period Andrew appears to become more important perhaps from the time of

Constantine II who retired to the monastery of St Andrews at Kinrimont in Fife. The later bishops of Alba were usually associated with St Andrews. There were also more local saints – Drostan at Deer, Serf at Loch Leven – with local churches dedicated to them. They had an important role in encouraging attendance at church, attracting pilgrims and in securing grants and donations towards the upkeep of their churches. The Life of St Margaret speaks of the crowds of religious people or pilgrims drawn to St Andrews, which were sufficient to warrant the provision of a regular ferry service to take them across the Forth at Queensferry.

The Church also offered things other than spiritual succour and health and welfare services, including administrative services based on the literacy of its priests in Gaelic or Latin. They produced Latin gospel books which formed the basis for worship, including The Book of Deer, Queen Margaret's Gospels and others now lost. They were also responsible for preserving the records of their society. These included king-lists, genealogies, annals, chronicles, records of grants and laws and poems. The few written records which actually survive from this period and which provide all our information about it were almost certainly maintained by clerics. The same men were probably also responsible for the transmission of reports about events in Alba to the wider world in Ireland, England and on the Continent. In this way the Church of Alba managed to preserve every scrap of information about the kingdom that survives to this day.

The Church in Alba has often been considered moribund during this period. It is difficult to know, however, if this impression, which is based on fairly limited evidence, is well-founded or not. The main source is The Life of St Margaret, which has a vested interest in portraying the Church in this way. The author of this work was clearly determined to portray his heroine as the saviour of the Scottish Church. He therefore had an incentive to exaggerate the faults of that organisation and to minimise its successes. In fact, he reports that 'she saw many things in Scotland were done contrary to the rule of faith and the holy custom of the universal church.' This statement, however, suggests that the failings of the Church in Alba amounted to no more than the preservation of ancient traditions that had been discarded elsewhere in Europe. The 'false customs' that Margaret sought to reform were exactly of this kind. They related to different observance of the Lenten fast, failure to take communion at Easter, different practices for celebrating the mass and neglect of Sabbath observance. The faults were regarded as serious by Margaret and other reformers, but were a sign of the isolation and conservatism of the Church rather than any fundamental decline. There is no mention of major faults within the Church itself, for example clerical celibacy, simony, vagrancy and other abuses of clerical life. This does not indicate a decadent or moribund Church and nothing in Margaret's reforms suggests this was the case.

If The Life of St Margaret is discounted, the suggestion that the Church of Alba was moribund seems to depend on a lack of evidence. There are few literary or other written records of any kind which survive from this period. There are similarly few architectural or monumental survivals. This does not prove, however, that such never existed in the first place. It is always dangerous to build arguments from a lack of data. Indeed, the zeal of the twelfth-century reformers who transformed the Church under King David I was itself responsible for most of the losses. They were so enamoured with their improvements that they disposed of old texts, buildings and monuments without a second thought. The evidence that remains about the early Church is therefore sketchy at best, and for that reason must be used with caution in any arguments. For example, a great deal has been made of the poor standard of the illuminations in The Book of Deer compared to the spectacular images in the earlier Book of Kells. This is hardly fair since both are individual works of art produced in completely different circumstances. It is simply not possible to judge whether either is representative of the rest of their kind. It is possible that other works produced at the time of The Book of Deer were fully equal to The Book of Kells. What can actually be argued from the limited evidence available?

A great deal of attention has focused on the few pieces of negative evidence which it is claimed proves the poor state of the Church in Alba. The focus has been on the supposed secularisation of church offices. This was an intermittent problem for all churches in the early medieval period and later. The hierarchy of the Church was after all recruited from the secular nobility and this brought a constant danger that family interest might conflict with the interests of the Church. St Cadroe was a member of the nobility, who had trained for war and been expected to inherit the family land before he became a priest. He proved able to put the interests of the Church before those of family, although not without conflict, but others were not. The detractors of the Church point to a vacancy in the succession to the bishopric of St Andrews towards the end of the eleventh century but there were similar vacancies in other countries too. There are perhaps more solid grounds for concern about the apparent secularisation of the abbots of Dunkeld. In 865 and 873 there are records of abbots who appear to be standard religious figures, but in 965 the Scottish Chronicle reports that Abbot Duncan perished in the Battle of Duncrub. The chronicler makes no remark about his presence or involvement. He may simply have been there to offer moral support but even if he had been involved in the fighting this would not necessarily have been out of place at the time. In Ireland abbots regularly participated in battles, some of which were conflicts between monastic communities. In the eleventh century, another abbot of Dunkeld, Crinan married a woman called Bethoc and their son became King Duncan I. He was later killed in battle at Dunkeld in 1045, possibly protecting his grandsons from Macbeth. He also is not an unusual figure for this period, either as a nobleman of Alba or as a church official in north-west Europe, but by the next century his lifestyle would be viewed as increasingly unnacceptable amid the new reforms. The general picture of the Church of Alba is not perfect by any means, but neither is it at variance with contemporary evidence from elsewhere, including Ireland and England.

There are also some positive indications about the Church in Alba with an important reform movement prominent in the monasteries. The *Celi De* – 'culdee' or 'servants of God' – movement had commenced in Ireland at the end of the eighth century. It was an attempt to return to the roots of Irish monasticism and emphasised a more ascetic monastic life with a focus on poverty, fasting and prayer. It looked back to the early saints and especially to those who retreated to islands for contemplation and prayer. Exactly when this movement crossed the sea to Alba is unknown, but the fact that it did so suggests that things were not ideal but that a willingness to change existed there too. The main culdee centre in Alba was at Loch Leven in Fife but others are known to have existed at St Andrews, Brechin and Abernethy. This reform movement appears to have been welcomed by the kings and senior bishops, who supported it with grants of lands, churches and rights. The *notitiae* in the Register of St Andrews Priory are a record of the grants made to the culdees of Loch Leven during the eleventh century. It is also possible that new construction at some important church sites was related to this movement, including the addition of round towers at Brechin and Abernethy. It has been suggested that the early fervour of this movement had been lost by the eleventh century and that by then the culdees of St Andrews and Brechin were little more than secular clerks. This was the inevitable fate of all ascetic reforms in time and does not mean that it had not been full-blooded in its early years. The culdees at Loch Leven were still considered worthy enough to receive grants from no less a zealot than Queen Margaret.

This entire social hierarchy, both secular and religious, was supported by the farmers. They produced the food surplus that provided the *cain* and *coinmed* for the *toiseachs*, *mormaers* and kings and for the priests, abbots and bishops of the Church too. It was their hard work on the farms spread across the lowlands and uplands of Alba that supported the rest of society. The agricultural economy was based on a mix of arable and pastoral farming. The arable farms were mainly concentrated in the eastern lowlands along the east coast and produced the corn and malt for bread and ale. The pastoral farms were situated in the uplands to the west and produced the horses, cattle, sheep and pigs that provided transport, meat, clothes, milk and cheese. The family that fostered St Cadroe were pastoral farmers who bred sheep and horses. The importance of this agricultural basis for the economy is confirmed by the eagerness to capture domestic animals and slaves during raids on enemy territory. In 1077 King Malcolm III captured the cattle of Maelsnechtai, *Mormaer* of Moray and hence deprived him of a great part of his resources, severely weakening him for a number of years. In 950 Malcolm I 'seized a multitude of people and many herds of cattle' from England and in 1070 Malcolm III returned from Northumbria with large numbers of stolen cattle and human captives. The livestock would add to the resources of the pastoral farmers while the slaves would provide agricultural labourers to work in the arable fields and to herd the livestock. In addition to their agricultural importance, the families of these farmers also produced the ordinary men and their equipment for the 'common army' of the kingdom and the majority of the worshippers that 'filled the church' as described by The Life of St Cadroe of Metz.

The kingdom of Alba was in many ways similar to many other early medieval kingdoms in western Europe in respect of its basic agricultural economy, its basic social structure, its Christian religion and its organisation for war. It was less advanced than its southern neighbour England, which was not only larger but also had many towns and a monetary economy at this time. It was more on a par with Ireland and Wales, where towns and a monetary economy were largely absent. It also had certain differences, however, from all its neighbours which would prove an advantage during the period covered in this book.

The kingdom of Alba was a single kingdom with one ruler on the model of England, but unlike Ireland or Wales. This political unity meant that its kings were more able to concentrate their energies on outward expansion rather than dissipating them in internal conflicts. As a result, the kings of Alba, like their English counterparts, were able to extend their territorial control by absorbing Strathclyde and part of English Northumbria. In contrast, contemporary Irish kings and Welsh princes still had to establish predominance over other independent kingdoms and so were involved in almost continuous power struggles. They often defeated a number of rival kingdoms only to find themselves opposed by others. It was rarely possible for them to subdue these other kingdoms for long enough to embark on more than short defensive or offensive campaigns against others, for example the Vikings or the English.

The kingdom of Alba also had uniquely mixed cultural origins compared to England, Ireland and Wales. It was now Gaelic in language, although this may conceal an initial bilingual phase, and it was superficially Gaelic in culture also, although, as noted above, it contained important elements from Pictish culture. It had been formed, not by the elimination of the Picts, but by their gradual assimilation. It was also in the process of assimilating the Britons of Strathclyde who were now subordinate to the kings of Alba and would fall increasingly under their influence. In contrast, the English, Irish and Welsh were, broadly speaking, more monocultural in the sense that they largely shared a single language and a related culture. It is true that England now included an element of Viking culture, but this was a closely related Germanic culture which was absorbed and assimilated fairly quickly.

The hybrid origin of the kingdom of Alba would be an important factor in its subsequent success. It would soon demonstrate its ability to assimilate other cultural elements from Strathclyde, Northumbria and, subsequently, Normandy with what appeared to be relative ease. The kings do not appear to have enforced a cultural norm on their subjects at this time but rather to have adopted their own model for others to follow. The important factor in recruitment to the kingdom appears to have been loyalty to the kingship rather than to any particular culture. It seems that this practice allowed the kings to adopt an independent cultural stance that drew in new subjects without excluding those who were not initially members of this culture. In contrast, the relatively unified cultures of neighbouring England, Ireland and Wales demanded a certain amount of conformity from others. This seems to have resulted in tension with outsiders, whose different culture was viewed as a threat especially if they assumed positions of power. In the period following the Norman Conquest, England, Wales and Ireland would all resist the Normans and their military aggression with varying success. Initially the kingdom of Alba appeared to follow this same path but it was able to switch to a policy of introduction and absorption under the leadership of its own kings. This controlled process and its previous history as a multicultural state allowed the kingdom of Alba to weather the Norman storm with relative ease.

3

A Scottish Constantine

Fortunately for the future of the new kingdom of Alba, a truly remarkable individual succeeded to the kingship in 900 on the death of Donald II. This was Constantine II, son of Aed or *Castantin mac Aeda*, Donald's cousin, who was at the time a relatively mature man of at least 22 and probably nearer 30. He would have been able to observe the activities of his predecessor and to learn something about what was required to rule. He certainly proved extremely able and a real survivor, going on to reign for forty-three years before retiring peacefully to a monastery to live out his final years before his death at a great age in 952. He would not meet an unnatural death in battle or at the hands of a rival and even in retirement was still able to offer advice to his successor. It was an extraordinary achievement at this time, when the lives of kings were often nasty, brutish and short, for an individual to dominate the political scene for more than half a century in this way.

In the year 900, however, all this lay in the future, and the young King Constantine II was immediately faced with a particularly dangerous Viking threat. The later Scottish sources claim that Vikings had killed his predecessor at Dunnottar, although the contemporary Annals of Ulster fail to mention this. They may have been seasonal raiders from the northern earldom of Orkney. The problem facing Constantine II would be of much greater significance. In 902 the Irish kings Mael Finnia of Brega and Cerball of Leinster defeated and expelled the Vikings of Dublin from Ireland. They were forced to abandon many of their ships and seek refuge elsewhere, most probably in the nearby Isle of Man. It was from this temporary but relatively secure refuge that they sought other opportunities for plunder around the Irish Sea. In 903, they launched attacks against Wales and north-west Mercia. It was probably also at this time that the colonisation of Galloway and north-west England by these Irish Vikings commenced. The later twelfth-century account contained in *Historia de Sancto Cuthberto*, or 'The History of St Cuthbert', reports the flight of an Englishman called Alfred, son of Brihtwulf, into the area around Durham from 'west of the mountains' during the episcopate of Bishop Cuthheard, which ran from 900 to 915. In the 870s Olaf had successfully exploited the Clyde Estuary to capture the fortress of Dumbarton and ravage Strathclyde and Fortriu. It seems likely that this profitable expedition of thirty years before influenced his descendants.

In 903, Ivar, grandson of the Ivar who died in 853, followed the same path up the Clyde past Dumbarton and turned north to invade Alba. He led a force, according to the near-contemporary Scottish Chronicle, made up of three large groups which plundered the sacred shrine of St Columba at Dunkeld. In the following year, 904, Ivar either returned or, perhaps having overwintered in Alba, resumed his raiding activities in hopes of repeating the successes of his predecessors here. One Irish source reports the death in 904 of an Aed, King of the Picts, who is otherwise unknown but who may perhaps have been a Viking puppet set up to rule in Fortriu. The Vikings were, however, opposed on this occasion by Constantine II and the men of Alba, who had been given time to organise. In preparation for the fighting the Fragmentary Annals report that Constantine fortified the morale of his troops by mustering them at St Columba's shrine at Dunkeld beforehand. There they took communion, fasted, prayed for the saint's intercession and distributed alms for the poor, no doubt including those who had suffered at the hands of the Vikings a year earlier. This astute action allowed Constantine not only to provide religious sanction for his army in its fight against the heathen Vikings but also to highlight the damage inflicted on the shrine. The men of Alba advanced to meet their opponents, fuelled with a desire for revenge. St Columba's crozier, a sacred relic that had apparently escaped the Viking raiders, was borne in the van of their army by clerics as a talisman. They encountered the Viking army in Strathearn and resoundingly defeated them, killing Ivar himself and inflicting a great slaughter on his men. They had inflicted a Christian retribution on the heathens in St Columba's name. Thereafter St Columba's crozier would be named *Cathbuiad* or 'battle-winner'. It would go on to bless the efforts of the men of Alba in future years. This great victory by Constantine would prove decisive in that the Irish Vikings never again attempted any serious intervention in Alba.

The successful elimination of this early threat to his rule effectively secured Constantine's throne and silenced any internal opposition. It also provided the Vikings and any other potential enemies abroad with a warning not to meddle with the new King of Alba. In the peaceful lull that followed this great victory Constantine sought to reinforce his links with the Church. In 906 he met with Cellach, Bishop of St Andrews, who was presumably now chief bishop of Alba in place of the bishop of Dunkeld. They met on the Hill of Faith near the royal monastery of Scone, which appears to be the site now known as the Moot Hill where later kings were enthroned. At this important royal centre King Constantine pledged to support the Christian faith in Alba and to protect the laws and rights of the Christian Church. This important agreement, which is recorded in some detail in the Scottish Chronicle, reaffirmed the already strong links between the king of Alba and the Church. It was an important part of the response by the men of Alba to the depredations of their heathen Viking enemies. This close relationship between Church and State would provide a key binding element in the development of the future enlarged kingdom.

In the period after Constantine's victory in 904, while the immediate Viking threat had been removed from Alba itself, the wider Viking threat remained. It was a common danger faced by the various Christian powers in Britain. In the period around 903, a Viking force led by Ingimund raided Anglesey and briefly seized control of Llanfaes. In response Cadel son of Rhodri collected an army and drove him out after some tough fighting. Ingimund then looked for a weaker target and occupied the Wirrall Peninsula in Cheshire. Aethelred, Lord of the Mercians, had initially permitted this occupation of a largely deserted area in the extreme north-west of Mercia on the basis that these Vikings would protect this region against others. It appeared clear subsequently that Ingimund intended to introduce more Vikings and occupy the deserted Roman site at Chester. In response, in 907, the Mercians led by Lady Aethelflaed, according to the Fragmentary Annals, but more probably by her husband, Lord Aethelred, collected a large army and garrisoned Chester. This effectively pre-empted Ingimund's plan and forced him to attack the fortress. The annalist provides a colourful account of subsequent events, describing how a fierce Viking assault on the fortress met a mixture of well-organised Mercian resistance and treachery within the Viking forces.

Following their expulsion from Dublin, the series of Viking failures, in Wales in 903, in Alba in 904 and in Mercia in 907, must have left them frustrated. They had proved unable to exploit a range of opportunities and must by now have been extremely short of resources. This was not to be the end of their marauding, however, since fate would soon present them with a new opening. In 910 Aethelred of Mercia defeated the Danes of York at Tettenhall, killing two kings and large numbers of their followers. This disaster for the Danes opened up a new field of opportunity for the Irish Vikings and they were quick to exploit it. If the dating of his coinage can be trusted, Ragnall, another grandson of Ivar, sailed with a large fleet for Northumbria in about 911. He probably travelled via the Ribble or possibly the Mersey rather than across the Forth–Clyde Isthmus. The usefulness of the latter route for the Vikings had probably been reduced following the defeat suffered by Ivar in 904. Ragnall captured York, killed or drove out the remaining Danish leaders and assumed control of York and their other conquests in northern England.

The seizure of York and its environs by Ragnall provided an important extension of power for the exiled Irish Vikings. It secured them control of the wealth accumulated over years of raiding and trading by their former Danish rivals. It provided access to the North Sea trading network with close links to their Scandinavian homelands, southern England and the wider Continent. The occupation of York provided the Irish Vikings under Ragnall with a secure base and ample resources for future operations, including a return to power in Ireland. There is some unique evidence of the wealth of York at precisely this time. In 1840 a lead-lined wooden chest, containing a huge hoard of silver was discovered buried near Cuerdale in Lancashire. It consisted of around 7,000 silver coins, large numbers of silver ingots and a great deal of hack-silver or fragments of silver jewellery. At around 40kg in weight, it was by a large margin the largest single hoard of Viking silver ever found outside Russia. The composition of the silver coins helps to date the hoard to around 905 and to associate it with the Vikings and more specifically with those from Dublin or, more probably, from York. The location of the find at Cuerdale on the Ribble valley route that runs between Dublin and York confirms this. The sheer number of coins minted in nearby Viking York that feature in the Cuerdale Hoard, at around 5,000 out of 7,000 or about 70 per cent of the total, would seem to favour a York origin.

A large number of possible scenarios could be devised to explain the deposition of this hoard, but none can be conclusively proved. The most that can be suggested is that the hoard was almost certainly not lost but rather deliberately concealed in circumstances of political uncertainty. A hoard of silver on this scale must have belonged either to an extremely rich individual or, more probably, to a wealthy group of people. In normal circumstances, it would have been kept at a fortified location like York or Dublin and, when in transit, it would have been accompanied by a large escort to protect it. It was almost certainly buried at Cuerdale while in transit since there is no obvious secure place nearby. If it had been accompanied on its journey by a large escort, it seems likely that someone would then have survived whatever emergency caused its burial to recover it. Instead, it was apparently accompanied by a smaller group, perhaps in the hope that its passage would go unnoticed. It was then buried when this small group encountered unforeseen problems and never recovered since none of the group survived whatever danger they faced. The hoard was therefore permanently lost to its owner or owners.

The triumph of Ragnall in capturing York and its wealth must have rung alarm bells across the rest of Britain about the danger presented by this new and aggressive Viking power. In southern Britain, the surviving Christian powers of Mercia and Wessex had come together in around 880 to form an alliance against the Danish Vikings. This alliance had brought rich rewards in the form of major defeats for the Danes of East Anglia at Holme in 903 and the Danes of York at Tettenhall in 910. In the face of this revived threat from York, it would perhaps not be surprising to find that a similar solution was tried in the north also, and indeed, it appears that the Mercians were looking for allies in the north at around this time. The admittedly late and highly coloured Fragmentary Annals contains some saga material that appears to confirm this. It records that 'Queen' Aethelflaed of Mercia made peace with the men of Alba and the Britons of Strathclyde so that whenever the Vikings attacked her they would assist her and vice versa. It goes on to relate that 'the men of Alba and the Britons fell upon the towns of the Northmen and destroyed and pillaged them.'

In 913 the Annals of Ulster record the death of Eadwulf 'king of the Saxons of the North' who was *Ealdorman* of English Northumbria. He was succeeded by his son Ealdred but his demise probably encouraged Ragnall, the new ruler of York to intervene in this region. According to the History of St Cuthbert, Ragnall invaded English Northumbria, defeated the English, who lost the best of their army, including Alfred, son of Brihtwulf, a tenant of St Cuthbert's church, and expelled *Ealdorman* Ealdred from his lands. The exiled Ealdred fled north with his brother Uhtred to seek refuge at the court of King Constantine II of Alba. This event is not dated but is indicated to have taken place at some point during the episcopate of Bishop Cuthheard of St Cuthbert's church at Chester-le-Street, who died in 915. It therefore happened at some point between 913 when Ealdred succeeded his father and 915 but cannot at present be more securely dated. The victorious Ragnall proceeded to allocate estates in English Northumbria to his followers, including former lands of St Cuthbert's church. In the process two Viking lords called Olaf Ball and Skuli were given lands at Eden and Billingham respectively, which had previously belonged to St Cuthbert. This seizure of church property by the heathen Vikings was greatly resented by St Cuthbert's clerks, who composed an edifying miracle story. This attributed Olaf's subsequent early death to the retribution of their aggrieved saint, as a lesson to future robbers who failed to respect the church.

In 914 Ragnall was faced with the threat from a new Danish fleet from Brittany under Ottar and Harold. This fleet had raided along both shores of the Bristol Channel earlier in the year. It had been defeated and Harold had been killed by the combined forces of King Edward of Wessex and Lady Aethelflaed of Mercia. The Danes had then turned northwards under the command of Ottar to contest control of the Irish Sea region with Ragnall and his Norwegians. Bard, son of Ottar, who had presumably replaced Harold, attempted to seize the Isle of Man but was opposed by the forces of Ragnall.

The result was a naval battle off the Isle of Man which ended with the death of Bard and the complete defeat of his force. Ragnall had emerged from this initial contest victorious but the danger was not over. The rest of the Danish fleet led by Ottar occupied Waterford in southern Ireland and proceeded to pillage widely in Munster for the following two years. The presence of the Danish fleet in this region, taking spoils that should have been his, could not be tolerated by Ragnall. In 917 Ragnall and his brother, Sihtric *Caech* or 'One-eye', moved to restore their own power and influence in Ireland and drive out these Danish interlopers. A period of sharp conflict followed before Ragnall finally seized Waterford and Sihtric reoccupied Dublin. This internecine fighting between rival fleets, although ultimately successful, kept Ragnall preoccupied with Ireland for several years, leaving his kingdom at York vulnerable to attack.

In 918 King Constantine II of Alba was ready to exploit the opportunity presented by this internecine fighting to intervene in English Northumbria. He did so, partly to assist the refugee Ealdred, to whom he may now have been connected by marriage (see Chapter 4, p. 91), but partly to increase his own power and influence. He was aware that Ragnall was preoccupied with events in Ireland and assumed, reasonably enough, that he would be unable to return before Constantine had secured his aims. In the absence of Ragnall and his forces, York and his other northern English conquests were more vulnerable than ever before. This fact was recognised by the men of York themselves, who apparently sought to take advantage of Ragnall's absence to surrender the city to Lady Aethelflaed of Mercia. To Constantine this must have seemed too good an opportunity to miss. He saw the prospect of securing control over English Northumbria in Ragnall's absence. If he could do so he would have a client region under *Ealdorman* Ealdred on his southern borders. He may even have considered the mouthwatering prospect of securing control of the rich commercial centre at York itself.

In 918 Constantine therefore took advantage of Ragnall's preoccupation in Ireland to advance into English Northumbria. He marched south under the protection of the *Cathbuaid*, the same crozier of St Columba that had brought him victory against the Vikings in 904. He was accompanied by the Britons of Strathclyde and the brothers Ealdred and Uhtred and was probably joined on the way south by the men of English Northumbria. He may have enjoyed some initial success on this expedition since the Fragmentary Annals mention 'Scots and Britons falling on the settlements of the foreigners' at about this time. The location of the subsequent battle at Corbridge suggests that Constantine had penetrated as far as the River Tyne at the very least. In addition to this northern pressure, the Vikings of York were also under pressure from the Mercians to the south. In 917 Lady Aethelflaed of Mercia had occupied Derby and, in 918, captured Leicester. Indeed, it is possible that this coordinated campaign was a product of their alliance against the Vikings. In the absence of their king and faced with the threat of war on two fronts, some of the local Danes approached Lady Aethelflaed offering to provide sworn pledges to submit to her direction. They probably hoped to avoid outright conquest by some form of submission. It is possible they made a similar approach to Constantine, but in the light of his military success it is likely that he rejected them out of hand.

This dire emergency and the open threat to York itself finally forced Ragnall to return from Ireland. In 918 a large army led by Ragnall and the earls Ottar and Gragabai (Krakabein) landed in northern England and came up against the men of Alba and their allies at Corbridge on the River Tyne in northern England. The Annals of Ulster include a fulsome report on the event as follows:

. . . Ragnall, King of the Danes and the jarls Ottar and Krakabein forsook Ireland and proceeded afterwards against the men of Alba. The men of Alba, moreover, moved against them and they

71

met on the bank of the Tyne in northern England. The heathens formed themselves into four battalions: a battalion with Gothfrith, grandson of Ivar, a battalion with the two *jarls* and a battalion with the young lords. There was also a battalion in ambush with Ragnall, which the men of Alba did not see. The men of Alba routed the three battalions which they saw, and made a very great slaughter of the heathens, including Ottar and Krakabein. Ragnall, however, then attacked in the rear of the men of Alba and made a slaughter of them, although none of their kings or *mormaers* was cut off. Nightfall caused the battle to be broken off.[6]

It would seem from this account that it was nightfall that saved Constantine from possible disaster. He took heavy losses to his men but Ragnall's forces had also suffered severe casualties.

It is interesting to note the tactics employed by Ragnall in this engagement. He appears to have kept back a large reserve under his own command, ready to intervene at a crucial stage in the fighting. It was this precaution that seems to have prevented Constantine from securing a complete victory and allowed Ragnall to secure a draw. It may possibly have been a tried and tested tactic or it may have been attempted following a recent incident in Ireland. On 22 August 917, Ragnall's forces were engaged by Niall *Glundub*, King of Ireland and his army near Cashel in Munster. The Viking army was apparently on the brink of defeat in this encounter when Ragnall arrived late with reinforcements and swung the battle back in his favour. This incident may have provided the inspiration for Ragnall's deliberate use of a similar tactic in Northumbria or it may be an earlier example of its use. In either case it shows a certain tactical flair and refutes the common idea that medieval warfare was always little more than a slogging match.

It should be noted that this account assumes that only one battle took place at Corbridge during this period. It is about time that the idea that two different battles were fought at Corbridge, between the same opponents and within a few years of each other, was finally discarded. This notion appears to have gained widespread acceptance on the back of Wainwright's article of 1950 entitled 'The Battles at Corbridge'. Unfortunately, the account offered by Wainwright relies on the misinterpretation of a late source which contains few reliable dates and does not offer secure evidence to support his argument. It also ignores his own advice that the invention of two or three different Ragnalls to reconcile complex sources from this period was an 'unnecessary complication'. This advice is very sound and should be applied when considering what actually occurred at Corbridge. If there is no solid evidence for two battles, why introduce this unnecessary complication?

A closer examination of the sources available makes it clear that there was, in fact, only one battle at Corbridge. This is the encounter described so vividly by the reliable Ulster annalist under 918 and quoted above. The Scottish Chronicle, composed around 975, also mentions only a single battle between Constantine and Ragnall, which also took place in 918 on 'the moors near the Tyne'. It seems indisputable that this is the same battle as that mentioned by the Ulster annalist. 'The moors near the River Tyne' is a fairly accurate description of the area around Corbridge. The Newcastle Tyne is such a well known landmark that there is no need to invoke the obscure Haddington Tyne simply to convert this into a separate event. The mention of a battle at Corbridge in northern English sources, including The History of St Cuthbert, supports this identification. They do not, contrary to the opinion of Wainwright and others, provide a secure date for this Corbridge battle. They only suggest that it occurred at an unspecified time after some events that took place during the episcopate of Bishop Cuthheard, who died in 915. They do not claim that the battle itself took place during Cuthheard's episcopate and it could therefore have happened in 918. This removes the main plank of

Wainwright's argument and means that there is no reason whatever not to accept that this battle at Corbridge is that reported by the Annals of Ulster in 918.

The fact that the three different sources that mention this battle take a different view of the result is not uncommon. It should not be taken as support for more than one battle. It is interesting nevertheless to note the differing views on the results of the Battle of Corbridge. The Ulster annals are fairly clear that this hard-fought encounter was a victory for Ragnall, though a pyrrhic one. The Fragmentary Annals and the Scottish Chronicle suggest a victory for the Scots. The History of St Cuthbert reports a defeat for the Scots even though this means by implication a defeat for *Ealdorman* Ealdred. It is clear that the spin doctors have been at work. What can a modern historian make of all this? It appears that one result of this encounter was that *Ealdorman* Ealdred and his brother were able to recover control over English Northumbria. In 920 The Anglo-Saxon Chronicle records that Ealdred participated in a submission to King Edward, the ruler of a newly united England. He did so alongside Constantine II and Ragnall of York. It is not, however, clear whether he did so as an independent ruler, which seems unlikely in view of his position, squeezed between his two more powerful neighbours. It seems most likely that he was a client of Constantine, who had probably secured his restoration following the clash with Ragnall at Corbridge in 918.

In the aftermath of the Battle of Corbridge there were a number of important changes in the political map of the British Isles. In December 918, King Edward of Wessex assumed control of Mercia following the deposition of his young niece Aelfwynn, daughter of Lady Aethelflaed. This brought an enormous increase in his power and made him, for the first time, an important figure in northern Britain. He now ruled an area that extended north to the Mersey and to the borders of the territory of King Ragnall of York. On 14 September 919 Sihtric *Caech*, King of Dublin and brother of Ragnall of York, defeated and killed Niall *Glundub*, King of Ireland in a battle at Islandbridge near Dublin. This victory temporarily improved the position of the Viking rulers of Dublin and York. The combined result of these events was to undermine the partial success achieved by Constantine in 918. The position of his new ally and subordinate *Ealdorman* Ealdred of English Northumbria was now potentially threatened by a Viking revival and the appearance of a new English power in the north. The potential challenge to King Constantine's new authority in this region was clear.

In the following year, 920, King Edward appears to have made an initial foray into northern politics. He was at Bakewell in Derbyshire building a *burh* near the northern borders of Mercia. He probably used the opportunity offered by his physical presence in the north to establish a firm basis for future relations with his new neighbours. The Anglo-Saxon Chronicle reports: 'And then the King of the Scots and all the people of the Scots, and Ragnall and the sons of Eadwulf and all who live in Northumbria both English and Danish, Norsemen and others, and also the king of the Strathclyde Welsh and all the Strathclyde Welsh chose him [Edward] as father and lord.' It is clear, however, that this interpretation of events is an English one and it is likely that matters were viewed rather differently by the other parties involved. It was probably seen from a Scottish or Viking perspective as a meeting intended to reach mutual agreement on boundaries and spheres of influence in the region. King Edward was now an extremely powerful ruler, but he had yet to demonstrate this power to his northern neighbours. Until he had done so there was no pressing reason for these men to submit to his authority in the way indicated by the Chronicle account.

It is far more likely that the Chronicle offers a carefully slanted interpretation of negotiations between Edward and his new northern neighbours. He would probably have sought to test the waters before seeing how far he could push each of them. He had more scope to coerce Ragnall of York, who was on his immediate border and most exposed to attack. He might have sought to exploit a common sense of English identity and a possible resentment of Scottish influence in his approach to the English of Northumbria. On his part, *Ealdorman* Ealdred may have welcomed closer ties with Edward in an effort to reduce the influence of both Constantine and Ragnall in his land. It is less likely that the Scots, who were more distant and had not yet felt the impact of southern English power, were prepared to submit in the same way. It is perhaps more likely that Edward's approach to them was to seek the confirmation or renewal of the earlier alliance struck between Alba and Mercia in 907. The Chronicle seems to indicate that English Northumbria and Strathclyde were independent powers when they submitted to Edward, but it is perhaps just as likely that they were subordinate to Constantine, or possibly even Ragnall, and took part as his subjects. It is important to remember that things are not necessarily what they seem in this source.

There would be no opportunity for King Constantine to assess the immediate implications of the creation of a united kingdom of the English before a series of deaths changed the position once again. In 921 King Ragnall of York died and was succeeded by his brother Sihtric *Caech*, who had been expelled from Dublin the year before. In the aftermath of this, Sihtric devoted his resources to recovering Dublin for his brother Gothfrith and had little time for affairs in northern Britain. In due course, Gothfrith was restored and entered Dublin later in the same year and commenced a series of raids across Ireland. This raiding absorbed all of Gothfrith's attention and resources, including perhaps the resources of his brother in York. In 924 King Edward of England himself died and was eventually succeeded after a period of internal dispute by his eldest son Athelstan. It appears that Athelstan had been raised at the Mercian court of his aunt Lady Aethelflaed and therefore, arguably, had a better understanding of northern affairs than his father.

In 926 Athelstan established an alliance with Sihtric of York, who was baptised as a pre-requisite for his entry into Christian society and subsequently married to Athelstan's daughter Edith. This brought Sihtric into the English King's circle and provided the latter with some influence at his court. It may also have offered Sihtric some reassurance against English aggression, at least in the short-term. This alliance, however, was a much more ambiguous arrangement as far as Constantine of Alba was concerned. It could be seen as another weapon being used by his English ally to keep the men of York subdued, but it could also represent a potential threat to Alba itself. If Athelstan strengthened his links with York, he might subsequently choose to ally with York against Alba. If this happened, Athelstan would pose a threat to Constantine himself and to his influence over English Northumbria and possibly even Strathclyde. It was a potentially dangerous departure from the previous hostility between the English kingdoms and the Vikings of York.

In 927 Sihtric of York died prematurely and his brother Gothfrith briefly abandoned Dublin in order to succeed him. The new ruler Gothfrith had lost his own son Halfdan only a year before and had surrendered control of Dublin when he left for York. He would rule as King of York for little more than six months. Immediately, King Athelstan exploited his relationship with Sihtric and Gothfrith's weakness as the newly installed king to intervene in York. He expelled Gothfrith from York, according to one version of The Anglo-Saxon Chronicle, and assumed direct control. A contemporary Latin poem in praise of King Athelstan, which celebrates his occupation of York in 927, confirms that King Constantine was still an ally of the English King at this point in time:

> Direct first of all our best wishes
> To the Queen, the prince,
> The distinguished *ealdormen* as well,
> The arm-bearing *thegns*.

Whom he [Athelstan] now rules with this
England made whole;
King Athelstan lives
Glorious through his deeds!

He, with Sihtric having died,
In such circumstances arms for battle
The army of the English
Throughout all Britain.
Constantine, King of the Scots,
Hastens to Britain:
By supporting the King of the English
Loyal in his service.[7]

The English occupation of York was quickly followed by Athelstan bringing under his rule, as the Chronicle has it, 'all the kings who were in this island', including Constantine and *Ealdorman* Ealdred of Northumbria. As in 920, the language of the Chronicle entry carries a highly charged political meaning. It deliberately seeks to exaggerate Athelstan's power and status. For example, the Chronicle suggests that these rulers had to 'renounce idolatry' despite the fact that most were actually Christian. This statement was clearly designed to damage their reputations in comparison with that of Athelstan.

The Chronicle goes on to say that Athelstan and these other rulers 'established peace with pledge and oaths in the place which is called Eamont on 12 July.' This seems to reflect what actually happened better than the rest of the entry. It appears that Athelstan met his new neighbours at Eamont Bridge with the object of reaching agreement about their common borders, following his recent occupation of York. In the Chronicle report, Constantine of Alba is mentioned but the ruler of Strathclyde is not, even though Eamont is on the border of Strathclyde rather than Alba itself. This perhaps

Dupplin Cross, Perthshire – a memorial to King Constantine, son of Fergus. (*Crown Copyright: Royal Commission on the Ancient and Historic Monuments of Scotland*)

Detail of infantry soldiers from the Dupplin Cross, Perthshire. *(Photo: W.E. Walker)*

Archway, probably from the royal palace at Forteviot where King Kenneth I MacAlpin died. *(National Museums of Scotland)*

St Columba's Shrine, Iona – an early target for the Vikings. *(Crown Copyright: Royal Commission on the Ancient and Historic Monuments of Scotland)*

Above and facing page: Pages from The Book of Deer, with Gaelic notes in the margin recording benefactions to the monastery. *(By permission of the Syndics of Cambridge University Library MS. Ii.6.32 folios 4v and 5r)*

Ri autem xp̄i ge
natio sic erat
cum ēēt disponsata ma
tēr eíus maria ioseph
antequam ̄ uenirent
inuenta ē in utero habēi
r̄ de sp̄u s̄co · ioseph autem
uir eíus cum ēēt homo iur
tur ⁊ nolet eam traduchī
uoluit occultē dimittēē
eum hēc autem eo cogitante
ecce angelus d̄ni in somnis
apparuit h dicēur ioseph
fili dauid noli timēē acci
pēē mariam coniugēn tua
qꝫ enim ēc ea nascetur de sp̄u
ēc ⁊ pariet autem filiū ⁊ uoca
bis no ē ihm ipse ẜ saluū facies

Robard colb[...]
in monnen[...]
buchan te[...]
ua ⁊ gen ga[...]
uara aben[...]
phurcc
⁊ donnca[...]
mc̄ sidug cor[...]
rech clenui[...]
morgainn[...]
nalnuhedbe[...]
⁊ca ni diei[...]
in norten[...]
⁊ mac col[...]
cilli ⁊ nece[...]
daua[...]pta[...]
onalnulib[...]
dolaudib an[...]
cūnit cēin[...]
dabach do[...]
inchindad[...]
gaidmand[...]
caibh alba[...]
cucodemn[...]
⁊a⁊ind cel[...]
laib ter hu[...]
broceinui oc[...]
mc̄ abb ua[...]
buaidy[...]
morgainn[...]
mc̄ donnch[...]

Id ⁊ sildi petan mc̄ donnchaid ⁊ malechin ⁊ da mc̄ matain
mathe buchan huli maradnaisse in helain :⁊

The Battle of Corbridge, 918, reported in the Annals of Ulster. *(Trinity College Library, Dublin)*

St Rule's Tower at St Andrews, where King Constantine II spent his retirement. *(Photo: I.W. Walker)*

Round tower at St Brigit's, Abernethy, where King Constantine II met St Cadroe *(Photo: I.W. Walker)*

Below: The Monymusk Reliquary, reputed to hold relics of St Columba. *(National Museums of Scotland)*

Round tower at Brechin, founded by King Kenneth II. *(Historic Scotland)*

St Serf's Island, Loch Leven, the site of a Culdee monastery which received gifts from several kings of Alba. *(Photo: I.W. Walker)*

The Govan Sarcophagus, reputedly the coffin of a king of Strathclyde. *(Crown Copyright: Royal Commission on the Ancient and Historic Monuments of Scotland)*

Sueno's Stone, Moray, which commemorates an important battle, now unknown *(Crown Copyright: Royal Commission on the Ancient and Historic Monuments of Scotland)*

Detail of battle scene, Sueno's Stone. *(Historic Scotland)*

The Moot Hill at Scone, probable site of Scottish royal inaugurations. *(Photo: I.W. Walker)*

Illustration of a Scottish royal inauguration from a later manuscript. *(The Masters and Fellows of Corpus Christi College, Cambridge)*

Opposite, above: Clifford's Tower, York, the site of a Norman castle which changed hands during Edgar *Atheling*'s campaigns. *(Photo: I.W. Walker)*

Opposite, below: Interior of Dunfermline Abbey, founded by King Malcolm III and Margaret. *(Photo: I.W. Walker)*

Initial page from a Celtic Psalter. *(Edinburgh University Library MS. No. 56)*

Queen Margaret's Chapel, Edinburgh Castle, built by one of her royal sons. *(Crown Copyright: Royal Commission on the Ancient and Historic Monuments of Scotland)*

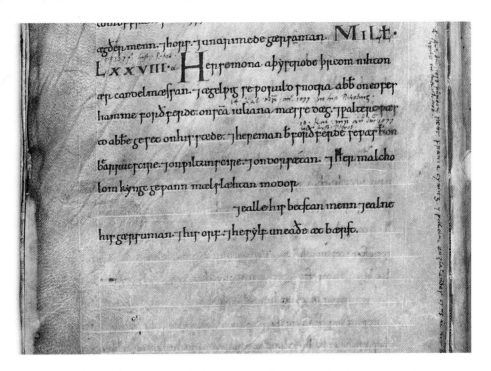

The defeat of Maelsnechtai in 1077 from manuscript 'D' of The Anglo-Saxon Chronicle. *(BL Cotton Tiberius B IV folio 85v)*

Original Charter of King Duncan II to Durham, 1094. *(The Dean and Chapter of Durham)*

Original Charter of King Edgar to Durham, 1105. This could almost be an English document except for mention of Edgar's kingdom and his subjects as 'Scots and English'. *(The Dean and Chapter of Durham)*

Seal cast of King Edgar *(National Archives of Scotland, RH 17/1)*

suggests that this ruler was subordinate to Constantine at this time and that the latter represented his interests. In contrast, *Ealdorman* Ealdred of Northumbria is mentioned separately, which may indicate a degree of independence from Constantine. Once again, it is far more likely to have been an agreement among, if not equals, then certainly independent rulers with their own agendas. It probably revolved around recognition of each others' current spheres of influence. It possibly included English recognition of Constantine's hegemony over Strathclyde in return for his recognition of English hegemony over York. In other words a recognition of the de facto position as a basis for future agreement or disagreement and change. The position of English Northumbria as noted above is less clear. Whatever the precise nature of the agreement reached, it appears to have been fair enough to last and the region had peace for the next seven years.

In 934 King Gothfrith of Dublin died and was succeeded by his young nephew Olaf, the son of his older brother Sihtric. The succession of this inexperienced youth effectively removed the immediate threat of Viking intervention in York. It is less clear, however, what caused Athelstan to repudiate his previous policy of alliance with the Scots and launch a major invasion of Alba. It may be that the current ebb in Viking power encouraged Athelstan to review his relationship with Constantine II of Alba. The later Chronicle of Melrose claims that it involved the breach of a treaty but it is hard to know whether this draws on early material or is simply speculation. It may simply be that the establishment of a common frontier brought tensions, possibly related to mutual cross-border raiding. It may have been the consequence of English attempts to seize direct control of English Northumbria. It is possible that *Ealdorman* Ealdred sought Athelstan's help in securing freedom from Scottish hegemony. If the cause of this invasion is ultimately unclear, its consequences are not. King Athelstan invaded Alba with a powerful land and naval force which included substantial contingents of Welsh and managed to reach as far north as Dunnottar. It was as a result of this huge campaign that Athelstan finally managed to secure the submission of Constantine King of Alba, whose unnamed son was apparently taken to England as a hostage for his future behaviour. It was at this point rather than in 920 or 927 that Constantine II became a man of the English King for the first time. A couple of charters of King Athelstan from this period include Constantine among the witnesses. This is certainly an indicator of his subordinate status at this point, but it may also indicate that Constantine himself was taken south to attend Athelstan's court at this time. Unfortunately, this is not confirmed by the chronicles, which might have been expected to make much of such an event.

This triumphant expedition was an extraordinary demonstration of power by the new English state and a terrible warning of their ambition. It was a shock to Constantine that the elimination of the Viking threat from York had brought a far greater danger in its wake. It resulted in a complete reversal of Constantine's earlier policy of alliance with the English kings against the Vikings. This policy had depended on mutual recognition of each others' spheres of influence, but Athelstan's campaign of 934 had effectively destroyed this. In these circumstances, Constantine was compelled to revise his policy and seek an alliance with his former enemies against Athelstan and the English. He therefore approached King Olaf of Dublin, who was eager to strike back at Athelstan and so restore his rule in York. The new aggressive policy of Athelstan had brought about the recognition of his hegemony across Britain based on his superior military power. It had also produced a negative reaction which took shape in the formation of a formidable coalition of defeated powers against him. The two men who had suffered most from English aggression, Constantine and Olaf, forged an alliance with the principal aim of defeating Athelstan and restoring their own power and influence.

The new allies Constantine and Olaf realised, as a result of their earlier experience of English military power, that they would not defeat Athelstan easily. They therefore put a great deal of thought and planning into how they might humble him. It would be three years before the allies were ready, but this preparatory period was not wasted. They spent the time carefully preparing a joint campaign in England, which was intended to force Athelstan to fight their combined armies at a disadvantage. It was hoped that where they had been unable to defeat him individually they could do so together. They also made great efforts to recruit allies from among those others crushed by Athelstan's rule. The Welsh poem *Armes Prydain* or 'The Prophecy of Britain' was composed in support of this recruitment campaign. It complained of Athelstan's levying of heavy tribute from Wales and urged the Welsh to rise up against him alongside the Scots and the Vikings of Dublin:

The warriors will scatter the foreigners [English]
As far as Caer Weir –
They will rejoice after the devastation,
And there will be reconciliation between the
Welsh and the men of Dublin,
The Gaels of Ireland and Man and Britain,

The men of Cornwall and of Strathclyde will be made welcome
    among us.
The Britons will rise again.[8]

Ultimately, the Welsh chose to reject these overtures on this occasion and when Constantine and Olaf eventually struck they did so without Welsh support.

In 937 the allies' plans were finally ready and King Constantine II and Olaf of Dublin launched their combined invasion of England. It appears from later accounts that Constantine had the support of his sub-king, Owain of Strathclyde. The invasion was clearly well coordinated and the two allies managed to achieve their objective of engaging Athelstan with the full strength of their combined forces. It is not clear whether Olaf sailed to join Constantine in the north and the two allies then crossed into English territory or if the allies invaded England separately and met at an agreed rendezvous. The former would have avoided any risk of Athelstan catching them and defeating them individually before they combined. Alternatively, if they had invaded England independently, Constantine from the north and Olaf from across the Irish Sea coast, they might have posed a quandary for Athelstan as to which enemy force to tackle first. What is clear is that the armies of Constantine and Olaf had combined at some point before they encountered the English army under Athelstan at a place called *Brunanburh*.

In spite of the spilling of a great deal of ink, the identity of this place remains elusive to this day. The best that can be said is that it probably lies somewhere in the northern half of England. This is unfortunate since it effectively prevents us from reaching any firm conclusions about the circumstances immediately preceding this important battle. If the location was conclusively identified it might, for example, be possible to identify whence and how the northern allies originally invaded, how far they had penetrated into English territory and, perhaps, how and where they had joined forces. It might also be possible to suggest whether they were in the process of advancing or withdrawing before the battle occurred. It might even provide an indication of what the allies had achieved, if anything, by their invasion. In reality, the current uncertainty about the location of this battle means that we can establish almost none of these facts.

What is beyond doubt is that the Battle of *Brunanburh* in 937 was a major engagement between two large armies. It features in a significant number of contemporary sources from Ireland, Scotland and England. It receives the prominence of a detailed entry in the Annals of Ulster, although the participation of Constantine and the men of Alba is completely ignored. The Anglo-Saxon Chronicle also chooses to distinguish this event but does so by incorporating a celebratory poem on the English victory. It contains the following details about the Scottish involvement:

There . . . the aged Constantine, the hoary-haired warrior came north to his own land by flight. He had no cause to exult in that crossing of swords. He was shorn of his kinsmen and deprived of his friends at that meeting-place, bereaved in the battle, and he left his young son on the field of slaughter, brought low by wounds in the battle. The grey-haired warrior, the old and wily one, had no cause to vaunt of that sword-clash; no more had Olaf. They had no need to gloat with the remnants of their armies, that they were superior in warlike deeds on the field of battle, in the clash of standards, the meeting of spears, the encounter of men, and the crossing of weapons, after they had contended on the field of slaughter with the sons of Edward.[9]

In contrast to accounts of the Battle of Corbridge, in 918 all the sources on *Brunanburh* are unanimous about the outcome. It was a disastrous defeat for the northern allies, Constantine and Olaf, and a major victory for Athelstan and the English. They are also in accord on the scale of the slaughter on both sides but especially among the Vikings and the men of Alba. On this occasion, the Old English poem contained in the Chronicle may perhaps offer a few hints about the course of the fighting. The poem describes how the English breached the allies' shield-wall and put them to flight. It follows this with a description of a mounted pursuit of the fleeing enemy that lasted all day. It is, of course, possible that these are no more than conventional expressions about a generic battle. The poetic account is completed with a list of the heavy casualties among the vanquished especially in the ranks of their leaders. It notes the deaths of five young kings, seven earls and a countless host among the Vikings and of Constantine's young son, kinsmen and friends and many others among the men of Alba. The Ulster annalist confirms the heavy Viking losses but adds that the English also suffered heavy losses. The English and Irish sources agree that Olaf of Dublin returned to Ireland with only 'a small company' or a 'few followers', respectively.

The victory achieved by King Athelstan of England at *Brunanburh* in 937 was clear and emphatic and it effectively ensured his immediate supremacy among the rulers of Britain. He had claimed in his charters since around 930 to be 'ruler of the whole island of Britain' and after this victory he could finally use this title with complete justification. It is clear that Constantine must have had to accept the restoration of his earlier subjection to Athelstan. The triumphant English realm would be secure against invasion for the rest of Athelstan's reign. The victory was incomplete in one respect, however, in that both Constantine and Olaf survived the defeat. They lived on to fight another day and this would prove a problem when Athelstan died within two years of his triumph in 939. The unexpected death of Athelstan on 27 October 939, so soon after this success severely undermined the English position of overlordship and none of his immediate successors could be considered rulers of the whole of Britain. In addition, when Athelstan died in 939 he had no heir and was succeeded by his much younger half-brother Edmund. This change was the exact reverse of that five years earlier in 934. The English kingdom was now in the hands of a young and relatively untried man, while a humiliated Olaf of Dublin was burning for revenge and stood ready to exploit this apparent English weakness.

The Battle of *Brunanburh* in 937 was perhaps decisive in another, previously unremarked, sense. It is notable that King Constantine II of Alba appears not to have joined the Viking attacks on England which raged between 940 and 943. There is no mention of the men of Alba in any of the fighting of this period, when the Vikings once again contested control of York with the English. In the earlier part of his long reign, Constantine had sought alliances against the dangerous Viking threat among the English rulers to the south. In about 907, he had allied with Aethelred and Aethelflaed of Mercia and in 920 he had renewed this arrangement with Edward of England. The alliances with English rulers had allowed him to extend his own influence southwards into Strathclyde and English Northumbria. On their side, the English rulers had been able to extend their authority northwards into Danish-controlled Mercia and Viking York. This mutually advantageous arrangement had reached a climax with the mutually satisfactory extinction of Viking York. It was King Athelstan's consequent strike against Alba in 934 that had forced Constantine to pursue an alliance with his former enemies, the Vikings. This had led to unmitigated disaster at *Brunanburh* and must have prompted Constantine to review his policy. He had been fortunate to escape the disaster himself and had lost his son Cellach, many of his kinsmen and friends and large numbers of his warriors.

In 938 the Scottish Chronicle reports the death of Dubucan, son of Indrechtach, *Mormaer* of Angus, who may have been an important supporter of Constantine. King Constantine himself was now an old man, in his sixties at least, and less able to lead troops into battle. The loss of his son Cellach at *Brunanburh* possibly left him with no adult heir to perform this duty on his behalf or to succeed him as king. The future of the kingdom would fall into the hands of others from the wider dynasty. The death of King Athelstan in 939 had effectively freed him from his earlier subjection to English overlordship. In these circumstances, there was little to be gained from supporting the Vikings and Constantine remained aloof from their further attempts to seize York. The conflict between the Vikings and the English that erupted in 940 absorbed all their energies and allowed Constantine the luxury of remaining at peace.

In 940, with some help from the local Vikings, King Olaf of Dublin finally regained control of York from the young King Edmund of England. He subsequently went on to conquer a large stretch of the East Midlands, including the *burhs* of Leicester, Lincoln, Nottingham, Stamford and Derby. This dramatically reversed the balance of power in northern England to the position before the English occupation of York in 934 and, arguably, before the English conquest of the northern Danish settlements in the 910s. It also removed the English presence on the borders of Alba, which eased Constantine's immediate problems, although a revitalised Viking York also raised the prospect of a return to the position around 910, when a powerful Viking kingdom at York was able to prey on both Alba and England. An early indication of what such a scenario might mean for Alba came in 941 when Olaf launched a raid deep into English Northumbria, devastating Lindisfarne and sacking St Baldred's church at Tyninghame in East Lothian. The wrathful Northumbrian saint was considered responsible for Olaf's sudden death soon afterwards. The Viking leader had showed no respect for the church and received a suitable heavenly punishment. It was perhaps only this saintly intervention that spared Constantine an invasion of his own kingdom.

The sudden death of Olaf in the midst of his hour of triumph in 941 transformed the situation once again. He was quickly succeeded by his cousin, another Olaf, the son of Gothfrith, who was nicknamed *Cuaran* or 'Sandal' but who proved much less successful. It was not long before King Edmund of England recovered and restored his authority over the East Midlands during 942 before applying pressure on Olaf *Cuaran* at York. The subsequent desperate struggles between the Vikings of York, under a variety of rulers, and the English kings absorbed their energies completely until 944. This left Constantine undisturbed and at peace during his final years. He was not apparently required or compelled to support either side in this bitter dispute. It was left to his successor Malcolm I to recognise the greater power of the English kings and to renew the alliance with them in 945.

The Life of St Cadroe of Metz, which was composed around 980 and describes events that occurred around 940 in the closing years of Constantine's reign, provides confirmation that the kingdom of Alba was at peace. It reports that Constantine was among those who urged Cadroe to remain in Alba rather than go on pilgrimage, probably to Rome. He was, however, eventually persuaded to assist rather than hinder the saint by Abbot Maelodair of St Brigit's monastery at Abernethy:

> . . . the king that ruled the land, Constantine by name, hastened to hold back the man [Cadroe]. Already part of the journey had been completed; and Cadroe had entered the church of the blessed Brigit to pray when a crowd of nobles and peasants filled the church . . . They all asked the man not to forsake his country. And turning to them he answered this only to the king and to all; he said 'I shall not forsake you since wherever I am I shall keep you in remembrance.' Then an outcry of the people arose. It happened that with the king had come a certain abbot called Maelodair. And he being a just man in counsel said: 'If we cannot prevail to turn this man from his design and wish, let us each as best we can render him help upon the way, that we may be sharers in the reward of his labours.' Then all competed to render assistance with gold and silver with clothes and horses; and they sped him with God's blessing; and conducted by the king himself, he came to the land of the Cumbrians.[10]

The Life also indicates in passing that Constantine retained control over the kingdom of Strathclyde. He personally escorted Cadroe to the border of Strathclyde and there commended him to his sub-king, Donald, son of Owain. In turn, Donald escorted the saint as far as *Loida* on his own border with Viking York before commending him to a man called Gunderic, who escorted him to the court of the Norwegian King Erik at York, who did not come to power until 947, implying a long stay in Strathclyde.

In 943 the aged King Constantine II chose to resign his kingship and retire to the monastery of St Andrews. He was certainly old and possibly infirm in body, although the Scottish Chronicle reports that he was alert enough in mind to urge his successor to invade England in 950. He spent the remainder of his years in relatively quiet retirement as a monk in the community at St Andrews. He had lost one son at *Brunanburh* in 937 and another was possibly still a hostage in England. The succession system in Alba, however, meant that he would be succeeded not by a son but by a member of another dynastic lineage. He had lived so long that it appears that, through natural or other losses in the various lineages, there was a relatively straightforward and undisputed succession. He was succeeded apparently without incident by Malcolm I, son of Donald or *Mael Coluim mac Domnaill*, who must have been at least 43 at the time and possibly older.

King Constantine II deserves to be remembered as the most remarkable of the early kings of Alba. He had taken part in three of the crucial battles of this period. In 904 at Strathearn, he had soundly defeated the last Viking attempt to subjugate Alba. In 918 at Corbridge, he had challenged Ragnall of York for hegemony over the remnant of English Northumbria in a hard fought battle. In 937 at *Brunanburh* he had been soundly defeated in alliance with his former enemies the Vikings against the rising power of King Athelstan of England. He had survived all these bloody encounters and had successfully preserved his kingdom intact. In 943 he surrendered to his successor, Malcolm I, a kingdom that had survived the worst that the Vikings could throw at it. It had emerged from heavy defeats at Viking hands under his earlier namesake stronger than before and better prepared to face the challenges ahead. It was now securely in control of the rich eastern lowlands of northern Britain from the borders of Moray in the north to the Firth of Forth in the south. It had secured a position of hegemony over the formerly independent kingdom of Strathclyde to its south-west. It had also begun to interfere in the affairs of the remnant of the former English kingdom of Northumbria. In the next sixty years Constantine's successors would seek to consolidate their position in the north and to extend their control and influence over the rich lands to the south.

4

The March to the South

In 943 King Constantine II, son of Aed retired and surrendered the throne to his cousin Malcolm I, son of Donald or *Mael Coluim mac Domnaill*. Constantine retired to the monastery of St Andrews but continued to take an interest in the fate of the kingdom. In 943 Malcolm inherited a kingdom which now extended from the borders of Moray in the north to the Firth of Forth in the south. It included hegemony over the sub-kingdom of Strathclyde under Donald, son of Owain and a looser and more intermittent hegemony over the *ealdormen* of Northumbria, the rulers of the northern remnant of this ancient English kingdom. In the north, the kingdom was bounded by the semi-independent region of Moray, presently ruled by a man called Cellach, and beyond that by areas under the domination of the Viking earls of Orkney. In the west, it nominally extended to the western coasts but most probably effectively ended in the central uplands, where it merged into a series of semi-independent lordships ruled by local Gaelic chieftains which themselves bordered coastal and island areas ruled by various semi-independent kings. In the south, it abutted the Norse kingdom of York beyond which stretched the newly unified and still fragile but nevertheless powerful kingdom of the English. In the next sixty years, the kingdom of Alba would expand from this core, especially to the south, as its kings sought to absorb their southern client states.

At the start of his reign, Malcolm was already a mature man in his forties and probably somewhat older. In spite of this, he still found himself in the shadow of Constantine's long and successful reign. He appears to have sought to establish his own reputation by extending his power northwards into Moray. The Scottish Chronicle reports that he invaded Moray and killed Cellach, who was most probably the ruler of this province strategically positioned between Alba and the lands under the domination of the earls of Orkney. It was an action which may have been informed by Constantine's recent lack of success in expanding southwards in the face of the rising power of the kings of England. This had produced some limited gains in Strathclyde but had provoked formidable retaliation under Aethelstan in 934 and 937. It may have seemed to Malcolm that it was safer to seek to expand his authority in the north instead.

The wisdom of Malcolm's action was quickly demonstrated when King Edmund of England exploited internal divisions among the Vikings to reoccupy York in 944. He expelled both of its current Viking rulers, the cousins Olaf *Cuaran* and Ragnall Gothfrithson, who subsequently fled to Dublin. King Edmund followed this up the following year by ravaging Cumberland, a name which appears to signify the region between the Rivers Solway and Ribble. He may have done so because it had offered an easy passage for the Dublin Vikings on their way to and from York. He did not seize this region himself but instead, according to The Anglo-Saxon Chronicle, he 'granted it [Cumberland] all to Malcolm King of Scots on condition that he should be his ally both on land and sea'. This partisan statement may in fact conceal an existing alliance between Edmund and Malcolm, which allowed them effectively to divide northern England between them. Thus Edmund seized York while Malcolm occupied Cumberland. It would not be surprising if, in reaction to the difficulties resulting from the previous enmity between their kingdoms, these two men had decided to test what profit might accrue from an alliance instead. If this was the case, it was clearly an arrangement which proved beneficial to them both.

In spite of the death of King Edmund in 946, this new alliance was probably renewed by his brother and successor Eadred. This suggests that it was regarded by both parties as a useful policy. It is reported, once again, in the partisan Anglo-Saxon Chronicle that '. . . the Scots gave oaths to him that they would agree to all he wanted.' The Chronicle once again chooses to interpret this arrangement in its own fashion as a submission by the Scots to the English King. It is, however, more likely that this is a result of the English writer's desire to portray this event in terms most flattering to his own king. There had been no major invasion of Scotland like that of 934 which might have triggered such an abject submission. It must therefore reflect, however distortedly, an agreement reached between the two kings with benefits for both. It seems likely that it was intended to deter any Viking attempts to restore their rule in York. It probably confirmed the status quo with the English occupation of York and the Scottish occupation of Cumberland. It is much less clear whether it dealt with the position in English Northumbria and, more importantly, if it did, what might have been agreed. *Ealdorman* Oswulf appears as a charter witness for King Eadred but is not mentioned in the submissions of this year unless the phrase 'all Northumbria' includes his northern portion.

In 947 Erik of Norway, who had been driven from his own kingdom by Hakon, a protégé of King Athelstan, briefly seized control of York. He was quickly expelled by Eadred but probably destabilised English control. In 949 Olaf *Cuaran* of Dublin, who had no doubt been roused from his lethargy by Erik's recent success, seized York. It appears that Malcolm, King of Alba invaded Northumbria in 950 and plundered it as far as the Tees. In the account of this raid contained in the Scottish Chronicle, he is said to have 'seized a multitude of people and many herds of cattle'. This raid may simply have aimed at securing plunder but wider motives are also likely. It may have been in response to Olaf's success, but if so, why did Malcolm strike at Northumbria, which was not under Olaf's rule? It is possible that the local English rulers had recognised Olaf's hegemony and that this raid was in retaliation. It is also possible that Malcolm decided to exploit the distraction offered by Olaf's intervention to enforce his own hegemony over Northumbria. The precise status of English Northumbria at this point is unclear. There was apparently no immediate response to Olaf's success from the English kings and this may have dissuaded Malcolm from more direct action against York.

The Scottish Chronicle suggests that the retired elder statesman Constantine, son of Aed was instrumental in guiding Malcolm's actions in 950. He had, after all, ruled Alba with great success for forty-three years and he probably still had supporters among the nobility. Constantine's opinions must have carried great weight, but whether or not Malcolm's aggression towards his southern neighbour during these years was actually incited by Constantine is uncertain. The old man had little reason to like the English, but equally he understood completely the reasons to avoid antagonising them. The author of the Scottish Chronicle knew that many people believed that Constantine had emerged from his monastic seclusion to lead this raid himself but was quite clear that this was untrue. It demonstrates clearly a perception that he continued to dominate the political scene in Alba, even from his retirement at St Andrews. He was perhaps a grey eminence behind Malcolm throughout the early years of his reign. If so, this must have been a considerable burden for Malcolm and was certainly one that no previous king had had to endure.

In 952, there was confusion in the restored Viking kingdom of York when the local nobles themselves apparently expelled Olaf *Cuaran* and welcomed Erik of Norway in his place. The reasons for this internal dispute are obscure but were probably connected to the rivalry between these two figures to rule this wealthy trading town.

This internal disruption probably encouraged Malcolm to intervene and he perhaps even hoped to secure control of York before Eadred was ready to do so. He may even have been encouraged by Constantine, as a final act before his death in this year. It must have seemed that King Eadred was continuing to ignore the Viking presence in York at this time. In fact, he was quietly working to undermine their independence. He arrested and imprisoned Archbishop Wulfstan of York, who had actively supported the Viking rulers for some time. It is possible that he may even have encouraged Malcolm to intervene.

It would appear from the Annals of Ulster that King Malcolm organised a substantial expedition against the Viking rulers of York in 952. The result of this invasion was a battle between the Scots, Britons and Saxons on one side and the Vikings on the other. The leaders of the opposing forces are not identified, but they can only be King Malcolm and either Olaf or Erik of York. It is difficult otherwise to work out how an encounter between precisely these opposing forces might have occurred at this time. The record clearly suggests that Malcolm commanded not only the men of Alba but also contingents under the sub-king of Strathclyde and, however unlikely it appears, from Northumbria. Unfortunately, King Malcolm was soundly defeated and forced to abandon any further plans he may have had to capture York himself. Malcolm's ambitious plans had come to nothing and he may even have inadvertently assisted King Eadred of England. The latter was now faced with a weakened King Erik in York and within two years would move to secure the town.

In 954 Malcolm, no doubt smarting from his defeat in the south two years previously, abandoned his activities on this front and turned north once again. He resumed his earlier strategy of expansion in the north at the expense of the rulers of Moray. Unfortunately, he was killed at Fetteresso near Dunnottar by men from the Mearns. The latter may possibly have been led by

Maelbrigte, *Mormaer* of Angus, the son of that Dubucan, who had possibly been a key supporter of Constantine II until his death in 938. Whether the killing occurred before or after the invasion of Moray is unknown, but the aftermath of an unsuccessful invasion seems to offer a more likely context for some kind of rebellion against the King. If Malcolm had indeed suffered a second major defeat, it would certainly have undermined his authority. In these circumstances, there was plenty of scope for malcontents, including supporters of rival lineages, to take action.

In 954, King Erik of York fled the town following a rebellion by the local nobility and the imminent approach of King Eadred of England and his army. According to a report preserved in a late source by Roger of Wendover, he appears to have headed north-west in an effort to reach the Irish Sea coast, possibly by way of Cumberland. He was betrayed and killed in a 'lonely place', usually presumed to be Stainmore, by a man called Maccus. The assassination was reportedly instigated by *Ealdorman* Oswulf of Northumbria, who may have been attempting to court the favour of Eadred. This was perhaps a natural development in the light of Eadred's increasing power at this time. The occupation of York placed Eadred on the borders of English Northumbria and offered a threat that could not be ignored. Oswulf had lost his only alternative protector with the death of Malcolm in the north in this same year. In addition, the defeat of his forces in company with those of Alba in 952, may have discouraged thoughts of holding on to that alliance. Oswulf was certainly richly rewarded for his action since Eadred appointed him *Ealdorman* of York in addition to his existing authority over English Northumbria. This possibly temporary change in allegiance – the *Ealdormen* had switched before – would, however, become something more permanent with the demise of an independent Viking York.

In spite of his relatively short reign of only ten years, in comparison with his predecessor Constantine, Malcolm I had proved to be a fairly successful ruler. He appears to have actively contained the potential threat from Moray in the north. He also made excellent use of his alliance with the English rulers to expand and consolidate his authority in the south. He secured or extended southwards the boundaries of his sub-kingdom of Strathclyde probably as far as Stainmore and secured hegemony over English Northumbria for a short time. He even intervened in the Viking kingdom of York, possibly with a view to seizing control of this rich prize, though ultimately unsuccessfully.

Malcolm was succeeded by a man called 'Edulb' or Idulf, son of Constantine or *Idulb mac Castantin*. He had probably waited in the wings for some time in hopes of succeeding his long-lived father and was probably well into middle age. It has been suggested that his name is derived from a Norse name like Hildulf. It is more likely to be a version of 'Ettulb', which features in the Annals of Ulster in 913 as the Gaelic equivalent for the English name Eadwulf. This suggests the intriguing possibility that he had an English mother and that she might have been a relative, perhaps a daughter, of *Ealdorman* Eadwulf of Northumbria who died in 913. If this suggestion is correct, it would be the first known marriage between the kings of Alba and the English. It might also throw more light on the relations between the kings of Alba and the *ealdormen* of Northumbria. They might have been based as much on close family ties as on alliance between two political entities. Such a marriage could have taken place during Ealdred's exile in Alba between 915 and 918. It would offer an added incentive for Constantine's invasion in support of Ealdred in 918.

It appears that early in his reign, King Idulf exiled Fothad, son of Bran, Bishop of St Andrews to the Isles. This information is contained in rather late sources, which place the event in 955, the first year of his reign. The action is attributed to a quarrel between the two but it must surely have been about something fairly fundamental to warrant such punishment. In view of the timing, it seems likely that the dispute concerned Idulf's refusal to endorse the agreement reached in 906 between his father and Bishop Cellach on the Hill of Faith at Scone. This fundamental contract between Church and State had probably been renewed by Malcolm on his succession, but Idulf may have had reservations. Whatever the exact cause it resulted in the expulsion of Fothad, who lived in exile for the rest of Idulf's reign and was only restored following his death in 962. The consequences of this for the Church in Alba are also unknown but may have been severe.

If King Idulf was indeed an Anglo-Scot, it might explain his more direct intervention in English Northumbria. He sought to build on his predecessors' unsuccessful efforts to secure control of this region. He wanted this control to be direct and personal rather than mediated through the *ealdormen*. He may even have felt that he had a right to rule there through his mother. According to the Scottish Chronicle, at some point during his reign, he seized control of Edinburgh from the English Northumbrians. This presumably included the surrounding area that would become known as Lothian, although the sources do not confirm this. The fortress is described in the Chronicle as having been 'evacuated and abandoned to the Scots'. This suggests that it did not succumb to direct assault, something which might have been difficult for the Scots to achieve. It was perhaps brought to submission by a process of raiding the surrounding region and hence cutting its supplies. Indeed, we know that Malcolm had probably been raiding in this same area in 950. Its surrender may even have been negotiated peacefully. A fortress like Edinburgh which was distant from the sea and possible supply would be vulnerable in this way. The loss of Edinburgh must have been a severe blow for *Ealdorman* Oswulf. It would also have been suitable revenge for his change of allegiance in 954. If Oswulf had ceased to be subject to the kings of Alba, he was no longer entitled to their protection and Idulf had no duty to respect his borders.

This important southward advance by Idulf is not dated in our sources but it might be attributable to the period of confusion that occurred after the death of Eadred in 955. He had been succeeded by his nephew Eadwig, the eldest son of his deceased older brother King Edmund. In 957, King Eadwig quarrelled with his younger brother Edgar and the English kingdom was subsequently divided between them, with Edgar ruling Mercia and Northumbria and Eadwig ruling Wessex. This uneasy settlement lasted until 959 when Eadwig died and Edgar succeeded to the whole kingdom. This partition effectively weakened English power and distracted the attention of its rulers for two years and it might have caused them to accept the loss of Edinburgh without retaliation.

In the wake of his success in occupying Edinburgh and possibly Lothian, King Idulf appears to have been equally active in the north. The Scottish Chronicle records the arrival of a force of Viking raiders in Buchan at some point during his reign. This event reveals the decline in the threat presented by the Vikings since the heady years of the 860s, 870s and 900s. In Alba by the 960s the Viking Age, that period when Viking armies had attempted to conquer large areas of the British Isles, was more or less over. The descendants of those early Vikings were still present in the northern and western islands, in the Isle of Man and in Ireland but they no longer had the power to subdue fresh kingdoms. They spent most of their time attempting to hold on to what they had. This did not mean that the kingdom of Alba was completely free from attacks, which continued into the thirteenth century. It was, however, no longer threatened with conquest. The new attacks were mainly local and seasonal in nature and usually directed at securing plunder.

In 962 Idulf was killed while fighting more Viking raiders in the north-east at Cullen in Banff. In the aftermath of his death, according to the Scottish Chronicle, Dub, son of Malcolm I or *Dub mac Mael Coluim* initially succeeded Idulf. He immediately restored the exiled Bishop Fothad to his position at St Andrews, although the latter would not enjoy his triumph for long since he died only a year later in 963. He was replaced as chief bishop of Alba by Maelbrigte, who ruled for some eight years. It appears, however, that Culen, son of Idulf or *Culen mac Idulb* was not content to accept the restoration of the kingship to the lineage of Malcolm and he subsequently collected support to contest the kingship. The result was an outbreak of civil strife between two claimants, Dub, son of Malcolm and Culen, son of Idulf. This conflict almost certainly drew on support from different factions among the nobility. The result was a period of misery for Alba described by The Prophecy of Berchan: 'Two kings after that, the pair plundering equally; white and black together, woe to him who shall take them in joint kingship.'

In 965 the Scottish Chronicle and the Annals of Ulster both report that the rival claimants and their supporters met in battle. The Chronicle locates the battle at Duncrub, which is near Dunning in Perthshire. It was an extremely bloody fight which cost the lives of a number of prominent men, including Duncan, Abbot of Dunkeld and Dubduin, *Mormaer* of Atholl. The sources, however, appear to disagree about the outcome. The Chronicle proceeds to state that Dub was expelled from the kingship and Culen reigned for a short while. In contrast, the Annals of Ulster imply that Dub continued to rule for another year until 966, when he was killed by 'the Scots themselves', presumably a reference to Culen and his followers. It was probably only after Dub's death in 966 that Culen finally succeeded to the kingdom.

In 966, the Annals of Ulster report that, Dub son of Malcolm was slain during an internal dispute and nothing more. A few rather later Scottish accounts of Dub's death appear to offer additional information, but it is not clear how reliable these might be. In these sources, it is suggested that Dub met his end at Forres at the hands of the men of Moray. Unfortunately, these sources also include a legend that his body was hidden under the bridge at Kinloss and that the sun would not shine until it was found and provided with a Christian burial. The accretion of such legendary material can only undermine our faith in the accuracy of the information found in these sources. It has been suggested that Sueno's Stone at Forres commemorates this encounter, and it certainly features something that might represent a bridge but there is no way to establish this and other battles have been suggested. In any case, Culen finally succeeded Dub in 966 but he would himself rule for only a few years.

In the same year of 966, King Edgar of England appointed Oslac as *Ealdorman* of York in an attempt to increase royal influence in the north. It seems that prior to this Edgar had been content to allow Oswulf and then Eadwulf, the successive *ealdormen* of English Northumbria, to rule York following the final expulsion of Erik in 954. The appointment of Oslac left Eadwulf, who was nicknamed 'Evil-child', with authority over Northumbria from the Tees to a place called Myreforth or Myreford. This is probably not the Firth of Forth but some so far unidentified location in East Lothian or Berwickshire. In the same year, The Anglo-Saxon Chronicle reports that a man named Thored, son of Gunnar ravaged Westmorland. He was probably the son of Edgar's faithful *ealdorman* Gunnar, who held lands in Yorkshire but whose area of authority as an *ealdorman* is unknown. Thored himself would eventually rise to replace Oslac as *Ealdorman* of York in 975 and to marry his daughter to King Aethelred of England. The Chronicle does not reveal the precise objectives of this raiding by Thored. It may have been intended to conquer Westmorland, an area nominally under English rule but largely independent until now. This region does not seem to have been recognised as part of the area known as Cumberland, which had been ceded to the Scots in 945. King Edgar perhaps sought to intervene in this area and encroach somewhat on Scottish territory while its rulers were embroiled in their civil war. It is possible that both events were part of a process whereby Edgar sought to increase his authority in these border regions.

In 966 Culen had finally secured undisputed control of the kingship following the death of Dub. He had a brief reign of five years which appears to have been uneventful, as far as can be told from the meagre sources that exist. The Scottish Chronicle notes a number of important deaths that occurred during his rule but provides no further information. In 971 Maelbrigte, Bishop of St Andrews died after an eight-year rule. He was succeeded by Cellach, son of Ferdalach, who would go on to rule the see for twenty-five years. In addition, Maelbrigte son of Dubucan, *Mormaer* of Angus died at some unknown date. He was probably the son of the Dubucan, son of Indrechtach, who had been *Mormaer* of Angus under Constantine before his death in 938. He may also have been involved in the killing of Malcolm I by the men of the Mearns in 954. This succession of a son to his father as *mormaer* of Angus offers some support for the notion of a hereditary element in succession to these important positions.

In 971 Culen, son of Idulf was killed in battle by the Britons of Strathclyde along with his brother Eochaid, according to the Annals of Ulster. The later king-lists offer some supposed background to this story, though it is difficult to know whether the additional information that they provide is accurate or not. They inform us that he had supposedly offended a man named Rhydderch, son of Donald, Sub-king of Strathclyde, by abducting and raping his daughter. In response, Rhydderch apparently attacked his overlord, King Culen while he was collecting tribute or taxes in nearby Lothian. In the process, King Culen and his brother Eochaid were killed. If this account is accurate, it offers in passing some interesting information on the situation in Lothian. This region had only been occupied by the men of Alba about ten years before. It was apparently still necessary for the King of Alba to collect the tribute of Lothian in person and while accompanied by a reasonably substantial military force. It seems that Rhydderch may have exploited the exposure of the King in this respect to exact his revenge.

This fate suffered by King Culen allowed Kenneth II, son of Malcolm or *Cinaed mac Mael Coluim*, the younger brother of King Dub, to seize his chance and take the throne. The information about his reign is meagre in the Scottish Chronicle, confused and possibly limited to the early part of his reign. This is largely because the main text ended in 972 and the final section on Kenneth's reign was added later. It consists of a brief list of Kenneth's achievements with only the barest indication of possible dates. This makes it extremely difficult to achieve a logical account of his rule. The Chronicle reports that Kenneth 'immediately plundered part of Britain'. It is possible that this indicates some form of retaliation against Rhydderch, who had killed Culen and does not again feature in the sources. It is likely that this was considered necessary by King Kenneth II in order to crush their rebellion and ensure the future delivery of tribute, rather than to avenge Culen. It also reports that Kenneth lost his infantry near Abercorn, but it is difficult to work out what precisely this means. It may be entirely unrelated since, if it was an encounter with the rebellious Britons, why did it take place in Lothian? It might be that an attempt was made to catch Rhydderch as he fled from the scene of the murder in Lothian.

It is next reported that Kenneth, at some unknown date after his succession, 'plundered England [*sic*]' as far as Stainmore, the River Clough and the pools of the Derwent. The area subject to these raids by Kenneth was in fact within Strathclyde and not England. It might therefore have been part of Kenneth's attempt to crush the British rebels involved in the death of Culen. It may equally have been an attempt to restore control of this area following the relaxation of royal authority during the recent civil war. It is an outside possibility that the reference to England is not an error and that this marked a belated Scottish response to the actions of Thored in 966. While the kings were distracted by their civil war, Thored had perhaps managed to occupy parts of Cumberland rather than simply raiding Westmorland. If this speculation is correct, then Kenneth may have recovered this area now by raiding what had briefly become English territory.

Kenneth is also reported to have fortified the banks of the fords of the Forth. It is once again not clear what this means, but it may refer to some form of construction work, possibly near Stirling. Alternatively, it may be linked to the Myreforth or Myreford reference in relation to the border with English Northumbria back in 966. It may, on the other hand, be connected to his dispute with the Britons. He could conceivably have built fortifications to protect Alba from British or English attacks. The references to British activities in Lothian and Abercorn appear to suggest actions extending beyond the boundaries of Strathclyde proper.

The Scottish Chronicle next reports that Kenneth proceeded to plunder England 'after a year' and carried off 'the son of the king of the Saxons'. This is another event that is extremely difficult to interpret in a sensible way. The most straightforward interpretation would be that the writer means a year after Kenneth's succession in 972. It is equally possible that it only means a year after the immediately previous event, the fortification of the fords, which is undated. If Kenneth had captured a son of the English King, it would certainly have been a major coup. It could provide the background to the subsequent negotiations between Kenneth and Edgar at Chester. Unfortunately, no English source records this important event and there is absolutely no confirmatory evidence that a son of King Edgar was captured by the Scots. It has been suggested instead that this entry preserves a garbled account of the handing over of a son of King Edgar as a hostage prior to Kenneth's attendance on Edgar at Chester in 973. This is unlikely, since all Edgar's three sons were extremely young at this time and indeed, according to The Anglo-Saxon Chronicle, the infant Edmund died in 972. It is much more likely that this source has confused a son of Edgar with an unnamed son of Eadwulf, *Ealdorman* of Northumbria. The latter might more conceivably have been captured during a raid into English Northumbria. In 913 the Annals of Ulster had mistakenly titled an earlier *Ealdorman* Eadwulf 'king of the Saxons'. This would certainly appear to be more likely, with the Scottish sources simpy exaggerating their king's success!

This wide range of activity, all of which is poorly dated, appears to have occurred early in Kenneth's reign. It probably provides some of the background or wider context to the famous meeting between King Kenneth II and King Edgar of England at Chester in 973. Unfortunately, the only accounts of this meeting which survive have been heavily politicised, even more than those of similar meetings in 920, 927 and 946, mentioned previously. This important event has also become a magnet for so much later legend that it is now difficult to disentangle what actually happened in 973. The later writers and propagandists have built it into a showpiece event intended to demonstrate English over-lordship throughout the British Isles. Whether any of this later legendary material has any basis in fact is now difficult to establish.

What is the story according to the earliest sources? The Anglo-Saxon Chronicle relates that in 973, King Edgar of England, the most powerful ruler in the British Isles was consecrated at Bath. He then 'took his whole naval force to Chester and six kings came to meet him and all gave him pledges that they would be his allies on sea and on land.' This account seems fairly straightforward and makes clear that this was a meeting of rulers to resolve relationships between states, not unlike those of previous years. In the Chronicle itself the six rulers are unfortunately not named. It is only in the twelfth-century account of John of Worcester that the 'eight' rulers are finally named. They include Kenneth, King of Scots and his Sub-king Malcolm, 'King' of Strathclyde. Another twelfth-century source from northern England relates that Kenneth and Malcolm were escorted to Chester by Oslac, *Ealdorman* of York, Eadwulf, *Ealdorman* of Northumbria and Bishop Aelfsige of Durham. The only possible difficulty with these names is that Malcolm was apparently not 'King' of Strathclyde in 973, since his father Donald did not die until 975. He may, however, have been representing his aged father, Donald, or perhaps the latter had resigned the kingship before 973 in order to go on pilgrimage.

The other rulers who were reportedly present at this Chester meeting were Magnus, son of Harold, 'king of many islands', Sifrith, an important but unplaced Viking ruler and Hywel and Iago, two important Welsh princes. They were all contemporaries who could therefore have been there and Chester was a reasonably convenient place for them all to meet. Kenneth and Malcolm, as noted above, could reach there relatively easily by land, travelling from either Cumberland or Lothian with their English escort. The Welsh rulers could easily reach there from their own lands beyond the River Dee. The Viking rulers could comfortably reach the port of Chester by sea from Ireland or the Isle of Man. It is certainly possible that a major summit like that depicted in the sources occurred. The prestige of King Edgar at this time and the likelihood of rich gifts for those attending would have made it attractive to these men.

The main focus of John of Worcester's twelfth-century account is on an unusual ceremony which he describes as taking place on the River Dee, near Chester. He relates that '. . . on a certain day, [Edgar] boarded a ship; having set them [i.e. the independent rulers who attended the summit] to the oars, and having taken the helm himself, he skilfully steered it through the course of the River Dee.'[11] This account has been widely accepted by later historians in spite of the fact that it is not mentioned in the earliest accounts. It certainly makes a great story, but it is surely no more than that: a story. It seems unlikely that these independent rulers would have been prepared to participate in such an event in the fashion described. It is surely unlikely that they actually rowed a ship themselves and equally unlikely that Edgar actually steered it in person. It would be unlikely for prestigious rulers like these to perform such menial tasks when they had others to do such things for them. It is more realistic to imagine that these rulers travelled together on the Dee in the same vessel and that Edgar stood on the platform in the stern with the others in front on the lower main deck. If this had happened, it might very well have seemed to observers, who recounted the story later, that King Edgar was being rowed by these other rulers. This would effectively reconcile the more fantastic aspects of this much later account with possible contemporary events.

It is clear that the accounts of this meeting at Chester, especially the later ones, have been carefully drafted to enhance the prestige of King Edgar. The formal agreement which was actually reached between Edgar and Kenneth at Chester is relatively easy to establish. It is unlikely to have involved a major submission by the Scottish ruler. There had been no preceding campaign into Scotland that might have prompted such a submission. The later northern source that provides details of the escort for Kenneth's journey to Chester, also suggests that King Edgar 'gave Lothian to Kenneth'. It seems, however, from the evidence of events above, that the kings of Alba had probably held this region since the 950s, occupying it while the English kings were distracted by other matters. It is possible that the Scots had lost it again during the civil war of the 960s, but there is no evidence for this. Indeed, the references to Scottish military activity around Abercorn and in Lothian in the 970s suggest that they still held it. It seems likely that the two rulers reached a formal agreement at Chester which confirmed Scottish possession of Lothian. The mysterious 'son of the king of the Saxons' may have been released in exchange. This would have done no more than recognise the status quo. It is also possible, though perhaps unlikely, that Edgar confirmed further Scottish gains beyond Lothian towards the Tweed.

It was probably at around this time that 'Kenneth gave Brechin to the Lord'. This appears to describe the foundation by Kenneth of a monastery at this location. It is possible that part of this still exists to this day in the form of the round tower now attached to the later medieval cathedral. The tower, whose main function was as a bell tower, is of a type then being constructed all across Ireland. If this surmise is correct, it demonstrates that Kenneth was building his monastery in the fashion then prevalent in neighbouring Ireland. The record of this monastic foundation is the final entry in the Scottish Chronicle. It is unfortunate that this native source reaches an end at this point. It is frequently infuriatingly cryptic, poorly dated and always sparse in detail but it provides a unique and fairly contemporary Scottish view of events for this period. Thereafter we are forced to depend largely on foreign or later sources for Scottish history at this time. As a result, the sources become patchy and incapable of providing anything approaching a complete account and the sequence of events is difficult to follow.

In 975 there occurred a couple of important deaths that would be significant for Scotland. The great King Edgar died and was succeeded by his young son Edward. The faction supporting Edward subsequently had *Ealdorman* Oslac of York exiled from England in the same year. He was replaced with the Thored, son of Gunnar, who had raided Westmorland in 966. It is unclear what lies behind this and it may simply have arisen from internal factional disputes. It is entirely possible that Oslac was considered weak and that Thored was viewed in contrast as a man of action. There is perhaps a remote possibility that it was linked to the earlier capture of the Saxon prince by Kenneth. If this was indeed a son of *Ealdorman* Eadwulf of Northumbria, then perhaps the latter blamed Oslac for not helping to secure his release. He may therefore have lobbied the new King and his supporters to secure Oslac's exile.

In 975 the Annals of Ulster and the Welsh annals both report the death of Donald, son of Owain, King of the Strathclyde Britons, during a pilgrimage to Rome. It is possible that Donald had relinquished his throne before 973, when, as we have seen, Malcolm appears as the 'king of Strathclyde' alongside Kenneth at Chester.

108

He may have resigned his kingship in order to go on pilgrimage. He may have been forced to resign it as a penalty for his failure to control or to punish his son Rhydderch in 971. In either case, he surrendered his kingdom to his son Malcolm, who may have succeeded him in 972. The Annals of Tigernach, which are another group of contemporary Irish annals, attribute a twenty-five-year reign to Malcolm when they report his death in 997, which would place his accession in 972. It is therefore probable that Donald actually set out for Rome in 972 or 973. If so, he may have died on his return journey in 975.

In 976 the Annals of Tigernach record the names of three Scottish *mormaers*. Unfortunately, nothing else is known about these men, who are Cellach, son of Findguine, Cellach, son of Bard and Duncan, son of Morgand. The annalist himself provides no further details whatsoever, not even mentioning that they died. It is possible that the rest of this entry was lost in the process of copying. It might be expected to go on to relate that the three men died, were killed in a battle or traveled somewhere – but there is nothing at all. The demise of three *mormaers* in a single year, if this is what this signifies, is unusual and, perhaps, suggests something other than natural causes. It might perhaps then be connected to the internal dispute over the kingship in the following year. The three are not mentioned in any other Irish sources and the ending of the Scottish Chronicle at around this time effectively removes the only possibility of learning more about these mysterious men.

In 977 the Annals of Ulster record that Olaf, son of Idulf or *Amblaib mac Idulb*, who was presumably a younger brother of Culen, was killed by Kenneth II. He is described by the annalist as 'King of Alba'. It can only be presumed that Olaf, who may have been impatient for power, had raised a claim to the throne in opposition to Kenneth. The fact that the annalist awards him the royal style may perhaps suggest that he had even had himself enthroned, although the title only appears in a later marginal note.

He had presumably been unwilling to wait for Kenneth to meet a natural death and perhaps attempted to overthrow him. It was perhaps a revival of the rivalry of the 960s between Dub and Culen. Unfortunately for him, it was Olaf who was killed in the resultant clash between them.

In 980, the Annals of Ulster record the Battle of Tara between the Irish under Mael Sechnaill, son of Domnall and the Vikings of Dublin and the Isles under Olaf *Cuaran*. The latter was the same Olaf who had attempted in vain to seize control of York in the 940s. The result of this encounter was a major defeat for the Vikings during which Olaf's son, Ragnall was killed and Olaf and his followers were expelled from Dublin. They are said to have fled to the Isles, presumably Man and the Western Isles of Scotland. It was not long after this that Olaf retired or, perhaps, was forcibly retired from the kingship. He was now in his sixties and spent his remaining years in the apparently reconstituted monastery of Iona. He had originally been baptised in 943 under the sponsorship of King Edmund of England and finally died a Christian in 981 and was buried in Iona. As in 902, the sudden influx of Vikings expelled from Dublin appears to have brought disruption to northern Britain. It would be surprising if it had not upset the local balance of power and there are certainly signs of disturbance in other entries from the Annals of Ulster. In 980, however, the disruption was limited to the western coasts and islands and hardly affected the kingdom of Alba itself.

In 986, a force of 'Danes' under a man called Guthfrith, son of Harold, who was probably a brother of the Magnus present at Chester in 973 and is later named 'King of the Isles', plundered Iona. The raiders killed the Abbot and fifteen elders of the monastery, which makes it clear that a monastic community had been revived there. In this case, Guthfrith may just have been indulging in normal raiding activity. On the other hand, this attack on Iona, which was presumably within his own sphere of authority, seems rather more purposeful. He may have attacked Iona in retaliation for its providing refuge to Olaf and his Irish Vikings. The focus of the subsequent activities of this force of Danes suggests internal strife between two Viking factions: those from Dublin who had been worsted at Tara, and those from the Isles. In 987 Guthfrith and his followers won a victory against some other Vikings in Man, perhaps those who had fled from Dublin, before being slaughtered themselves in a counterattack and suffering 360 casualties. In 989 a severely weakened Guthfrith returned to his home in the Isles where he was killed during a raid on Dalriada. This defeat was presumably inflicted by local Scottish forces who may or may not have acknowledged the authority of Kenneth II of Alba. This internal dispute reduced the potential threat presented to Alba by both of these Viking groups.

In 995, the Annals of Ulster record that 'Kenneth, son of Malcolm, was treacherously killed by his own people'. He had ruled the kingdom fairly successfully for nearly twenty-four years. The later king-lists name his assailant as Finella, the daughter of an earl, presumably a *mormaer*, Cunthar of Angus and place his death at Fettercairn. He is portrayed as the victim of a personal attack launched in revenge for his killing of Finella's only son. The assassination may, however, have been prompted by supporters of his rival and successor. Cunthar, *Mormaer* of Angus was perhaps not the first leader of that province to be implicated in the killing of a king from the lineage of Donald II. In 954 Maelbrigte of Angus may have led the men of the Mearns in killing Kenneth's own father King Malcolm I, perhaps in support of the lineage of Constantine II.

If Constantine III, son of Culen or *Castantin mac Culen* did indeed benefit from this murder he would not live to enjoy his prize for long. The treacherous killing of Kenneth II appears to have revived the struggle for the throne between the descendants of Dub and Culen which had been such a feature of the 960s and which had been revived briefly in 977. It once again inaugurated a period of intense competition for the kingship between these rival lines. In 997 the Welsh annals report that Malcolm, son of Donald, King of the northern Britons of Strathclyde died after a reign of twenty-five years. He was presumably succeeded by his brother Owain, although this is not mentioned in the sources. In the same year the Annals of Tigernach record a battle between the two Scottish factions. In this fighting, the recently installed King Constantine III, son of Culen was killed with many others at Inveralmond by Kenneth, son of Dub or *Cinaed mac Dub*, who subsequently assumed the throne as Kenneth III.

In 999, the Irish 'Annals of the Four Masters, although a very late compilation, appear to offer some evidence of a new feud over the kingship. They report that Dungal, son of Kenneth was killed by Gillacomgain, son of Kenneth. This encounter involved a struggle between cousins from different branches of the descendants of King Donald II, who appear to have quarrelled over the succession to the kingship so recently seized from the lineage of Constantine II. Unfortunately, the existence of two different Kenneths, one from each of the rival lines, and the lack of any other reference to these two characters, makes it impossible to be sure which party benefited from this victory. It does indicate, at least, that the propensity for feud was becoming ever more prevalent with each faction attempting to gain the advantage and eliminate its rivals. Indeed, the greater frequency of violent clashes between these groups is graphically indicated by the annal entries. The frequency of such events in 995, 997, 999 and 1005 suggests an intensification of the rivalry over the kingship.

It seems that the increasing distance in terms of relationships between the rival lines produced a parallel increase in the likelihood of violence between them. In the early period, when the claimants were brothers or close cousins, the amount of violence was perhaps tempered or restrained by the relative closeness of the relationship between them. In subsequent years, as the relationships between the rival lines became more distant, there was less of a family connection to restrain the potential for violence. The distant cousins of the 990s such as Constantine III and Kenneth III had to go back three or more generations to establish a close family connection. It was increasingly like having two or three rival dynasties with no family link between them at all. The increasing estrangement of the various branches fuelled their rivalry and made the competition for the prize of the kingship increasingly violent.

In 1000, according to The Anglo-Saxon Chronicle, King Aethelred of England 'went into Cumberland and ravaged very nearly all of it; and his ships went out round Chester and should have come to meet him, but they could not.' Instead they launched a series of raids against the Isle of Man. At this time Aethelred was struggling to cope with renewed Viking attacks along the coasts. He was consequently anxious to secure some positive results to counter his failure against these Vikings. The attacks on Cumberland and Man have often been considered as attempts to strike at the Vikings themselves. The Chronicle entry, however, makes it clear that the Isle of Man was not originally a target. Instead Cumberland was the real objective that Aethelred intended to strike against and it was currently subject to the kings of Alba. He may have hoped to seize this region to compensate for his poor performance elsewhere and perhaps restore his popularity. The current state of internal dissension within Scotland may have encouraged him to adopt this plan. He may have seen it as an easy way to secure an English victory.

In 1005 the simmering tensions between the rival dynasties of Alba exploded into violence once again. The Annals of Ulster report another battle between the Scots, during which Kenneth III, the son of Dub, was killed by Malcolm, son of Kenneth II or *Mael Coluim mac Cinaeda* at Monzievaird near the upper River Earn. The victor subsequently assumed the kingship in place of his dead rival as Malcolm II. This battle was to prove decisive in ending a period of intense internecine conflict that had begun almost ten years earlier. It brought to the throne a man who would actively work to confine the succession to a single line and so end this sort of conflict permanently. It is probably the case that others had already sought to do this before, but none had been successful. Malcolm may have been doing this for selfish reasons, but his achievement would ultimately prove beneficial to the kingdom as a whole.

In the period of sixty years between 943 and 1005, the kingdom of Alba was actively consolidated and expanded by a series of rulers. It had become a single unified state with a mixed culture based on its Picto-Scottish origins. It had effectively secured solid control over a sub-kingdom of Strathclyde and its rulers based in the Clyde Valley. It had further extended this control southwards into the region of Cumberland and the borders of Westmorland. It had also expanded southwards across the Firth of Forth into the rich farming lands of Lothian, which had previously been part of English Northumbria. It had also, more importantly, secured recognition of this expansion from the powerful kings of the English to the south. It had also intervened in the semi-autonomous region of Moray. In the face of powerful English competition it had tried but, so far, failed to secure control over the rest of English Northumbria. It was not prepared to abandon this attempt and would yet achieve further success. This was remarkable progress for a state that had frequently been hindered by its alternating succession especially in the last ten years. While this system had ensured the succession of the adult rulers necessary to engage in the kind of military struggle to expand the kingdom, it often resulted in fierce competition between rival claimants which could sometimes explode into civil war. This was often wasteful and debilitating and distracted kings from their efforts to expand their sphere of authority.

In the same sixty years from 940 to 1005, the kingdom of Alba had witnessed significant changes elsewhere in Britain. It had seen the rise to dominance of the kings of England over southern Britain and the complete absorption of Viking York on its own southern border into an expanding England. It had managed, however, to avoid a similar fate itself and to hold onto its own dependant regions of Strathclyde, including Cumberland, and Lothian in spite of the presence of the powerful kingdom of England to the south. The kings of Alba had achieved this relative success by reaching an acceptable modus vivendi about respective spheres of influence with their English counterparts. They had had to surrender for the present their claims to the rest of English Northumbria to achieve this. They had managed all this in spite of bloody internal conflicts over the succession to the throne. It was an impressive achievement for a small kingdom with limited resources.

5

The Great King and the Exiled Prince

I t had been over a century since the first appearance of the kingdom of Alba by that name in the records. It had then been a new and vulnerable political entity surrounded by dangerous enemies. In the century that followed, it might have seemed that very little had changed on a superficial level. The Vikings once again posed a threat to the British Isles as a new wave of raiders and invaders arrived from Norway and Denmark towards the end of the tenth century. Fortunately, the ambitious leaders of these new Vikings concentrated on the higher rewards to be secured by attacks on the rich English state to the south. They left the poorer Celtic states of Scotland, Ireland and Wales more or less alone. The Vikings who had settled on the northern and western fringes of Alba remained a feature of the local scene but were no longer a major threat. The Britons of Strathclyde and the English of Lothian were now subject peoples under Scottish hegemony, a hegemony accepted, at least for the present, by the English kingdom to the south.

It was, in fact, the kingdom of England itself that presented the greatest potential threat to Alba in 1000. Fortunately, its kings were based in the far south where most of their lands and wealth were concentrated. They considered the Welsh a more convenient target for their aggression. They seldom bothered about the Scots who were so far removed from their vital centres in the south. They were, also, preoccupied with the renewed Viking threat at this time. The

English had the potential to threaten Alba when they were free from other dangers or distractions, as under Athelstan in 934. In other circumstances, and especially in periods of weakness, they made it a priority to defend their heartland in the south.

In contrast, the kings of Alba were increasingly drawn towards their own eastern and southern areas close to England, where most of their lands and wealth were concentrated. They were thus ideally placed to exploit English weakness to extend their own power southwards. The kings of Alba had already exploited the advantageous position of their southern power centres to establish control over Strathclyde and Lothian. They had, however, been unable to secure York because of its closer proximity to the English power centres. The south-eastern location of their own power centres, however, presented a risk when England was strong and free to intervene in the north. The English could easily reach the power bases of the kings of Alba, which were relatively close to the border. The vulnerability of the kingdom of Alba had been made clear by the ease with which Athelstan had been able to penetrate into the heart of it in 934.

In 1005 King Malcolm II, son of Kenneth II or *Mael Coluim mac Cinaeda* had secured the throne after killing his cousin and rival Kenneth III at Monzievaird on the upper Earn and was probably in his twenties or thirties when he secured the throne and would go on to have a long reign of almost thirty years, longer than any other king since Constantine II. He succeeded to a kingdom which had been disrupted for the previous decade by fighting between three rival factions. This must have weakened the kingdom and exposed it to external attack. It was fortunate that England was unable to exploit this weakness as a result of its preoccupation with Viking raids during most of this period. The Vikings were similarly preoccupied with raiding in wealthy England and showed little interest in Alba. In spite of the recent debilitating shedding of blood among the royal lineages, Alba remained a significant power in northern Britain. It continued to exercise lordship over the sub-kingdom of Strathclyde and to rule over the former English region of Lothian. The new king had removed or silenced his internal rivals but still faced a number of potential problems including the presence of the formidable English kingdom to the south.

A series of circumstances now conspired to free Malcolm from external threats too. In the first place King Aethelred of England would remain distracted for over a decade by his problems with the Vikings, which would eventually culminate in the conquest of his kingdom by Danish rulers in 1016. He would never be in a position to repeat his invasion of Cumberland in 1000. In 1005 the Annals of the Four Masters report the death of Ragnall son of Guthfrith, King of the Isles, who presumably had ruled the Western Isles since 989 in succession to his father. The death of this ruler appears to have produced a power vacuum in the west that drew in the earls of Orkney. The resultant struggle for control effectively eliminated a potential threat to Malcolm from the west for a number of years. In 1006 Aelfhelm, *Ealdorman* of York and his two sons were killed by agents of King Aethelred. This severely weakened the English position in the north following the rise to power of Malcolm as King of Alba.

The confusion in Northumbria opened up a tempting opportunity for Malcolm to retaliate in response to the earlier English raid on Cumberland. He was currently free from other distractions and wasted no time in attacking. In 1006 he invaded northern England at a most opportune moment, immediately after the death of *Ealdorman* Aelfhelm and when *Ealdorman* Waltheof of Bamburgh was old and infirm. This may have been a simple raiding campaign designed to secure military success and the associated booty early in the new king's reign. It is possible, however, that it was a full-blown attempt at the conquest of English Northumbria. This last possibility is perhaps suggested by the attempt to besiege and take Durham itself. A straightforward raid had no need to attempt this and, indeed, would normally avoid such fortified locations. The result of Malcolm's invasion, according to the Annals of Ulster, was a battle between the men of Alba and the English in which the former were defeated and a great number of their nobles left dead.

The fullest account of Malcolm's attack is provided by a badly misdated and almost certainly confused account found in a later twelfth-century source called *De Obsessione Dunelmi*, or 'The Siege of Durham'. This reports that:

> Malcolm, King of Scots, son of Kenneth, having gathered an army from all Scotland, devastated the province of the Northumbrians by fire and slaughter and surrounded Durham in a siege . . . Waltheof, who had been Earl of Northumbria, shut himself up in Bamburgh. He was in fact of great age and so too old to be able to make a stand against the enemy . . . Seeing the land devastated by the enemy and Durham besieged, and his father unable to act, the young warrior [Uhtred] gathered the army of the North-umbrians and the people of York, no small force, and killed almost all the Scottish host: whose king himself barely escaped by fleeing with a few men. He [Uhtred] had the heads of the dead made more presentable with their hair combed, as then was the custom, and transported to Durham; there washed by four women, and fixed on stakes round the walls . . . Hearing of this King Aethelred called the aforementioned young man to him, and while his father, Waltheof, was still living, gave him as reward for his prowess and the way in which he fought, his father's earldom, adding the earldom of York.[12]

The twelfth-century account is certainly unreliable in terms of the date of 965 offered for this event in the text. It may also include an element of confusion with a later attack on Durham by Malcolm's own son Duncan in 1039. It is entirely understandable that local traditions about two separate attacks on Durham which both resulted in Scottish defeats became confused in the period between their occurrence and their description in the twelfth century. The contemporary and accurate Annals of Ulster prove conclusively that a battle between the Scots and the English occurred in this year and that the Scots were beaten. It is true that this source does not mention Durham or use the term 'siege', but that is no reason to reject the subsequent tradition entirely.

In spite of dubious aspects of one of the main sources for this episode, it is clear that Malcolm was heavily defeated. The disastrous outcome of this invasion might have ended Malcolm's reign then and there. Instead, it seems that the bloodletting of the last decade, which included among its victims no less than four adult members of the dynasty, had left few suitable alternative candidates for the kingship. The increased threat of Viking attacks, especially after 1007, also alleviated the danger of any English counterstroke. This serendipity allowed Malcolm time to recover and restore his position. In fact, the actions of others across the British Isles improved Malcolm's position dramatically over the next decade. In 1008 the latest Viking crisis, which would culminate in the Danish conquest of England, compelled Ealdorman Uhtred of Northumbria to focus his attention on matters nearer home. He was unable to exploit his victory at Durham but was instead forced to submit to Danish rule in 1013. In 1014, Brian Boru, King of Ireland fought and heavily defeated the King of Leinster and the Vikings from Dublin and the Isles, at the Battle of Clontarf near Dublin. Sigurd, Earl of Orkney, who had managed to seize control of the Western Isles following the death of Ragnall, son of Guthfrith in 1005, was among the fatalities. The Vikings of the north and west were left leaderless for many years as rivals fought for control of Sigurd's territories and another potential threat to Malcolm evaporated.

The Annals of Ulster record the interesting information that a certain Donald, son of Eimen, son of Cainnech, *Mormaer* of Mar fell alongside King Brian Boru at Clontarf. It is perhaps worth speculating on the possible reasons for the presence of this Donald in the Irish camp. He may simply have been a military adventurer seeking an outlet for his martial energies in foreign wars. He would not be the first or the last Scot to do so and might foreshadow the later appearance of the 'gallowglas' or Scottish mercenary soldiers. He might have been fostered with an Irish family and therefore been obliged to fight alongside them. The custom of fostering was prominent in Gaelic tradition. He could have been an exile driven out of Scotland for some misdemeanor and now seeking favour and the chance to return. More intriguingly perhaps, he might have been a member of a Scottish force which had been sent to assist Brian Boru in his war against the Vikings. The presence of Earl Sigurd of Orkney on the Viking side makes it not unlikely that Malcolm might want to assist Brian in some way. This would be an example of the principle that 'the enemy of my enemy is my friend'. This is certainly an intriguing possibility but must remain no more than that.

In 1016 Malcolm, King of Alba was in a commanding position once again. He had survived a heavy defeat at the hands of Uhtred of Northumbria at Durham in 1006. He was apparently still free of rivals at home. He had been freed from any possible Viking threat by the death of Earl Sigurd of Orkney and the defeat of the Dublin Vikings at Clontarf in 1014. He was in no immediate danger from the south, where the English and the Danes were involved in a destructive war for control of the kingdom of England. This conflict had drawn *Ealdorman* Uhtred into its maelstrom and left the northern borders of English Northumbria exposed once again. In 1016, indeed, a vacillating Uhtred would be executed by Cnut for changing sides too often. This offered an unprecedented opportunity for Malcolm, who was probably anxious to restore the prestige lost at Durham.

The consequences of this situation were almost inevitable and Malcolm, King of Alba seized the opportunity to invade English Northumbria again. The result on this occasion was, fortunately for him, much more favourable. It is recorded only in much later English and Scottish sources, the former reporting that 'A great battle was fought at Carham between the Scots and the English, between Uhtred, Waltheof's son, Earl of Northumbria and Malcolm, King of Scots, the son of Kenneth. And with him in the battle was Owain the Bald of the Britons of Strathclyde.' *Historia Dunelmensis Ecclesiae*, or 'The History of the Church of Durham' adds the information that this conflict involved 'an endless host of Scots' and that 'the entire people from the River Tees to the Tweed with their nobility, almost wholly perished . . .' The latter clearly involves an element of exaggeration but does perhaps provide a flavour of the scale of this defeat for the English.

The battle at Carham, which appears to be such an important event in Malcolm's reign, has been the source of considerable controversy among historians. The problem starts from the fact that it is not mentioned in any contemporary sources, Scottish, Irish or English, but first appears only in much later twelfth-century English sources. The main points of contention relate to when the battle actually happened and which individuals were involved in it. The confusion surrounding these issues has resulted in a number of sometimes elaborate reconstructions of the event, usually designed to justify the particular date allocated to this battle by a single twelfth-century source. There is, in fact, very little need for all this angst about what should be a relatively simple solution to this apparent problem.

The Battle of Carham is recorded only in a few late sources which may or may not be related to each other. The sources that offer a date for the battle are consistent in placing it in 1018. This point is clear. Unfortunately, one of these sources, the *Historia Regum* or 'The History of the Kings', a set of annals based on a version of The Anglo-Saxon Chronicle and attributed to Simeon of Durham, also names the main protagonists as Malcolm, King of Scots, Owen of Strathclyde and Uhtred, son of Waltheof, Earl of Northumbria. This is where the difficulty arises. Other contemporary and more reliable sources report the deaths of two of these three men a couple of years before 1018. The Welsh annals place the death of Owain of Strathclyde in 1016, two years after the battle of Clontarf, which occurred in 1014. The main Anglo-Saxon Chronicle reports the execution of *Ealdorman* Uhtred of Northumbria taking place before Easter in 1016. The latter death is also reported by The History of the Kings itself under 1016, in flat contradiction of its own report on Carham, two years later, in 1018. How could these two dead men have fought at Carham in 1018? This is the crux of the problem.

There have been many attempts to reconcile these facts or resolve this problem. Unfortunately, these have sometimes involved considerable distortion of the few facts supplied by nearly contemporary sources or, in some cases, the ignoring of these altogether. The presence of Owen and Uhtred at Carham is often ignored. They are arbitrarily replaced by other leaders, who could have been there if the battle had happened in 1018, without any evidence whatsoever in support of the presence of these others. In other cases, the accurate contemporary records of the deaths of these two individuals in 1016 are dismissed and their lives are artificially extended to allow them to participate in a battle two years later, in 1018. It is surely unacceptable to ignore or distort the few facts that exist in this fashion. Instead, the facts must be deployed in such a way that the majority are preserved and that the most reliable and contemporary are accorded preference.

In the case of the Battle of Carham the real problem comes down to one basic question: whether reliance should be placed on the year date of 1018 attributed to the battle, or on a number of facts that were part of the collective memory of the event. In the early medieval period, a calendar date associated with an event is open to error, involving the simple addition or loss of a pen stroke or strokes in the Roman numeral used. This all makes such dates more prone to be unreliable, with errors of one or two years relatively common. In contrast, the names of famous leaders who participated in a particular event are more likely to be preserved in the collective memory. It remains true, even in our own times, that most people find it much easier to recall the participants in great events rather than the precise date when the events happened.

In this context it is surely more sensible to discard the date of 1018 for the battle at Carham than to reject the information about those who participated in it. The Battle of Carham was therefore most probably fought early in 1016 between Malcolm, King of Alba and his sub-king, Owain of Strathclyde on one side and Uhtred, *Ealdorman* of Northumbria on the other and the latter was decisively defeated. There are other reasons in support of placing Malcolm's invasion of England and this battle in 1016 rather than two years later. In 1016 the English kingdom was in complete chaos with English and Danish armies competing for supremacy. This was surely the perfect moment for Malcolm to launch an invasion of the north of England. In 1018, by contrast, the Danes had emerged victorious and King Cnut was in control of England.

If the precise date of the battle of Carham has proved difficult for historians to agree on, the result is not generally disputed. The Siege of Durham reports that Eadwulf *Cudel* or Cuttlefish succeeded his brother Uhtred as *Ealdorman* of Bamburgh and proceeds to state that: 'he ceded them [the Scots] by firm treaty the whole of Lothian to make amends. In this way Lothian was added to the kingdom of the Scots.' This concession perhaps influenced those who described Eadwulf as a 'cowardly man'. He had plenty of reason to be fearful with the victorious Scots to his north and a victorious and vengeful Cnut, with his ally Jarl Erik ruling at York, to the south. It must have seemed to Eadwulf that he had little choice but to concede territory to the Scots. There is some dispute about exactly what territory was ceded to Malcolm after the victory at Carham. It is supposed by some that Lothian itself was finally secured for the

Scots, but this had almost certainly already been achieved by 973. It is possible that this hegemony might have been lost after 1006 and was now restored, but there is no evidence for this. It seems more likely that Malcolm was able to extend his authority southwards as far as the Tweed. This might have happened in the immediate aftermath of the fighting. It was not perhaps formally conceded and accepted by the English kings until rather later, perhaps in 1020 or more probably 1033.

In addition to the conquest and occupation of more of English Northumbria, the convenient death, whether in the Battle at Carham or not, of Owain, Sub-king of Strathclyde allowed Malcolm to complete the absorption of this subject kingdom. He brought this area under direct Scottish rule for the first time. The precise arrangements for this are unclear but there are perhaps some intriguing possibilities. In 1034 the Annals of Ulster record the death of a man called Suibne, son of Kenneth, King of Galloway, a man otherwise completely unknown. In light of the name of his father, Kenneth, it is perhaps conceivable that he might have been a relative of Malcolm II, King of Alba. It is unlikely that he was a brother of King Malcolm himself. He could perhaps be a son of Kenneth III, who had been offered the rule of this area to prevent him claiming the kingship itself. Unfortunately, there is no further mention of this Suibne or his descendants. Another possible fate for Strathclyde might be implied by a late source which makes reference to Malcolm's great-grandson Malcolm III as the son of the 'Prince of the Cumbrians'. If this source records an accurate tradition, it may signify that Malcolm may have appointed his own grandson Duncan to a position of authority in Strathclyde. Whatever the precise arrangement, Malcolm was now secure to the south with a greatly expanded kingdom. This achievement was facilitated because Cnut, the new Danish king of England, had a strong interest in keeping Malcolm quiet while he secured his own wider Scandinavian empire. He was probably therefore prepared to accept the significant concession to Malcolm that the loss of English Northumbria beyond the Tweed represented.

In 1020 an internal dispute flared into life in the semi-autonomous northern region of Moray. The Annals of Ulster and the Annals of Tigernach both report the killing of Findlaech, son of Ruadri. The Ulster annalist describes him incorrectly as 'King of Alba' while Tigernach refers to him more properly as *'mormaer* of Moray'. He was killed by his nephews, the sons of his older brother Maelbrigte. This appears to have been an internal dispute, which probably arose from the operation in Moray of a similar system of succession to that affecting the throne of Alba itself. It seems that all adult male relatives of previous rulers were also able to claim this title. It would not be surprising if this sort of dispute was exploited by King Malcolm to extend his authority into Moray. It is possible that Macbeth, the son of the murdered Findlaech, sought refuge with Malcolm. He is later described by the chronicler Marianus Scotus as the *dux* or 'commander' of King Duncan, Malcolm's grandson and successor, which suggests some kind of service relationship between them. It is not clear when this might have developed but it may not be fanciful to suggest that its origins lay in the refuge and assistance provided to Macbeth by Malcolm at this time.

The focus on the region of Moray that is a feature of the Annals of Ulster between 1020 and 1032 is unique. It was not the first time that kings of Alba had engaged with the local rulers of Moray. The Scottish Chronicle records some earlier contacts, usually of a hostile nature. There is, however, no sign of these earlier contacts in contemporary Irish annals. The prominence of Moray at this point seems to suggest that relations between Alba and Moray had moved into a new phase which was of interest to Ireland. It was clearly a period of increased contact and probably of increased tension between these two polities. The use of the title 'King of Alba' for some of the rulers of Moray may provide a reason for this. In Irish texts the hostile relations between Moray and Alba may have been interpreted, however inaccurately, as a contest for domination in Alba. In contemporary Ireland, rival dynasties were contending for wider rule over Ireland and beginning to employ the title 'King' or 'High-king' of Ireland. It would be perfectly natural for an Irish annalist to report an apparently similar conflict in Alba in the same terms.

In 1027 the Annals of Ulster report that Dunkeld in Scotland was completely burned. The annalist offers no further information about this event which could have been accidental or deliberate. If it was deliberate, it could have resulted from internal dispute or external invasion, in the latter case possibly by Vikings or the men of Moray. In 1027 Dunkeld would have been a particularly appropriate target for anyone at loggerheads with King Malcolm. It was probably administered by a man called Crinan, Abbot of Dunkeld, who had married King Malcolm's daughter, named in later sources as Bethoc. The couple had a son Duncan, who was King Malcolm's grandson and would eventually become his heir. This Duncan would be old enough by 1034 to succeed his grandfather and he must therefore have been born before 1027. If King Malcolm was harbouring Macbeth, a claimant to the *mormaerdom* of Moray, it is possible that the rulers of that land sought to strike back at him. In these circumstances, an attack on Dunkeld, the power base of Crinan and the probable location of King Malcolm's heir, would be highly appropriate. This is little more than speculation but interesting nonetheless.

In 1029 the Annals of Ulster record the death of Malcolm, son of Maelbrigte, son of Ruadri, who was the *mormaer* of Moray. The Annals of Tigernach provide an addition in the form of the mistaken title 'King of Alba'. This repeats the earlier use of this mistaken title by the Ulster annalist himself in 1020 and, as noted above, it may provide evidence for the Irish perception of the nature of the struggle between Moray and Alba at this time. The tension between these two regions and their rulers seems to have been fuelled by mutual interference in each other's succession. In this context, the Irish use of the style 'King of Alba' for the rulers of Moray represents their own interpretation of the political situation in Alba. In 1029 the death of Malcolm of Moray brought his brother Gillacomgain to power and this man represented a more direct danger to King Malcolm II. He had married a lady called Gruoch, a descendant of Kenneth III, and their son Lulach had inherited a claim to the kingship of Alba itself. This sequence of events can only have encouraged Malcolm to intervene directly in support of his protégé Macbeth.

In 1031, according to The Anglo-Saxon Chronicle King Cnut 'went to Scotland and the king of the Scots surrendered to him, Malcolm and two other kings Macbeth and Eachmargach'. It also reports that Malcolm 'became his man, but he observed it but a little time.' As so often before in the Chronicle, this represents an English view of the event, which offers a specific interpretation of what happened. The court poet of King Cnut, Sighvat the *Skald* also records this event: 'The most famous princes in the North from the midst of Fife have brought their heads to Cnut; that was to buy peace.'[13]

This probably represents a renewal of the earlier alliance between Alba and England by Malcolm and Cnut. It probably focused once again on the agreement of respective borders and spheres of influence. It seems likely that Cnut accepted Malcolm's direct rule over Strathclyde, including Cumberland, and his occupation of former English Northumbria north of the River Tweed. In response, Malcolm probably recognised Cnut as King of England, Denmark and Norway, including English Northumbria south of the Tweed. The presence at this meeting of Macbeth, who was not *mormaer* of Moray at this point but only a claimant to that title, and Eachmargach, King of Dublin and the Isles suggests some interesting wider possibilities.

The current rivalry between Malcolm II and the rulers of Moray was probably reaching a head at this time. The death of Malcolm, *Mormaer* of Moray in 1029 and the maturity of Macbeth surely meant that an invasion of Moray by King Malcolm was increasingly likely. The fortuitous opportunity of a meeting with Cnut in 1031 was possibly utilised to complete the preparations for this planned invasion. The presence of Eachmargach might then be explained by Malcolm's desire to secure naval allies, who could attack Moray from the north or west. The meeting with Cnut would then provide an opportunity to secure Cnut's neutrality in the contest and reassure him that this action would not disrupt his wider rule across the North Sea. On his side, Cnut was possibly pleased to find a safe outlet for the aggression of the Vikings of Dublin outside his own empire.

In the wake of his success in absorbing Strathclyde and English Northumbria as far as the Tweed and following the agreement with Cnut, Malcolm was now ready to deal with Moray. In 1032 the Annals of Ulster report that Gillacomgain, son of Maelbrigte, *mormaer* of Moray was burned along with fifty of his men. This was surely the successful outcome of Malcolm's sponsorship of Macbeth and invasion of Moray. The burning was most likely carried out by Macbeth himself or on his command but with the support and endorsement of King Malcolm. It eliminated a dangerous threat from Gillacomgain's son Lulach and restored Macbeth to his father's office of *mormaer* of Moray. It probably also placed the candidate of Malcolm, King of Alba in charge of this important northern province and, at least for the immediate future, secured its loyalty to the southern king. If this interpretation of these events is correct, it represents the first time that the kings of Alba secured control of this important region. It may also explain Macbeth's later appearance as *dux* or 'commander' of King Duncan of Alba. This must have been the crowning achievement of King Malcolm's reign. He had been triumphant in the south by 1020 and was now similarly triumphant in the north.

King Malcolm II was now getting old. He had been born some time before 995 and was therefore at least 40 and probably much older in 1032. He certainly had a brother active as early as 999. He now had to consider the future of his greatly enlarged kingdom. He had secured his expanded southern borders in treaties with Cnut and extended his lordship northwards into Moray. He was friendly with the rulers of Dublin and the Isles and possibly Orkney. This was a real achievement by Malcolm which built on the successes of his predecessors. The one real question mark that remained concerned the succession to the kingship on his death. King Malcolm had no surviving sons but Duncan, a young grandson through his daughter Bethoc. He had had to fight hard against the adult members of no less than two rival lines to secure his own succession. This problem would be all the more acute for his own young successor. There is no evidence that such a succession had previously been acceptable. It seemed highly likely that Duncan would be pushed aside by rival adult claimants, who considered their own claims to be superior. It was therefore essential and increasingly urgent for Malcolm to act to prevent this.

In 1033 the Annals of Ulster report that the unnamed grandson or 'son of a son' of Boite, son of Kenneth III was killed by King Malcolm. It is also possible that this entry relates to a person referred to as 'M', perhaps standing for Malcolm, son of Boite rather than to a grandson. This appears to have been part of Malcolm's efforts to eliminate rival claimants. He was almost certainly attempting to clear the way for the succession of his own grandson Duncan. If the assumption made above is correct, namely that Suibne, son of Malcolm was a member of a rival line, then this might reflect another aspect of the same process. Malcolm may have persuaded Suibne not to claim the throne itself by handing him rule over Galloway. In either case it appears that Malcolm's actions were sufficient to neutralise any rival claimants from the other royal lineages. Contrary to previous custom he would indeed be succeeded by his own grandson.

Malcolm II, son of Kenneth, King of Alba finally died peacefully on 25 November 1034 apparently at Glamis. The precise date is provided by Marianus Scotus, a contemporary Irish or Scottish monk who was living in Germany but who appears to have been well informed about events in Scotland. The Annals of Tigernach describe King Malcolm II as 'the honour of Western Europe'. He had certainly had a long and highly successful reign of almost thirty years. He had finally completed the absorption of the sub-kingdom of Strathclyde after the demise of its last ruler, Owain, in 1016. He had secured the control of English Northumbria as far as the Tweed, following his victory at Carham in the same year. He had successfully installed his own candidate, Macbeth, in the northern *mormaerdom* of Moray in 1032. He had worked hard to secure, to eliminate or to buy out rival claimants from other royal lineages and hence limit the succession to his own line. Finally, he had managed to pass his kingdom on to his own grandson, Duncan in 1034. This was the first case of direct succession since the time of Kenneth MacAlpin himself and it would set an important precedent for the future.

On 30 November 1034, according to Marianus Scotus, Duncan I, son of Crinan or *Donnchad mac Crinain* was enthroned as King of Alba, probably at Scone, in succession to his maternal grandfather only five days after the latter's death. Duncan was not the kindly old man portrayed by Shakespeare, who has badly distorted the popular view of eleventh-century Scottish history. He was in fact a much younger man who had a lot to prove as successor to his successful grandfather. Against customary practice he had been promoted to the kingship by the actions of his grandfather, King Malcolm II and probably enjoyed the active support of his father Crinan, Abbot of Dunkeld. In spite of this, the haste with which he had been enthroned, only five short days after his grandfather's demise, suggests a certain amount of anxiety about whether his succession might be opposed. It appears, however, that the enthronement went smoothly and there are no signs in the sources of any immediate opposition. There exists an assumption, based largely on Shakespeare, that Duncan was a weak king but the sources suggest otherwise. He ruled without recorded incident for more than five years before encountering difficulties.

In 1040, the twelfth-century History of the Church of Durham reports that 'Duncan, King of Scots, came with enormous forces and besieged Durham and laboured greatly to reduce it, but in vain. For a great part of his cavalry was slain by those who were besieged; and he fled away in confusion, and in his flight lost all his infantry killed. And their heads were carried into the market-place, and set up on stakes.' This event is dated to 1040, by reference to the regnal year of King Harold I of England and the episcopal year of Bishop Edmund of Durham, although a set of late Durham annals places it in 1039. Unfortunately, there is no easy way to resolve this discrepancy satisfactorily, but the allegation of The History of the Church of Durham that Duncan's death, which is firmly dated to August 1040, followed 'not long afterwards' perhaps points to 1040. It is possible that this attack was not unprovoked since The History of the Kings reports that Eadwulf, son of Uhtred, *Ealdorman* of Northumbria raided Cumberland shortly after his succession in 1038.

The twelfth-century account of this second disaster at Durham contains some points of similarity with that which befell Duncan's grandfather, King Malcolm II in 1006. On that previous occasion, Malcolm also besieged Durham and suffered a severe reverse. In both cases the Scots lost many men and the heads of their dead were impaled on stakes. The similarities suggest the possibility that subsequent memories of these events have perhaps become somewhat confused or conflated. This does not necessarily mean, however, that there were not indeed two separate attacks on Durham since there are also differences between the two accounts. There is no doubt that Durham and its wealthy church of St

Cuthbert presented an attractive target for the kings of Alba and a potential source of rich plunder. In addition, the capture of this important fortified position on the winding course of the River Wear might also secure the surrender of the surrounding region, later known as St Cuthbert's land. The failure of Malcolm before Durham in 1006 may even have encouraged Duncan to attempt its capture to avenge his grandfather's defeat.

There was another more important difference between the two Scottish defeats at Durham. In 1006 Malcolm survived his disastrous defeat and went on to rule with great success for a further twenty-eight years. In contrast, Duncan was not to be so fortunate and, not long after his humiliation at Durham, he would be dead. In 1040 the Annals of Ulster report that 'Duncan, son of Crinan, King of Alba was killed by his own people.' This was a familiar tale and customarily referred to the outcome of a violent dispute over the succession between rival royal lineages. If this had indeed been the case, then King Malcolm's efforts to clear a path for his grandson had clearly come to nothing. In fact, the contemporary account of Marianus Scotus reveals that this was not the case. He reports that King Duncan was slain, possibly at Pitgaveny near Elgin, on 14 August 1040 by his *dux* Macbeth, son of Findlaech. The Latin word *dux* used by Marianus usually signifies a military commander of some sort and, if used in this specific sense, might imply that Macbeth held a senior position in Duncan's court. In this particular context, it may, however, simply represent a translation of the Gaelic term *mormaer*, a position that also involved military leadership.

The precise circumstances of this killing are unclear. It is possible that Duncan was killed in battle while invading Moray. He may have turned against Moray in an effort to expunge his recent defeat in the south with a victory in the north. It is equally possible that he was murdered during a tour of the region, possibly made at Macbeth's invitation. Macbeth may have chosen to exploit an opportunity to challenge the King and improve his own position. It is, however, possible to trace the likely source of tension between Macbeth and King Duncan, the son of his former mentor and ally Malcolm II. It undoubtedly lies in the recent marriage of Macbeth to Gruoch, the widow of his cousin and rival Gillacomgain. This happened at some point after 1032 and most probably after Malcolm's death in 1034. Gruoch is another figure who, as 'Lady Macbeth', has suffered at the hands of Shakespeare. The marriage appears to have produced no children but it brought Macbeth a stepson, in the person of Lulach. The action of Macbeth in offering refuge and support to this young boy was a direct challenge that Duncan could not ignore. It resulted in a clash between these former allies and led Duncan to his fate.

The murder of a king by one of his *mormaers* was not an unknown event in this or earlier periods. What is unique on this occasion is that Marianus goes on to state that Macbeth then 'succeeded to the kingdom'. This was the first time that someone from outside the rival royal lineages succeeded to the kingship. One or two of Macbeth's predecessors in Moray were titled 'King of Alba' in some of the Irish sources, but there is absolutely no evidence to assume that any of them ever held the throne of Alba. The succession of Macbeth therefore calls for some explanation. This has usually revolved around theories that Macbeth was related in some fashion to one or other of the royal lines, the most common suggestion being that Macbeth had a claim through his mother, Donada, supposedly a daughter of Malcolm II. There is, however, absolutely no contemporary evidence for this and it only appears in much later sources. It seems likely that it was an invention of later writers, who sought to explain Macbeth's otherwise inexplicable succession. If this suggestion is correct then Macbeth had no personal claim to the throne of Alba.

It was in fact Lulach, Gruoch's son by her previous marriage to Gillacomgain, who possessed a claim to the throne. It was a claim at least as credible as that held by King Duncan himself. Lulach was the *nepos*, i.e. the nephew or grandson – in this case almost certainly the grandson – of Boite, and so a descendant of Kenneth III. In this context, Macbeth might be regarded as acting on behalf of his young stepson Lulach, who was probably too young to claim the throne himself. Macbeth may even have adopted Lulach to facilitate his action. There is, however, a wider possible explanation for this unusual succession and it reflects the success of Malcolm II in eliminating or excluding alternative lineages. In 1040 there were simply no suitable adult males in any of the three royal lineages capable of succeeding to the throne. It is well known that King Duncan left behind two infant sons, Malcolm and Donald, who were incapable of rule. But what about the other two lineages?

The adult male descendants of Dub and Kenneth III had been eliminated with the killing of Boite's son or grandson in 1033 and, possibly, the death of Suibne in 1034. In 1040, no adult members of this line were available to claim the throne, with Lulach being a child of around eight or nine years. There were apparently other descendants of Dub in existence although they were probably not adults in 1040. It is now generally accepted that the later MacDuff earls of Fife were descendants of this royal line. It is presumed that they surrendered their claim to the kingship in return for rich lands in Fife, a position of primacy among the other Scottish *mormaers* or earls and the right to enthrone the king at Scone. It is not known exactly when this transition might have occurred but presumably before the first recorded appearance of Constantine MacDuff, Earl of Fife in 1095. The abandonment of their claim, if it did occur at this time, effectively removed one line of this rival royal lineage from the competition for the throne.

The other rival lineage, the descendants of King Aed, are usually assumed to have died out with the killing of Constantine III in 997. There is no evidence to support this assumption but there is some, admittedly meagre, evidence to suggest otherwise. This relates to the appearance in the twelfth century of a family known as the

MacHeths, who fairly consistently challenged the descendants of Malcolm II for the kingship. There has been a great deal of speculation about their origins and the nature of their claim, much of it highly inventive. The reality is surely much more straightforward – that they were indeed the descendants of King Aed or Heth – and it is a mystery that this connection has not been widely accepted. It provides the simplest reason for their frequent challenges to the descendants of King Malcolm II. The fact that there is no mention in the sources of this lineage between Constantine III in 997 and the first mention of the MacHeths in 1157 seems to have discouraged the adoption of this solution. This is certainly a long gap but the sources for this period are so thin that it is probably less significant than it seems. It is possible that the MacHeths simply had no adult males ready to challenge for the kingship at crucial moments in the succession, including in 1040. It is also possible that an attempt was made to buy them off on the model of the MacDuffs. If so, it was on this occasion only partially successful. The later association of the MacHeths with Ross might suggest a location where they were offered lands and authority in return for a surrender of their claim. There is, however, no evidence for this suggestion and it certainly did not prevent the MacHeths from challenging for the kingship. It may of course be that subsequent descendants regretted the choice of their ancestors or were disappointed by the position and wealth obtained and decided to revive their rights.

If this scenario is correct, it appears that Macbeth successfully exploited the absence of adult candidates from the three royal lineages to seize the kingship. This was in itself a significant achievement but he also went on to hold onto it for nearly seventeen years. He was clearly a remarkable man who managed to persuade the *mormaers* and nobles of the kingdom to accept his usurpation. If he had been the *dux* of Duncan's armies, he might have established precisely the kind of close connections with these men that would have smoothed his path to the throne. A slightly later contemporary, Earl Harold Godwineson, who had been the *dux* of King Edward the Confessor, would similarly exploit his wide connections to secure the throne of England. It was not impossible for a powerful and determined individual with no recognised claim to exploit the absence of recognised adult claimants to seize the kingship. It may be that the later accounts used by Shakespeare, which suggest that Macbeth was a usurper, were not entirely without foundation.

It is clear from the sources that Macbeth, son of Findlaech or *Macbethad mac Finnlaech*, became King of Alba in 1040. What is far from clear, however, is how far his authority actually extended and what happened to the young sons of King Duncan. It is generally assumed that Macbeth controlled the whole of the kingdom of Alba, including its new southern territories of Strathclyde and Lothian. In fact, it is only possible to establish for certain from the sources that survive that he controlled the old core of the kingdom north of the Forth–Clyde line. He was presumably enthroned at Scone although no source confirms this. He is otherwise associated with Dunkeld, Loch Leven, Dunsinane and, finally, Lumphanan, all of them located within the original kingdom. He is never found in association with the southern regions of Strathclyde or Lothian. This may simply be a consequence of the shortage of sources, but it may also be because these areas were outwith his control. If this assumption is correct, the question of who did control this area remains open and will be discussed further.

There is little information in the sources on the fate of Duncan's two young sons, Malcolm and Donald. They are completely absent from the contemporary record between 1040 and 1057 and later sources offer little additional information about their whereabouts. It is only the fourteenth-century *Gesta Annalia*, attributed to John of Fordun, that reports that Malcolm sought refuge in England while Donald went to the Western Isles and it is difficult to place much reliance on this. It is possible to reconstruct any number of possible scenarios to fill this gap but this adds little to our knowledge without support. They could have sought refuge with supporters in Scotland or in exile abroad in England, the Orkneys, the Western Isles or even Ireland, or indeed a combination of these.

In 1045, the Annals of Ulster report 'a battle between the men of Alba themselves in which Crinan, Abbot of Dunkeld, fell', while Tigernach adds that 180 men were lost with him. This might support the possibility that the two young princes may have sought refuge with their grandfather, Crinan, Abbot of Dunkeld. This would be a natural refuge for the two princes and this report might reflect an attempt by Crinan to seize the kingship on behalf of his grandsons. It is perhaps more probable, however, that it represents an attempt by Macbeth to eliminate the last source of opposition to his rule. If this latter assumption is the case, it shows that not everyone was reconciled to Macbeth's rule.

In the aftermath of the death of Crinan of Dunkeld, there is no further indication of any threat to Macbeth's rule. Indeed, in 1050, he is reported by Marianus Scotus to have visited distant Rome on pilgrimage, which certainly suggests that he felt his throne to be secure in his absence. If this is the case, where was Malcolm? There appear to be three possibilities. Firstly, he fled to England in 1040 and remained there until his return with Earl Siward in 1054. This is the most obvious assumption and it is the one usually adopted. Secondly, he was sheltered by his grandfather Crinan but following his death in 1045 sought refuge in England. This is also an assumption that fits the few facts that are known. Lastly, he had been appointed by his father to rule in Strathclyde and possibly Lothian under a suitable adult guardian. He subsequently managed to retain control of this region while Macbeth ruled the main part of the kingdom to the north of the Forth–Clyde line. It must be admitted, however, that there is no contemporary evidence for any of these scenarios.

It is established that Malcolm understood English, which suggests that he spent a lot of time among English-speakers and so either in southern Scotland or England. He knew English well enough to be able to communicate with his English-speaking wife and to act as her translator. He may have become more familiar with English-speaking Northumbria and England itself than with his homeland. How did this affect him? He was the first king of Alba with detailed first-hand knowledge of his southern neighbours. He was able to observe their rich culture and sophisticated administration. He would be followed by other Scottish monarchs in this path, most notably by his own son, David I, but also by David II and James I. In some sense all these men were influenced by their experiences in England and it would be surprising if Malcolm were an exception. He probably admired and absorbed aspects of English culture and administration. He also had an important advantage in relation to his own future subjects in Lothian. He would be the first king of Alba with a direct linguistic and cultural connection to his English-speaking subjects. This must have helped him to secure the loyalty of these southern areas during his struggles against Macbeth and Lulach and their northerners. He would be so comfortable with these English-speakers that he would later establish his main power base among them around Dunfermline and Edinburgh.

If it is not clear where exactly Malcolm was during the fourteen-year period from 1040, it is clear that he sought and secured English assistance to pursue a claim to the kingdom. He had not lost the desire to recover his paternal inheritance and he worked hard in exile to secure English assistance to recover his throne. The death of Crinan had removed a vital source of support within Scotland and thereafter Malcolm would need outside assistance to restore his fortunes. It is possible that Malcolm may initially have tried to exploit memories of his great-grandfather's alliance with Cnut to seek support from the latter's son and successor Hardecnut. He may even have attempted to portray King Duncan's invasion of 1039 as being directed against Harold I, Hardecnut's deadly enemy in order to curry favour. It seems unlikely that he sought support from *Ealdorman* Eadwulf, with whom his father had been in conflict only the year before. In 1041, however, Earl Siward of York killed Eadwulf and assumed control of all of Northumbria. It is likely that Malcolm found him more sympathetic and it was ultimately Siward who promoted Malcolm's cause in 1054.

It was, however, not until some fourteen years later that Siward's support finally took concrete form. In the years immediately after 1040 there were many other more important matters to preoccupy Siward. In 1042 Hardecnut died and was succeeded by King Edward the Confessor; between 1043 and 1047 England faced the threat of a Norwegian invasion; and from 1048 until 1053 a series of internal disputes broke out among the English nobility. A late set of Durham annals reports that Siward invaded Scotland and expelled Macbeth in 1046, but this receives no confirmation in contemporary sources and it may be a misplaced reference to events of 1054. It was not therefore until after 1053 that Siward was finally able to apply his own and royal resources, in the shape of royal *huscarls*, to support Malcolm's cause. The expedition itself or, at least, the involvement of the royal *huscarls* may have been prompted by Macbeth's provision of shelter to some Normans expelled from England in 1053. It is unlikely that Siward provided his assistance without some form of concession on Malcolm's part. The most likely price for English support was the surrender of Cumberland to Earl Siward. The text of 'Gospatric's Writ' indicates that Earl Siward held control over Allerdale in Cumberland at this time. It seems most likely that it fell into English hands in this way since there is otherwise no record of its physical seizure by the English.

On 27 July in 1054 The Anglo-Saxon Chronicle reports that '. . . Earl Siward proceeded with a large force to Scotland, both with a naval force and a land force, and fought there with the Scots and routed the king Macbeth and killed all the best in the land and carried off a large amount of plunder such as had never been captured before.' The Annals of Ulster report the same encounter and the resultant heavy casualties of 3,000 Scots and 1,500 English. The savagery of the fighting is also revealed by the number of prominent casualties listed in the sources. The English lost Earl Siward's son Osbeorn and his nephew Siward and Dolfin, son of Thorfinn Mac Thor of Allerdale, and a number of *huscarls*. The Scots lost the exiled Norman knights Osbern Pentecost and Hugh. Unfortunately, none of the contemporary sources mention the site of this battle. It is located at Dunsinane in Angus only in much later sources and the basis for this is unclear.

The consequences of this toughly fought battle in 1054 are also unclear. The English army certainly returned home with more plunder than ever before but also with heavy losses. They appear to have considered it a success and this is confirmed by the balance of losses noted in the Annals of Ulster. The English victory does not appear, however, to have ended Macbeth's rule which continued until 1057. It must, however, presumably have secured some form of advantage for Malcolm. He does not appear to have been recognised as king at this stage but perhaps he gained control over more territory. It has been suggested that he already held the southern regions of Lothian and Strathclyde and this latest success, if correctly located at Dunsinane, may have brought him control of Fife, Strathearn and Angus. He may also have secured control of his grandfather's former base at Dunkeld. This sort of advance would find him in control of a significant and rich area of the kingdom. It would leave Macbeth with a much smaller area immediately to the south of his heartland in Moray. If Malcolm had not made some headway following this encounter it would be difficult to explain Macbeth's downfall only two years later.

The English invasion was not repeated, so either it had achieved its purpose or the English were discouraged from further action by their heavy losses or the death of Siward in the following year. Malcolm himself was not dissuaded by the loss of direct English support, but continued the struggle on his own. It is possible that he sought an alternative ally in the person of Earl Thorfinn of Orkney. This northern ruler is sometimes considered an ally of Macbeth because they both visited Rome in 1050, but little more is reliably known about him. The career of Thorfinn is not covered by contemporary sources but is related in the *Orkneyinga Saga*, compiled nearly two centuries later. The Norse sagas are literary entertainments rather than historical texts. They focus on exciting stories and interesting characters and not reliable historical facts and sound chronology. This makes them even more unreliable than other late sources and they should generally be avoided unless supported by more historical texts. A number of historians have, for example, attempted in vain to identify the fictional character Karl Hundason with various historical figures, including Malcolm II, Duncan I, Macbeth, Lulach and Malcolm III, but this is probably a futile exercise. The saga relates that Malcolm married a daughter of Thorfinn, although there is no contemporary support for this. If this did indeed happen, then Malcolm may have received Viking support against Macbeth. It is possible that Thorfinn found the expanded power of his southern neighbour Macbeth troublesome. If Macbeth was under pressure on two fronts this could certainly help to explain his final defeat in 1057.

On 14 August 1057, according to Marianus Scotus, Malcolm finally caught up with his rival Macbeth and killed him at Lumphanan on the fringes of Moray. The Annals of Ulster, for once, mistakenly record the death of Macbeth in 1058, after that of Lulach. There appear to be two possible scenarios that might explain the location of this killing. Macbeth had held an area north of the Tay since 1054 until a recent defeat by Malcolm forced him to retreat northwards, where he was caught at Lumphanan before he could reach safety in Moray. Alternatively, Macbeth had retreated into Moray some time before but was now attempting to advance south to resume the struggle and restore his fortunes. The defeat and death of his rival should have secured the kingship for Malcolm, but this did not in fact happen. On the contrary, the contemporary sources indicate that the kingship was assumed by Lulach, Macbeth's stepson and the candidate of the MacDuff lineage. This occurred in spite of the fact that Malcolm appeared to be in control of much of Alba, including the royal inauguration site at Scone. How did this happen?

It appears that Lulach was, like Macbeth, based in Moray, which appears to have been the main territory still controlled by their supporters in 1057. In contrast, the royal inauguration site at Scone appears to have been deep within territory controlled by Malcolm. If this was indeed the case, it would be difficult for Lulach to arrange an inauguration before retreating north to meet his end in Strathbogie only months later. If, however, Lulach had not undergone inauguration at some point he would surely not feature in the king-lists and Malcolm would be recognised as king instead. What is the answer to this conundrum? It was suggested earlier that Macbeth was a usurper unrelated to any of the lineages of Alba, who sought to bolster his lack of a claim by the adoption of Lulach. If these assumptions are valid, then it may be that Macbeth had arranged the formal inauguration of Lulach as his successor at some point during his own reign. Although there is no precedent for this in Alba itself, there were earlier precedents from Mercia and the Frankish kingdoms. In particular, if Macbeth felt that his rule was becoming undermined after 1054, he might have inaugurated Lulach as his co-ruler to secure the backing of the MacDuff lineage. This would account for the appearance of Lulach in the king-lists despite the likelihood that he probably never exercised rule much beyond the confines of Moray.

There is perhaps a small piece of evidence that might support the suggestion of joint kingship in this period. The Annals of Ulster use the title *ri Alban* or 'King of Scots' for every Scottish king between the first use of the name 'Alba' in 900 and 1130. There are only three exceptions to this rule: Macbeth in 1058, Lulach in 1058 and

Malcolm in 1093. These three individuals and no others are uniquely referred to as *ardrigh Alban* or 'Over-king' or 'High-king of Scots'. This title was used in Irish texts to indicate a superior king ruling over other minor kings. In the kingdom of Alba, however, there were no other kings and the title of 'King' was therefore more appropriate. The use of the title *ardrigh* for these three individuals suggests the existence of other kings to whom these individuals might be superior. This might be appropriate in a situation where Macbeth ruled alongside Lulach but in a superior role. This would not appear to explain the use of this title for Lulach or Malcolm, but perhaps a solution lies in an otherwise unknown agreement between Malcolm and Lulach. If Malcolm controlled the south of Alba and Lulach the north, they may have agreed to rule jointly in the short term while each gathered strength to continue the fight. It is entirely possible, however, that the use of this specific title between 1057 and 1093 represents no more than a quirk of the scribe who originally compiled this section of the annals.

According to Marianus Scotus, it was not until 17 March 1058 that Malcolm was finally able to eliminate Lulach by killing him in battle at Essie in Strathbogie. It was only now, following the elimination of all his rivals, that Malcolm was finally able to claim the undisputed title of King of Alba. He had had to fight hard for the kingship against not one but two rivals. He had spent nearly eighteen years in the pursuit of his paternal inheritance. This represented a great part of his young life and a major investment of time and money. He was now intent on holding on to the prize, but only time would tell how successful he would be. It was nevertheless a significant achievement for a man who had been an exile in 1040. He had secured English aid to sponsor his initial return in 1054 but this had been withdrawn after the death of Earl Siward in 1055. Thereafter he had had to carry on the struggle alone. In spite of this he had ultimately triumphed. He was now the sole ruler of the kingdom.

6

Malcolm, King of Alba

On 17 March 1058, Malcolm III, son of Duncan or *Mael Coluim mac Donnchad* found himself undisputed King of Alba, following the killing of Lulach, his last remaining rival from the MacDuff lineage. There is no surviving account in the historical record of Malcolm's inauguration as King of Alba. It is not even certain when it took place, although John of Fordun, writing in the fourteenth century, dates it to 25 April 1057. If Fordun is correct, and this is by no means certain, it seems that Malcolm was inaugurated before he had disposed of either of his rivals. He was presumably also in temporary control of the region around Scone at this point, since otherwise he would not have been able to hold the ceremony. In spite of the lack of evidence, it is nevertheless almost certain that some form of ceremony marked Malcolm's assumption of the kingship.

The precise nature of the royal inauguration ceremony in the eleventh century is unknown. It has been suggested that an inauguration scene appears on Sueno's Stone near Forres beneath the cross, but it is now so badly worn that it is impossible to be certain. In the absence of any useful contemporary evidence, it may be possible to suggest some of the key elements of the ceremony from reports of later examples. The first Scottish royal inauguration for which a detailed account survives is that of Alexander III at Scone in 1249, which is also described by John of Fordun:

... earls, namely ... Fife and Strathearn, and many other nobles led [the King] to a cross standing in the graveyard on the east side of the church. There they set him on the royal throne adorned with silken cloths woven with gold and the bishop of St Andrews assisted by the rest, consecrated him king as was fitting. The king himself sat down on the royal throne or stone, under whose feet the earls and other nobles, on bended knees, cast their cloaks. And lo, when these things had happened, a certain highland Scot, suddenly fell on his knees before the throne and with bowed head, saluted the king in [his] mother tongue, 'God bless, [the king's name] king of Scots ...' and speaking thus he read the genealogy of the kings of Scots up to the end ...[14]

This event occurred almost two centuries after Malcolm's time and is recorded in an even later source but such ceremonies are often by their nature conservative. It is likely that elements of it had survived over a long period of time. It can therefore usefully be examined for evidence for the kind of inauguration practised in Malcolm's own time.

It is almost certain that, as in 1249, the ceremony that marked Malcolm's assumption of the kingship also took place in the open air at Scone and probably on the site now known as the Moot Hill. It is clear that Scone was an important royal centre from the very origins of the Picto-Scottish kingdom in the early 800s and, possibly, for much longer. It is described in The Prophecy of Berchan as Scone of 'the high shields' and Scone of 'the melodious shields', obscure terms which probably refer to the ancient acclamation rituals of, respectively, raising a new king on a platform of shields to show him to the people and striking spears against shields to celebrate a new king. The Moot Hill is probably the same site referred to in the Scottish Chronicle as the 'Hill of Faith', where King Constantine II struck his deal with Bishop Cellach of St Andrews in 906.

The inauguration ceremony itself, as in 1249, almost certainly consisted of inauguration or enthronement rather than coronation, which was not introduced until 1329. The new king was probably seated on a throne or stone, or possibly a combination of these, which represented the wider kingdom. This custom has some similarities with certain Irish and Dalriadan ceremonies, and may possibly signify the marriage of the king with his kingdom. The ceremony almost certainly also included the recitation in Gaelic by a *sennchaidh* or historian of the king's genealogy. This remained a feature of the ceremony in 1249, when the use of Gaelic suggests that it was an early survival from before 1097 at least. A succession system which selected its kings from three alternate lineages descended from early kings would have required reliable proof. The royal genealogy provided the necessary confirmation that this was the true king by placing him in the line of descent from Kenneth MacAlpin and beyond.

The role of others in the ceremony is perhaps even more difficult to ascertain. In the eleventh century, the new king was probably led to the throne or stone and placed on it by a *mormaer*, the equivalent of the earls of 1249, and probably by the *mormaer* of Strathearn alone. The role of this important secular figure was probably to acknowledge that the new king controlled this vital central region of Alba, formerly known as Fortriu. Indeed, the wider kingdom of Alba was sometimes known by the name of this region in Irish sources in its early years. In 1249 this role had been usurped by the Earl of Fife, while the Earl of Strathearn, although still present, no longer had any clearly defined function. It was probably only after Malcolm's time that the earls of Fife took over this role, probably as compensation for their surrender of the claim of the MacDuff lineage to a place in the succession. This possible change between Malcolm's time and 1249 highlights the fact that, while some elements of the ceremony demonstrated considerable continuity over time, others were subject to change.

The role performed by the Christian Church in the royal inauguration ceremony of Malcolm's time is much less clear. It seems unlikely that, after nearly 400 years, the Church would not have secured a role in this important ceremonial by the eleventh century. Adomnan's account of St Columba anointing Aidan of Dalriada, even if it exaggerates Columba's role, suggests that senior clerics were already alive to the issue in the 690s. Abbot Ailred of Rievaulx reports that David I in 1124 'so abhorred those obsequies which are offered by the race of Scots in the manner of their fathers upon the recent promotion of their king that he was with difficulty compelled by the bishops to receive them.' This appears to suggest some unfamiliar or barbaric elements in the ceremony, but it should perhaps be seen as an example of cultural snobbery rather than evidence of pagan ritual. It should be remembered that St Margaret's biographer portrayed the entire Scottish Church as backward in many respects. The Scottish bishops, who finally persuaded David I to undergo the ceremony, clearly did not regard it as pagan. The agreement of 906 between Bishop Cellach and King Constantine II, struck on the Hill of Faith at Scone itself, may have included provision for a clerical role in the royal inauguration, if this did not already exist. It would seem most likely that this involved at the very least a blessing of the new king. It perhaps also included an oath by the new king to maintain the agreement of 906 between the clerical and secular authorities.

Whatever the precise nature of the ceremonial and the exact date, King Malcolm III was inaugurated on the Hill of Faith at Scone. He would prove to be a worthy successor of his great-grandfather and namesake Malcolm II. He would reign for thirty-five years, which was longer than Malcolm II and over a strong and stable kingdom. In 1058, of course, none of this was apparent and Malcolm had just returned from a long period in exile. He had had to fight for the kingship, initially with English assistance but subsequently on his own. He had nevertheless managed to triumph over his rivals Macbeth, the northern usurper from Moray, and Lulach, the candidate of the rival MacDuff lineage. It had taken him four years to secure his rule and he remained vulnerable for the immediate future.

In the period immediately following his victories over Macbeth and Lulach, Malcolm preserved his early alliance with England in spite of changes there. In 1059, a late Durham source reports that King Malcolm, escorted by a great body of men led by Tosti, Earl of Northumbria, Cynesige, Archbishop of York and Aethelwine, Bishop of Durham, visited King Edward in England probably in recognition of his military and political support. He may have met his future bride Margaret at this time but, if so, there is no record of this. It is likely that this visit involved discussion and agreement on common borders in line with many similar meetings in the past. It seems likely that it endorsed the border changes that Malcolm had been forced to accept as the price for English aid in 1054, namely the surrender of Cumberland. It is known that Siward had controlled Allerdale in Cumberland during his time as earl and there is no evidence to suggest that it was lost until after the Norman Conquest in 1066. It seems likely that Malcolm was still involved in consolidating his hold on the kingdom of Alba and could not therefore afford any disturbance on his southern border.

In 1061 Malcolm appears to have exploited the absence of Earl Tosti in Rome to launch a raid against Lindisfarne. This raid may perhaps be a sign that two years on Malcolm felt that he had secured his rule in Alba and felt sufficiently confident to risk irritating his former allies in the pursuit of plunder. It has been suggested that this raid is, in fact, clear evidence of the severance of Malcolm's alliance with England and with Earl Tosti specifically. It is important to note, however, that this raid occurred during the absence of Tosti in Rome and that good relations were apparently quickly restored through negotiations on Tosti's return. It has also been suggested that this attack marks the restoration of

Cumberland to Scottish control. The raid, however, was directed at Lindisfarne rather than Cumberland and there is no evidence in the sources of any border changes until after 1066. It is possible that the raid was prompted by a local dispute initiated in Tosti's absence by the family of the old Northumbrian earls. It would become clear from subsequent events that relations between Tosti and some members of this dynasty were not always friendly. They may have exploited his absence to pursue personal grievances against Malcolm, who controlled some of their ancestral lands in Lothian. The Scottish raid would then represent Malcolm's retaliation rather than his own initiative. There is no evidence of any personal animosity between Malcolm and Tosti, who were blood brothers, and only five years later Malcolm would welcome the exiled Tosti at his court.

In 1063, the English launched a major invasion of Wales that involved forces drawn from Northumbria and led by Earl Tosti himself. It seems unlikely that Tosti could have taken part in this invasion if King Malcolm had represented a hostile threat in the north. The result of this invasion and the subsequent fate of the Welsh ruler, Gruffydd ap Llwelyn, offered an object lesson in the fate of those who stood against the English at this time. It must have reinforced in Malcolm's mind the wisdom of a continued alliance with Tosti and the English. Indeed, it appears that relations between Malcolm and his southern neighbours remained friendly for the rest of King Edward's reign. If there had been tension between Malcolm and the English it might have been expected that he would have sought to exploit the Northumbrian rebellion of 1065 for his own ends. There is, however, no evidence that he did so and Malcolm would not seek to interfere in English affairs until 1068.

It was not until 1066 that Malcolm's relations with England would enter a new phase. The fundamental changes in the English political situation which occurred in that year and were outside Malcolm's control would be responsible for this. The exile of Tosti,

Malcolm's blood brother would be swiftly followed by the death of King Edward, Malcolm's ally, the brief succession of King Harold II Godwineson, an unsuccessful Norwegian invasion of England and, finally, the Norman Conquest. What role, if any, did Malcolm play in these great events? He appears, very wisely, to have managed to remain neutral amidst these political storms. It is true that he offered refuge in the summer of 1066 to the exiled Tosti, but he did not offer to aid him to any significant extent to restore his fortunes in England. There was no Scottish invasion of Northumbria either in support of Tosti or his Norwegian allies.

In the summer of 1066, the exiled Tosti sought refuge in Scotland after the abject failure of his raids on the east coast of England. It seems unlikely that this is what he originally intended although it may have been prepared as a fall-back position. He knew that Malcolm, his blood brother, would at the very least offer him shelter. It is much more difficult to fathom Malcolm's purpose at this time. He may simply have offered Tosti shelter on the basis of their relationship. He may also have viewed this as a potential political opportunity. He could perhaps use the threat of intervention on behalf of Tosti to negotiate the restoration of Cumberland. In the end Malcolm decided to offer him refuge and supplies, but nothing more. It was left to Tosti himself to seek more powerful and more willing allies elsewhere. He turned to King Harald of Norway, who was eager to restore his fortunes following the dismal end of his long war with Denmark.

It is not clear whether Malcolm supported the subsequent alliance between Tosti and the Norwegians and their combined invasion of England. It would surely be dangerous for Malcolm if Harald of Norway managed to surround him by seizing control of England. He would face Norwegian power not only to the north and the west but also to the south. He may have been content to distract them from targeting his own kingdom. He did not challenge the southward passage of the Norwegian fleet along the Scottish east coast, but it is unlikely that he could have prevented this in any case. What appears to be clearer is that Malcolm remained aloof from the subsequent invasion of England. There is no evidence that any Scottish forces were involved in the fighting around York or in the disaster at Stamford Bridge that followed. There King Harold II of England surprised and defeated the Norwegians, killing both King Harald and Tosti. Whatever Malcolm's intentions, the result probably worked to his advantage. He had managed to avoid both the danger of Norwegian encirclement and a potentially costly commitment to either side. It seems likely that Malcolm remained neutral thereafter with a victorious English king to the south. He was, in any case, in no position to influence the momentous events that took place at Hastings. He had simply to await the result like many others across Europe.

The victory of William of Normandy at Hastings and his subsequent coronation as King of England probably came as a surprise. It is likely that Malcolm was unsure of what this might signify for him and his kingdom and that he initially opted to await developments. The recent series of dramatic events in England made assessment of the political situation very difficult. In the immediate aftermath, Malcolm had lost his former allies in England. He lacked any connection with the new Norman rulers but even greater changes would follow. It is, however, probably fair to say that the Norman Conquest would not only change English history but also transform Malcolm's relationship with England. This did not happen overnight, however, but became clearer over a number of years as the full implications of the Norman Conquest gradually became apparent.

It was not, in fact, until some two years later in 1068 that events in England altered Malcolm's attitude of watchful neutrality. An important consequence of the Norman Conquest had been the vacuum in royal authority in the north of England. The authority of King William I was effectively restricted to southern England for the first years of his reign. He sought to exercise influence in distant

Northumbria through a series of ad hoc appointments. The resulting combination of weak central authority and conflicting local claims encouraged dissent and lawlessness in the area. A series of rulers – Morcar, Marleswein, Copsi, Oswulf, Gospatric and Edgar *Atheling* – all attempted to control the region with varying levels of local support and royal backing. There was a danger that the resultant unrest might spread to Malcolm's own territories, but it also offered an opportunity for him to intervene in Northumbria. In earlier times, Malcolm's predecessors had exploited similar circumstances to extend their authority southwards. He was now secure enough at home to be able to contemplate the same.

In the summer of 1068, King William finally decided to intervene in Northumbria himself. After a year spent as a captive in Normandy, Edgar *Atheling* had managed to escape and seize control of Northumbria. He probably hoped to use the Northumbrians to restore his fortunes and reclaim his lost kingdom. The Northumbrians were the most volatile and combative people in the kingdom. He probably considered himself safely beyond William's reach there, but he was mistaken. King William reacted quickly to this threat by marching north to York, defeating the English and building a castle. An unprepared Edgar retreated before him and along with a number of English exiles, including Marleswein and possibly Gospatric, sought refuge in Scotland. This provided Malcolm with vital intelligence and opened up a range of opportunities for him.

The most important of these exiles were without doubt Edgar *Atheling*, the true heir to the English throne, and his sister Margaret. Edgar had briefly been acknowledged as successor to King Harold II in October 1066 although he was never actually crowned. He had a solid claim to the English throne through his blood relationship to King Edward the Confessor and his descent from King Edmund Ironside. The presence of this important royal figure at his court offered King Malcolm some mouthwatering political prospects which he was not slow to pursue. It was in many respects a reversal of Malcolm's own situation in 1040 when he had been the exile dependent on English aid. He almost certainly exploited his position as host to persuade Edgar to allow him to marry his sister Margaret. The Anglo-Saxon Chronicle reports that Edgar 'opposed it [the marriage] for a long time' and it was not a great match from the viewpoint of the English. They might have expected Margaret to marry a major royal or princely figure from Europe rather than this – in their view – minor regional potentate. In reality, force of circumstances meant that Edgar and his family were in a very weak position in 1068. They were dependent on King Malcolm's support and assistance for their future. The Chronicle explains: 'The king [Malcolm] pressed her brother [Edgar] and he said "yes" and indeed he dared not do anything else.' The marriage, which probably occurred in late 1068 at Dunfermline in Fife, finally secured King Malcolm's active sponsorship for Edgar's cause and his plans to invade England.

It is difficult to exaggerate the importance of this single event for subsequent Scottish history. Its importance, however, did not lie in the introduction of English and Continental culture and manners into Alba, despite the emphasis placed on this by Margaret's contemporary biographer and later historians. It was important because it placed Malcolm III, King of Alba and his descendants and successors at the very centre of political events not only in Britain but across the Channel. He had been transformed almost overnight from a fairly minor figure of no more than regional importance into one of the key players in Western European politics. The activities of King Malcolm would no longer be restricted to skirmishes over border adjustments in Northumbria and Cumberland but would involve the future of the English kingdom itself. It was an amazing transformation with unlimited potential achieved by an obscure king on the edge of the civilised world.

The marriage allied Malcolm to Edgar *Atheling*, the sole legitimate claimant to the English throne. Although Edgar was currently a landless exile, the same had once been true of King Malcolm himself and of Edgar's uncle, Edward the Confessor. Malcolm had returned from exile to secure his birthright and Edward had survived the Danish conquest to claim his throne. There was every reason to suppose that Edgar would survive the Norman Conquest to recover his kingdom in a similar fashion. It is important to remember that in 1068 Norman rule was still far from secure and remained restricted to the area of southern England within the immediate reach of their military forces. A single defeat or the death of one man might end it all as it had for King Harold II at Hastings. Malcolm was the brother-in-law of the future king of England and would no doubt receive an appropriate reward in due course. At the very least, he might expect territorial concessions, in Northumbria perhaps. The possibilities open to Malcolm seemed endless: Edgar might be restored to the English throne with Malcolm's support; Edgar might be installed as ruler of Northumbria and Mercia with William holding on to Wessex – the result of other disputes over the kingship; or Edgar might be installed as ruler of an independent Northumbria. If any of these possibilities transpired, Edgar would be in a position to reward Malcolm for his support with money or territory. He might also be expected to maintain good relations with his brother-in-law, providing Malcolm with a secure border.

There were also other more distant possibilities that must have occurred to Malcolm. If Edgar was killed or died childless, then Malcolm and Margaret would hold the future of the English claim in their hands, through their descendants. They would carry the claim of the old English dynasty descended from Alfred into the future. The children of Malcolm and Margaret would not be named in Gaelic and, in the case of the sons, after earlier kings of Alba. They were named, uniquely at the time, in English and, in the case of the sons, after previous English monarchs – Edward, Edgar, Aethelred and Edmund. The purpose was clearly to emphasise their English royal heritage. It was not the result of any whim or fashion or Margaret's supposedly dominant personality. The royal couple were preparing a dynasty to assume the rule of the English kingdom at some future date. It is possible that a more immediate result of the marriage may have been the agreement of Edgar to the restoration of Cumberland to Malcolm. It certainly fell into his hands sometime after 1066 and before 1070. It may have been offered in lieu of a dowry for Margaret, since Edgar may not have been in a position to offer anything more substantial at the time.

In view of Malcolm's new stake in the future of England, it is hardly surprising that he focused most of his attention on affairs in England for a long period after 1068. He probably paid much greater attention to his southern borders and to his southern neighbour than had any king of Alba before him. This new priority may also have influenced his pattern of residence within his own kingdom. Malcolm appears to have spent more time in southern parts of the kingdom, notably formerly English Lothian, than any of his predecessors. He appears to have spent a lot of time in the area around Dunfermline and Edinburgh, which offered better access to the southern borders than the old heart of Alba around the Tay and Earn. It also offered easy access to Continental trade which passed up the east coast from England. The greater use of Lothian by Malcolm was no doubt prompted by the practical need to be close to his important southern border. It was also, however, a more central location within the expanded kingdom of Alba. It enjoyed excellent communication links by water across the Forth, as witnessed by the development of the royal ferry at Queensferry.

On 28 January 1069, Robert Comyn, King William's nominee as earl of Northumbria was killed at Durham with around 900 men and this initiated a major Northumbrian rebellion. It is possible that this action may have been encouraged by Malcolm and Edgar from the safety of Scotland, but it was probably spontaneous. It did, however, prompt Edgar to resurrect his claim and he entered England to lead the Northumbrians, including Marleswein,

Gospatric, Siward *Barn*, Archill and the sons of Karl, southwards to capture York and its Norman castle. He secured York and rule over Northumbria, probably as a precursor to invading the rest of England. He paused to collect more forces and encourage further rebellion, but he delayed too long. In contrast King William reacted decisively and marched north early in the spring to surprise Edgar, rout his forces and sack York, including its Minster. Edgar was forced to flee back to safety in Scotland with his brother-in-law, Malcolm at some point after 11 May 1069.

In the autumn of 1069, sometime between 15 August and 8 September, a Danish fleet arrived in the Humber estuary. The English exiles led by Edgar *Atheling* and including Marleswein, Waltheof, Gospatric, Siward *Barn*, Archill and the sons of Karl marched south from the Scottish border to join the Danish fleet in planning the capture of York. The late account of William of Malmesbury suggests that there may also have been a Scottish contingent with this force. It seems clear from the coordination of their activities that Edgar and the Danes had previously been in contact. On 11 September, Archbishop Ealdred of York died and was buried in the Minster church probably shortly before the combined English and Danish forces occupied the city. On 19 September, according to John of Worcester, the Norman castle garrison in York fired the city to deprive the English and Danes of any useful shelter in attacking the castles. This tactic failed and the combined Anglo-Danish forces defeated the Normans and destroyed both their castles on 21 September.

It must have appeared to Malcolm at this point that many of the political hopes arising from his marriage to Margaret were close to fulfilment. He had already secured the restoration of his control over Cumberland. In England Edgar *Atheling* had now seized control of Northumbria, including York. He had also opened negotiations with earls Edwin and Morcar, who retained wide authority in the West Midlands and who could be instrumental in his achieving control

159

over Mercia. He was closely allied to a large Danish royal fleet which could offer him an invaluable source of trained troops. In effect, Edgar was now ideally placed to launch an invasion of southern England alongside his Danish and English allies in the spring of 1070. The authority of King William and his Normans was restricted to the south and they still faced hostility in the south-west and across the Midlands. The whole Norman position was fragile in the extreme. If Edgar managed to advance south in spring 1070 with the English and Danes behind him almost anything might happen.

King William was all too aware of the dangers presented by this uprising. He chose once again to strike first during the winter of 1069. It was a tactic often employed by William to catch his opponents off-balance and one already used against Exeter, the Mercians and Edgar in 1068. He marched north rapidly to catch Edgar and his Danish allies unprepared and was completely successful in this. The Danes had crossed the Humber in their ships to take up winter quarters in Lincolnshire, leaving the English unsupported in York itself. William deployed troops to confine the Danes in their marshy retreat while he continued towards York. In spite of a three-week delay when the English defended the river crossing at Pontefract, he still managed to recapture York and expel the English leaders before Christmas. The surprised English had little choice but to withdraw from York and take refuge in camps in the open countryside, according to Orderic Vitalis. William remained in York over Christmas while his troops devastated in brutal fashion the surrounding shire in pursuit of the English in their camps. On 11 December, Bishop Aethelwine and the clerks of Durham hastily abandoned their church, taking the body of St Cuthbert with them, in anticipation of William's advancing further north. They made their way north to Lindisfarne where they presumably felt they would be safe from William's wrath.

In early 1070, a frustrated William duly advanced further north into Northumbria after the English rebels. He spent fifteen days camped near the Tees where Waltheof surrendered in person and Gospatric did so through proxies. The latter was subsequently appointed earl of Northumbria. In January 1070, King William continued his raiding northwards to Hexham on the Tyne before returning to York and then setting out across the Pennines to Chester. In the meantime the hungry Danes remained confined to Lincolnshire, where Norman forces were able to restrict their foraging quite effectively. In the face of imminent starvation the Danes sought terms from William and, in return for the immediate delivery of food supplies and a substantial pay-off, agreed to leave the area in the spring. In spring 1070 King William plundered the English monasteries of their wealth, partly in order to buy off the Danes. The latter finally left England on 24 June 1070 but only after plundering the monasteries of Ely and Peterborough with English help. This entirely sensible deal for the Danes effectively abandoned their English allies to their fate.

The collapse of the Danish alliance and the loss of support that followed William's savage harrying of the north forced Edgar to return to Scotland. It was clear that Edgar *Atheling* had consistently underestimated King William and hence had been unprepared for the swiftness of his counterstrokes. It was also clear that King Malcolm himself could not support Edgar's restoration solely with his own limited resources. It required either strong support from the restless English population or powerful Danish assistance. It seemed increasingly apparent that the former was effectively restricted by an active Norman response which quickly crushed any dissent. The Danes had proved to be untrustworthy allies who were pursuing their own aims rather than those of the English. In these circumstances, it was inevitable that Edgar and his followers had little option but to withdraw until the situation improved.

At some point, most probably in spring 1070, Malcolm led a large army of Scots from Cumberland into Northumbria. This force ravaged the whole of Teeside and neighbouring areas, including

Cleveland, Holderness, County Durham and Wearmouth. This Scottish raid is portrayed in the twelfth-century account featured in The History of the Kings as an example of state terrorism of the worst kind with no political objectives whatsoever. It certainly appears to have fallen on lands already devastated by King William during his previous harrying. It is reported that Earl Gospatric responded with a counter-raid into Cumberland before retreating and shutting himself up in his stronghold at Bamburgh where he was safe from any Scottish retaliation. This suggests that the Scots pillaged as far north as Bamburgh, although this is nowhere mentioned in surviving sources. It is possible that Malcolm's intention, however harsh it might seem to us, was to punish this region for deserting his brother-in-law Edgar and submitting to William. He appears to have targeted the lands of the earldom of Northumbria and the bishopric of Durham and may therefore have been specifically punishing the defection of Earl Gospatric and Bishop Aethelwine. If The History of the Kings is correct in reporting the presence of Edgar and his family at Wearmouth in 1070, which is by no means certain, it is even possible that Malcolm launched this raid to protect Edgar from betrayal by his former allies, including Gospatric. It is also possible that the failure of the English uprising encouraged Malcolm to try to extend his own direct control from Cumberland into Northumbria. He had previously focused on consolidating his hold on Cumberland, leaving Edgar to pursue the conquest of Northumbria and England. The self-evident failure of Edgar may have induced him to attempt to seize Northumbria himself. The absorption of Northumbria would certainly be pursued by his successors into the thirteenth century. It seems likely that this Scottish raid ended before 25 March 1070 when Bishop Aethelwine and his clerks returned to Durham with the body of St Cuthbert. It seems unlikely that they would have done so unless it was safe.

In its twelfth-century account of this Scottish raid, The History of the Kings portrays Malcolm as the villain of 1070. 'He [Malcolm] ordered his troops no longer to spare any of the English nation but either to smite all to the earth or to carry them off captives.' It then proceeds to relate the kind of apocryphal atrocity stories common to wars throughout history. This account does not, however, appear to reflect more contemporary opinion in this respect and it may have been influenced by subsequent Scottish raids from the 1130s. In contrast, the contemporary Anglo-Saxon Chronicle does not even mention Malcolm's raid but clearly identifies the actions of King William as the main cause of the devastation inflicted on Northumbria. There must also have been some destruction inflicted by the English and the Danes, although admittedly this is likely to have been on a lesser scale. The History also contains a story about how Malcolm captured Edgar *Atheling* and Margaret at Wearmouth in 1070 during his raid and that the marriage to Margaret took place thereafter. This tale is also contradicted by the contemporary Chronicle which indicates that Malcolm and Margaret were already married by then. This suggests that the twelfth century account in The History should be treated with some caution and is not necessarily entirely accurate in his portrayal of events and that earlier sources, if available, should be preferred.

In 1071 the Mercian leaders, Edwin and Morcar, found themselves increasingly isolated and under pressure from King William, following his raids on Chester and Stafford in 1070. They finally started to look for allies in a serious way, instead of standing alone as they had done until then. Edwin, Earl of Mercia supposedly intended to seek support from Malcolm and possibly Edgar *Atheling*. He was, however, betrayed by his own men and killed by the Normans before he could reach the Scottish border. It seems unlikely that his mission would have been a success in any case. King Malcolm was already tied to Edgar and may have been increasingly reluctant to challenge a successful William. It appears that Morcar, Edwin's brother had chosen a different course. He sought refuge on the Isle of Ely with Hereward and his followers, who had remained behind after the departure of the Danes in the summer of 1070. In 1071 Aethelwine, the deposed Bishop of Durham and Siward *Barn* sailed from Scotland to Ely to join Morcar and Hereward there. They were possibly representatives of Edgar *Atheling*, who may once again have been in the process of seeking allies. Once again, King William struck swiftly to crush this latent rebellion and imprisoned its leaders, apart from Hereward who escaped.

In 1072 King Malcolm's eager hopes of only three years ago had been dashed following the series of English defeats in 1068, 1069, 1070 and 1071. The departure of the Danes, however unreliable they had proved to be, must also have been a major blow. The prospect of Edgar's restoration to the English throne had clearly vanished with them. The existence of an independent north under native English rule had also faded following William's raids and Gospatric's defection. King Malcolm had managed to retain control over Cumberland and he continued to shelter large numbers of important English exiles, including Edgar. He would now have to fall back on his own resources. He could seek to extend his own authority over Northumbria, perhaps with the tacit support of these exiles. In contrast, King William appeared to have finally silenced native rebellions with his brutal northern campaign of 1070. He had managed, for the time being at least, to buy off the Danes in 1070. He had crushed the last organised English opposition at Ely in 1071. He had no intention of leaving Malcolm and his dangerous nest of English rebels alone to plan further invasions or insurgencies. He could not ignore the continued presence on his northern frontier of his main rival Edgar *Atheling*. He may also have been concerned by the additional threat offered by the birth of a son, named Edward, to Malcolm and his English wife Margaret, which must have occurred at about this time.

At some time after 15 August 1072, King William invaded Scotland with a land and naval force like Athelstan before him. He led his army to the Forth but, according to The Anglo-Saxon Chronicle, 'there he found nothing that he was any better for.' This suggests that Malcolm, like Constantine II, when faced with such overwhelming force, chose to withdraw before it and adopt a scorched earth policy. In the end Malcolm met William at Abernethy on the Tay where, according to the Chronicle, he 'made peace with King William and was his vassal and gave him hostages'. This appears to be an abject surrender by Malcolm, who was certainly under intense pressure. It was, however, probably more in the nature of a compromise reached after a stalemate. William had been unable to achieve the kind of significant military success that had brought him control of England. He had failed to penetrate as far north as Athelstan in 934. He would soon have to retreat and needed some form of concession to justify his expedition. On his side, Malcolm could not oppose William's superior force openly but was keen to get rid of him as soon as possible. It was this that brought them together to treat for peace. On his return to England, William deposed the unreliable Earl Gospatric, who fled first to Scotland and then to Flanders, presumably to join Edgar *Atheling*. He also built a castle at Durham to control this region and to protect his new appointee, Walcher, Bishop of Durham.

The agreement reached at Abernethy in 1072 represents another occasion when each side probably placed a very different interpretation on what the agreement actually signified. It was clear that Malcolm submitted to William's superior force but what this implied was open to different interpretation. The Anglo-Saxon Chronicle clearly suggests that the Normans interpreted this as a formal feudal submission, which acknowledged William, King of England as the superior lord of Malcolm, King of Alba. In contrast, Malcolm probably viewed the submission as a practical and temporary acknowledgement of English superiority with no long-term consequences. It was viewed by the Scots in exactly the same light as the temporary submission of Constantine II to Athelstan in

934. This difference of interpretation, which was partly cultural in origin but also political, would result in problems in the longer term.

In the short term, the Treaty of Abernethy confirmed that Malcolm had been forced to acknowledge William's military superiority. The presence of William's army near Abernethy in the heart of Alba was ample witness to this. The surrender of hostages by Malcolm in the shape of Duncan, his eldest son from his first marriage, recognised his temporary inferiority. It also appears that Malcolm was forced to expel Edgar *Atheling* from his kingdom and he went to Flanders at some point before 1074. This all seems fairly one-sided; but it was not a complete success for William. There were restrictions on what William was able to achieve at Abernethy, which are important signs of limits on his power. They indicate that it was not entirely a case of abject surrender by Malcolm. For example, Malcolm was not compelled to hand Edgar over to William. In addition, he remained married to Margaret and kept his infant son Edward, who held a claim to the English throne. King Malcolm could present this as a success, even though William held his eldest son, Duncan as a hostage.

In the aftermath of the Norman invasion of 1072, Malcolm was compelled to review his policy in relation to England. He could no longer ignore the fact of the Norman Conquest. King William was now secure and dominant throughout his new kingdom. The long run of Norman military successes in 1068, 1069, 1070, 1071 and 1072 and the expulsion of English nobles and clerics from lands and offices had left William apparently unassailable. In addition Malcolm's brother-in-law, Edgar *Atheling* had proved himself either unlucky or inept and incapable of promoting in an effective way his strong claim to the English throne. In these circumstances, it was no time for Malcolm to throw good money after bad and he therefore abandoned, temporarily at least, both his support for Edgar and his own designs on the north of England. He had not entirely given up on these goals and probably intended to resurrect them when circumstances appeared more favourable. He could afford to bide his time until his son Edward and the brothers that would follow him were old enough to raise their own claims.

On 8 July 1074 Edgar *Atheling* returned to Scotland from Flanders, accompanied by Gospatric. King Philip of France sought to exploit Edgar's claim to threaten William and invited Edgar to come to France. Unfortunately, Edgar was shipwrecked on the shores of England. He had to return to Scotland through hostile territory in a bedraggled state. This latest debacle persuaded Malcolm to convince Edgar to abandon his claim to the throne and submit to King William. It may be that Malcolm wanted simply to reduce tension with his powerful southern neighbour by removing this major source of irritation. It could also be that he sought to open up a path for the future claims of his own son Edward by convincing Edgar to resign his own apparently hopeless claim. It was perhaps a signal of future interest in the English succession that Malcolm, probably in 1074, appointed Gospatric as Earl of Dunbar in English-speaking Lothian. According to The History of the Kings, Malcolm endowed the new Earl with 'adjacent lands in Lothian', which may possibly have been lands formerly held by Gospatric's ancestors when they ruled this region before its loss to the Scots. This appointment was made 'until more prosperous times should come' or perhaps until King Malcolm could secure Northumbria or, through his sons, England itself. Earl Gospatric might then perhaps expect to regain the lands in Northumbria that he had lost to the Normans.

In the period between 1066 and 1074 a large number of refugees had arrived in Scotland from England. They ranged from major leaders, such as Edgar *Atheling*, Earl Gospatric, Earl Waltheof, Bishop Aethelwine, Marleswein and Siward *Barn*, right down to ordinary people fleeing Norman oppression or taken captive on Scottish raids. A large number of these refugees were only seeking temporary refuge in Scotland and subsequently moved on, but many remained permanently. The ones who remained were often unable to return home to a Norman-dominated England for one reason or another. The most important of these was Edgar *Atheling*, who frequently sought refuge in Scotland but who ultimately became a peripatetic figure travelling widely in north-west Europe and the Mediterranean. Earl Gospatric intermittently sought refuge in Scotland and Flanders before finally returning to Scotland to receive the earldom of Dunbar and to found a dynasty. Bishop Aethelwine of Durham took refuge in Scotland but returned to England to captivity and death in 1071. The clerk Thurgot of Durham apparently arrived in the household of Queen Margaret and went on to become Bishop of St Andrews. Marleswein fled to Scotland following the failure of the Northumbrian uprisings and apparently settled there. Eadwulf Rus would flee to Scotland after the killing of Bishop Walcher of Durham in 1080 and was subsequently buried at Jedburgh. The many ordinary refugees may have been unable or unwilling to return to devastated or appropriated lands. They may have been granted new lands, possibly in Lothian, by the Scottish King. The poor captives had no choice in the matter but according to The History of the Kings were settled as slaves all across Scotland. This influx of English speakers must have reinforced the English identity of Lothian and other lowland areas of Scotland.

In 1077 King Malcolm had been free of political entanglements in the south for three years and was therefore able to turn his attention to Moray in the north. Maelsnechtai, the son of Lulach, Malcolm's old rival for the kingship, was in his twenties at the very least by now and so old enough to claim the throne of Alba. He was a member of the MacDuff lineage and the son of a king. He therefore represented a clear threat to Malcolm's position and that of his entire family. If he managed to impose his claim, which was by no means an unlikely event, he could effectively end Malcolm's hopes for expanding Scottish territory or advancing a claim to the English throne. This was a threat that could not be ignored and Malcolm did not ignore it. In 1077 he launched a surprise attack on Moray which appears to have caught Maelsnechtai completely unawares. The man himself managed to escape the trap but Malcolm succeeded in capturing his mother, his key supporters, his treasure and his cattle. The last were a major element in the wealth of the upland pastoral communities of Alba, as in Ireland. This dramatic coup must have effectively crippled Maelsnechtai for some time thereafter. He would find it difficult to pursue his claim without his key supporters and without wealth to secure allies.

This raid on Moray is recorded in the 'D' version of The Anglo-Saxon Chronicle, which had a northern origin and records a number of other Scottish events. The Scottish entries are usually connected with the exiled English royal family and its activities. The Chronicle otherwise shows no interest in Scottish events unrelated to Queen Margaret's family. The entry for 1077, however, is unique and appears to have more in common with entries in the contemporary Irish annals than with anything found in this English source. It has no connection with England and is not comparable with other Scottish references, which are connected with the English royal family. The original manuscript version of the entry also contains a number of gaps. It is almost as though the writer were unable to read or fully understand his source material and left space for it to be completed later but never returned to it. Is it possible that the compiler was making use of a Gaelic source here? If so, he perhaps had problems with the text or its translation and so left gaps. If we had the full entry or knew where it had originated, it might tell us a lot about the background to the compilation of the 'D' version of the Chronicle, which shows such an interest in Scottish affairs.

The success in Moray might possibly have provided Malcolm with the opportunity to intrude his own men into this area. It had been a policy pursued by his great-grandfather and namesake, Malcolm II when he sponsored Macbeth in the 1030s. This is a hypothesis that might explain one of the mysteries of later Scottish history. The

MacHeth dynasty reappeared in the twelfth century as rivals of the kings with a base in Ross. They were descendants of the royal lineage of Aed from the tenth century. They may possibly have been intruded into Ross by Malcolm after his victory over Maelsnechtai of Moray in 1077. They were perhaps originally placed there to monitor and subdue the region but, like Macbeth before them, chose instead to adopt their own independent line. In the twelfth century, following the final elimination of the Moray dynasty, they would revive their ancient claim and rise up to challenge Malcolm's descendants for the kingship of Alba itself.

In 1079 King Malcolm chose to exploit tensions between King William and his eldest son Robert to resume his raids on England. He may possibly have used this opportunity to test the waters for resurrecting his plans to seize control of Northumbria. He invaded England with a great army at some point between 15 August and 8 September. He ravaged Northumbria as far as the Tyne, killing many hundreds of people and taking much treasure and many captives. It appears that Malcolm was almost unopposed and it seems likely that he was accompanied by Earl Gospatric I of Dunbar or his son, who would have had the advantage of invaluable local knowledge. The Earl of Northumbria at the time was Bishop Walcher of Durham, who signally failed to protect the area from the raiders. Indeed, it seems probable that the subsequent murder of Walcher on 14 May 1080 by the Northumbrians was due to his ineffectual performance in 1079. Eadwulf Rus, the man most implicated in the murder of Walcher subsequently fled to Scotland. King William clearly could not ignore these twin disasters and sent his newly reconciled son Robert to invade Scotland. The latter managed to advance as far as Falkirk, 'which he reached without accomplishing anything', according to The History of the Kings. On his return in the autumn, Robert built a castle at Newcastle on the Tyne. This was probably a less successful invasion than that of five years earlier and the parties probably chose to make peace at an earlier stage.

In 1085 a couple of important deaths probably caused Malcolm
to review the royal succession in Alba. The Annals of Ulster report
that Maelsnechtai died of natural causes with no further
elaboration. The surviving sources provide no information about his
career after his defeat by Malcolm in 1077. This death appears to
have removed the only adult rival from the MacDuff lineage who
could possibly challenge the succession of Malcolm's sons. This
undoubtedly improved the prospects of the succession falling to his
sons without dispute. The Ulster annalist also reports the unnatural
death of a man called Donald, son of Malcolm but once again
provides no further details. He was presumably a son of King
Malcolm by an earlier marriage and possibly a full brother of the
Duncan taken hostage by King William in 1072 and still held in
Normandy. If this assumption is correct, it seems likely that the
death of this Donald removed an obstacle to the succession of
Edward, the son of Malcolm and Margaret. It was probably now
that King Malcolm formally indicated that Edward would be heir
presumptive to the Scottish throne.

In 1087 William, King of England and Duke of Normandy, died
in France and his dominions were divided by his sons. He was
succeeded by his eldest son, Robert as Duke of Normandy and by
his second son, William as King of England. The two brothers
quickly showed themselves to be rivals for control of their father's
legacy and a fierce struggle for supremacy soon commenced that
lasted for many years. Robert, Duke of Normandy quickly released
Duncan, eldest son of Malcolm from his long captivity in
Normandy. He had no reason to keep Duncan imprisoned since he
had no border with Malcolm and no interest in holding a hostage to
ensure his good behaviour. In fact, he had reason to consider King
Malcolm a potential ally against his brother William II, King of
England. The newly released Duncan apparently chose to remain
with Robert in Normandy rather than return to Scotland. It seems
that his long sojourn in Norman custody had persuaded Duncan of

the merits of Norman culture and society. He had perhaps been influenced by contact with Norman culture in the same way as his exiled father had earlier been influenced by English culture. If King Malcolm had already made Edward, his son by Margaret, heir presumptive, as suggested above, there was nothing for Duncan to return to. He had few prospects with Malcolm and Margaret and their children in control of the succession.

In 1091 King Malcolm's initially peaceful relations with King William II were disrupted. In that year, King William had invaded Normandy in an attempt finally to dispose of his troublesome older brother, Duke Robert of Normandy and so to secure their entire patrimony for himself. It appears that Duke Robert had offered Edgar *Atheling* refuge and support. King William quite naturally viewed Edgar as a threat to his hold on the English throne. Indeed, Duke Robert probably encouraged Edgar to resurrect his claim to the English throne to use against his younger brother. In the end, King William was reconciled with Robert and as part of their reconciliation Edgar *Atheling* was expelled from Normandy. As so often before, Edgar fled to the court of his brother-in-law Malcolm in Scotland. In May 1091, King Malcolm invaded Northumbria, either to exploit King William's absence in Normandy or perhaps to avenge Edgar's expulsion from Normandy. Malcolm managed to ravage a great part of Northumbria until, opposed by local forces, presumably led by Robert de Mowbray, Earl of Northumbria, he was forced to retreat across the border with his spoils. In response to this invasion, King William returned from Normandy in September to invade Scotland with an army and navy in emulation of his father in 1072. Unfortunately, a storm on 29 September destroyed the fleet and left King William unable to supply his troops. He therefore advanced no further than the border, while Malcolm, secure from the sea, brought his own army forward into Lothian to confront him. In fact, there was no invasion but a stand-off, during which Edgar *Atheling* and Robert of Normandy acted as mediators. A temporary truce was patched up between the two kings and Edgar was reconciled to King William II or, perhaps, surrendered into his custody. Unknown to King Malcolm, however, William II was only seeking time in which to prepare a more purposeful riposte.

In 1092 King William II invaded Cumberland, seized Carlisle and expelled a man called Dolfin, who according to The Anglo-Saxon Chronicle ruled this region. He has been identified as the brother of Earl Gospatric II of Dunbar and son of Gospatric of Northumbria or as an otherwise unrecorded relation of the Dolfin killed in 1054 in the fighting against Macbeth. In either case – and the former seems more likely – he was almost certainly the local representative of King Malcolm in Cumberland. This dramatic act effectively ended a long period of Scottish rule in this region, which probably commenced in 1068. King William went on to construct a castle at Carlisle and to introduce southern English peasants, either to settle a devastated and deserted region or, possibly, to replace expelled Scots. It was clear that William intended to hold onto Cumberland on a permanent basis. This blow represented a serious loss to Malcolm, who must by now have been in his sixties. He was an old man with his mind increasingly focused on the future of his dynasty and kingdom. He had an adult heir, Edward and other children, but was perhaps anxious to bequeath them an undiminished kingdom. The loss of Cumberland deprived his successors of an easy invasion route into the heart of Northumbria and placed English forces closer to the western regions of his own kingdom.

It appears that Malcolm tried at first to negotiate over Cumberland with King William rather than immediately to counterattack. This caution has been seen as unusual by some but it should not really be surprising. Malcolm was old and, therefore, more reluctant to resort to military action and perhaps he was also fearful of English power. This cautious approach proved vain, however, and almost a year passed without any significant progress, while William built his castle at Carlisle and settled Cumberland. In August 1093, King Malcolm made a last-ditch attempt to negotiate with William in person at Gloucester. The willingness of Malcolm to enter England to treat with his opponent indicates his desperation to secure a deal. He had not negotiated a similar agreement from outside his own territory since the distant days of 1059. The two men finally met on 29 August but the result was a fiasco. King William chose to interpret Malcolm's willingness to come to him as a sign of weakness, which in a sense it was, and exploited this fact to humiliate him. William set unreasonable terms for the restoration of Cumberland by seeking full homage from Malcolm, perhaps for his entire kingdom. This was clearly too much for Malcolm to concede and he therefore returned to Scotland empty-handed and angry.

Malcolm now had no alternative to taking military action to redress this blow to his prestige and to seek the restoration of Cumberland. In late 1093 he therefore invaded Northumbria, accompanied by his heir, Edward and his second son Edgar. He may have decided that this expedition offered an opportunity for Edward and Edgar to command the Scottish army, or perhaps Malcolm himself was so old that he required their presence in order to command effectively. In either case, it was a dangerous risk to take and it would turn out badly for the Scots. The invasion was in full swing when Earl Robert of Northumbria sprang a carefully prepared trap. On 13 November 1093, King Malcolm was surrounded and killed by the Northumbrians at Alnwick along with his eldest son and heir, Edward. In the wake of this disaster, the Scottish army quickly withdrew in some disorder from England. Only three days later, on 16 November, an already sick Queen Margaret died in Edinburgh after hearing the terrible news from Alnwick from her son Edgar, who had escaped the rout. The consequence of these three important deaths in such a short space of time was to plunge the carefully arranged Scottish succession into chaos. King Malcolm had a number of other sons, including

Edgar, but the loss of the recognised heir meant that they were all potential candidates for the kingship. The chaos that ensued has meant that the solid achievements of Malcolm's reign have often been overlooked or ignored.

King Malcolm's most important achievement was the integration of the English-speaking southern territories into the expanded kingdom of Alba. He was the first king of Alba to have a real connection with his English-speaking subjects. The kings preceding him remained Gaelic lords, with the possible exception of Idulf, and their rule was based essentially on military conquest and subjection. They were viewed as alien outsiders by the English inhabitants of these areas and the two sides had no cultural and little political connection. In contrast, Malcolm was obliged by the circumstances of his exile in 1040 to adopt a very different approach to these people. As a political exile, whether in Lothian, Strathclyde, Northumbria or England itself, Malcolm desperately needed support from wherever he could get it. He needed support at first simply to survive but later to restore his fortunes and enforce his claim to the kingship. He therefore turned, not unnaturally, to these English-speaking areas of the kingdom for support. It was these same areas that might favour the English intervention that he also needed to obtain. This approach eventually produced a common bond between Malcolm and his English-speaking subjects that his predecessors had lacked.

The first step in this process was to learn the language and Malcolm was the first prospective king of Alba, as far as is known and with the possible exception of Idulf, to be able to speak English. He therefore had an immediate advantage over his predecessors in being able to communicate directly with his English-speaking subjects and to cultivate the kind of direct relationship between a king and his subjects that already existed in the old heartlands of Alba. He was in a real sense in a position to be 'their king' where his predecessors had been foreign overlords. It is not recorded in the surviving sources but it seems highly likely that Malcolm exploited this connection to canvass and secure the support of the English-speaking population of Lothian for his claim to the kingship. It was after all in the interests of these people to have someone in a position of power over them who understood their language, their culture and their needs.

This highly astute political move provided Malcolm with a secure base in Lothian from which to launch his attempt to take the throne of Alba. It also offered him a solid core of supporters who would back him against all comers and who were unlikely to desert him for a Gaelic rival. In contrast, the main support for Macbeth and Lulach came from the far north in Moray. It was unlikely that these Gaelic lords would be able to offer the English-speakers of Lothian the kind of advantages offered by Malcolm. The men of Lothian were also likely to be more sympathetic to his introduction of English military forces, which might not prove quite so popular with the men of Alba themselves. Malcolm therefore had a source of solid support for his restoration even before his English-backed invasion of 1054. He was also, however, assured of a solid basis of support even when direct English backing was withdrawn following the death of Earl Siward in 1055. This support from Lothian on its own could not guarantee his succession as King of Alba, but it went a long way to doing so.

In 1068 King Malcolm undoubtedly reinforced this initial connection when he married Margaret, a member of the exiled English royal house. As a result, he allied himself directly to the old English dynasty and associated himself with all its traditions. He had in effect transformed his kingship from a Gaelic into a Anglo-Gaelic one, a transformation confirmed by the birth of sons who inherited this dual culture. He had also provided a new focus for the loyalty of his English-speaking subjects which could draw on traditions of loyalty to English rulers. The people of Lothian now had an English Queen to support in addition to their English-speaking King, and after 1072 they would have part-English heirs with English names too.

There was another important aspect of Malcolm's bridging of the gap between the Gaelic kings and their English subjects. He had managed to achieve this task without losing the support of the original Gaelic inhabitants of the kingdom. He remained the son and heir of King Duncan I and the namesake and great-grandson of King Malcolm II. He does not appear to have faced any opposition from his Gaelic subjects to his closer relationship to his English subjects. The difficulties faced by Malcolm's half-English sons in this respect after his death in 1093 will be discussed more fully in the next chapter. They appear to be more related to the disastrous end of Malcolm's reign, with the deaths of Malcolm, Margaret and their eldest son Edward and to traditional Gaelic succession patterns, than to any true anti-English feeling.

The tragic deaths of King Malcolm III, his wife and their eldest son within a few days of each other and the resulting confusion has effectively concealed the great successes of Malcolm's long reign of thirty-five or more years. As a result of this tragedy Malcolm's legacy has been largely forgotten. He unified his infant kingdom as never before, drawing its Gaelic and English subjects into a multicultural Scottish kingdom. The marriage of Malcolm and Margaret and the birth of their Anglo-Scottish descendants played a key role in this process. He subdued the independent region of Moray for most of his reign and probably began the process of undermining its local rulers that came to fruition in the reign of David I. He developed closer relations than ever before with English rulers. He extended the scope of Scottish international contacts as never before to include Norway, Flanders, Normandy and the rest of the Continent. He shifted the centre of the kingdom of Alba southwards from Strathearn and Angus to Fife and Lothian. It was not a bad achievement for a man who had once been an exiled prince with no prospects.

7

A New Kingdom?

On 13 November 1093 King Malcolm's own careful plans for the succession collapsed with the death of his designated heir, Edward. It is reported that Edgar, who had also been in the army that invaded England in late 1093, managed to escape the fate that befell his father and elder brother. He immediately hurried back to Edinburgh with the remnants of the defeated Scottish army, ostensibly to convey the news to his ailing mother. He had time to tell her of the tragic events of 13 November before she succumbed to her illness and died on 16 November 1093. This is the account given in The Life of St Margaret, but it was surely just as important for Edgar to return to Edinburgh to secure his succession to the throne of the kingdom. If so, the death of his mother so soon afterwards and the state of the defeated army may have deprived him of his opportunity. Instead the deaths of King Malcolm, Queen Margaret and Prince Edward, their intended heir initiated a period of contention.

There were alternative candidates: Donald *Ban* or 'the Fair', King Malcolm's younger brother, who was now in his sixties, and Duncan, Malcolm's son by his first wife, who was in England. The men of Alba naturally preferred an adult ruler and found one ready to hand in Malcolm's brother, Donald *Ban*. He appears to have been largely forgotten in all Malcolm's plans for the succession. He now stepped forward, or was perhaps thrust forward, from the obscurity of the sources to centre stage. Indeed, Donald would have been the obvious choice to succeed Malcolm under the traditional succession system, which opted for the best available adult male. It seems that in the crisis following Malcolm's death the men of Alba sought comfort in a return to familiar practices. In 1093 Donald *Ban* had the clear advantage over Duncan that he was already present in the kingdom. It seems that there were no challengers from the lineages of MacDuff and MacHeth, possibly because Malcolm had already eliminated them or bought them off to clear a path for Edward. In November 1093, Donald III *Ban*, son of Duncan I or *Domnall Ban mac Donnchada*, duly succeeded to the kingship of Alba.

In 1093 The Anglo-Saxon Chronicle reports that the new king, Donald III, 'drove out all the English who were with King Malcolm'. This has been viewed as solid evidence for an anti-English reaction among the Gaelic lords of Alba led by Donald as the champion of the old order. This appears, however, to be stretching the interpretation of these words a little too far. In the first place, who exactly were the English who were driven out? It is clear that English-speaking Lothian was not emptied of its population. It is possible but unlikely that this refers to the expulsion of those English who had settled in Scotland since 1066, including Earl Gospatric II of Dunbar. They were probably too numerous, however, and there is no sign of large numbers of refugees moving south into England. It is much more likely that it refers to those Englishmen prominent in Malcolm's court itself. It is probable that Donald exiled Edgar and the other sons of Malcolm and Margaret who were his rivals. It was a logical next step to exile their supporters, many of whom would have been English. They may have included Edgar *Atheling*, whose whereabouts at this time are otherwise unknown. There is, however, another factor in this account. The Chronicle was an English source with an interest in English affairs, including those of Queen Margaret and her children. It is therefore more likely to report the impact of events on the English in Alba than the natives. This Chronicle therefore chooses to mention the English who were expelled because it was interested in them. This does not mean that Gaelic supporters of Malcolm's sons did not also suffer at Donald's hands.

The surviving sources tell us almost nothing about King Donald III *Ban* after he succeeded his older brother late in 1093. He has usually been considered a Gaelic reactionary chiefly on the basis of the Chronicle account already noted but this is hardly conclusive proof of a general anti-English sentiment. He is reported by the late fourteenth-century chronicler John of Fordun to have spent his exile during Macbeth's reign in the Western Isles. It is not at all clear, however, whether any reliance whatever can be put on this statement. If he was subsequently buried on Iona this may confirm a more traditional outlook, but this does not necessarily equate with an anti-English policy. He did not seek to prevent the burial of his brother King Malcolm III and his wife, Queen Margaret in their new church at Dunfermline. The only certain fact about Donald *Ban* is that he was successful in claiming the throne in opposition to his young nephews, the sons of Margaret. He might then have expected to enjoy the remainder of his already long life in peace while his young nephews grew to maturity and plotted their return. Instead, Donald found himself faced with an immediate challenge from another quarter.

In late 1093 or early 1094, The Anglo-Saxon Chronicle reports that Duncan, son of Malcolm III, who had effectively been excluded from the succession, was in England at the court of King William II. He was last noticed in Normandy in 1087 when Duke Robert released him from custody and knighted him. The presence of this almost forgotten claimant to the Scottish throne in England at this time may not have been entirely fortuitous. In 1092 William II had, after all, seized control of Cumberland from King Malcolm and had subsequently refused to negotiate with him. He must surely have anticipated that this might provoke a war with the Scots and that in this event it would be very useful to have a threat to wield against

Malcolm. In these circumstances, William II would have found Duncan a very useful pawn indeed. It was probably therefore no coincidence that he was already at the English Court when Malcolm and his heir Edward died and Donald seized the kingship.

It appears that Duncan, son of Malcolm, who had spent the last twenty years as a hostage in Normandy and England, was now a thorough convert to Anglo-Norman culture. He already had a wife and children, who would be mentioned in his charter to Durham. He had made no effort to return to Scotland in 1087 and had probably already been excluded from the Scottish succession in favour of his half-brother Edward. In 1094 he was persuaded to resurrect his claim to the Scottish kingship, either independently or more probably by King William II. Duncan would launch his claim with the assistance of a group of Anglo-Norman adventurers. It is unlikely that Duncan had any wealth or resources of his own for this purpose and William's hand must be suspected behind this venture. It is likely that William II had already secured Duncan's support for possible action against Malcolm III in 1093. The English King naturally preferred to promote this candidate, who was completely in his debt, rather than any of Malcolm's sons by Margaret, who additionally carried an embarrassing claim to his own English throne. The Anglo-Saxon Chronicle reports that Duncan had done formal homage to William II in return for English support. The sons of Margaret were left to decide whether or not to support their half-brother, and Edgar appears to have done so at least in the short term.

In May 1094, probably shortly before launching his invasion of Scotland, Duncan issued a charter to Durham Cathedral. The original of this, the first known Scottish charter, survives in the archives at Durham to this day and provides some rare evidence about Duncan and his brief reign. This document, which was drafted by a scribe of Durham Cathedral itself, describes Duncan as *Rex Scocie* or 'King of Scotland'. It shows that Duncan was acting with the support of his 'brothers', more properly his half-brothers, the sons of Malcolm and Margaret and Edgar appears in the witness list. The purpose of the charter was to secure the support of St Cuthbert for his campaign by making concessions to the church of Durham. It grants to Durham some lands in East Lothian and the services due from those lands, which had formerly been due to Bishop Fothad of St Andrews, who according to the Annals of Ulster had died in 1093. Duncan's propitiation of St Cuthbert may also have been intended to foster support within Lothian itself. In this context the witness list includes a man called Wulfgeat the White of Duddingston, who was presumably ready to support Duncan's candidacy. The population of that region continued to demonstrate an attachment to St Cuthbert and his church in spite of the intrusion of the bishopric of St Andrews into this area. The numerous subsequent Scottish charters involving the grant of Lothian lands to Durham amply demonstrate this connection.

The majority of the other names in the list of witnesses to this first Scottish charter are unidentified. They probably consist of members of the Anglo-Norman personal retinue recruited by Duncan to help him secure the throne. If so, many were probably killed in the course of the various misfortunes that befell this short-lived king and had no chance to make any other impact in the sparse records. The few who do appear elsewhere may include Aelfric, who is possibly the man who went on to become butler to Kings Edgar and Alexander I. It might also perhaps be worth considering the possibility that the man called Ulf who appears on the witness list might be the Ulf, son of King Harold II who had spent years as a hostage in Normandy but who had been released by Duke Robert of Normandy in 1087. Is it possible that Duncan and Ulf, who both suffered this fate, became friends during their time in custody and on their release worked together to seek their fortune? It is an interesting idea and there is currently no other record of Ulf after 1087. The appearance of a man named Malcolm in the witness list suggests some Gaelic support for Duncan but the origins of this individual are otherwise unknown.

In spring 1094, Duncan II, son of Malcolm, King of Scotland, used the military backing supplied by William II to expel his uncle Donald *Ban* and secure the kingship. This success would prove short-lived, however, since his uncle Donald remained alive and at large. It appears that Duncan's Anglo-Norman supporters somehow offended local sensibilities and there was a severe reaction against them. The Anglo-Saxon Chronicle reports that King Duncan was attacked by some of his own subjects, probably from north of the Forth, and nearly all of his Anglo-Norman military escort were killed. Duncan himself escaped with a few men but was subsequently forced to promise not to bring English or French troops into the country. It seems that he was not personally rejected in spite of his long absence and his Anglo-Norman cultural outlook. It was his use of foreign troops that caused offence. This elimination of Duncan's military support badly weakened his position. It was probably as a result that, on 12 November 1094, Duncan II was treacherously killed by Maelpetair, son of Malcolm, *Mormaer* of Angus, at Mondynes in the Mearns. The Annals of Ulster suggest that Duncan's betrayal was engineered by his uncle Donald and his half-brother Edmund, who subsequently assumed some form of joint rule over the kingdom. It is possible that Edmund was, initially, a supporter of Duncan alongside his brother Edgar but subsequently struck a deal to betray his half-brother to Donald in exchange for a share of the kingdom. It is possible that Donald III, King of Alba ruled north of the Forth while Edmund perhaps ruled English-speaking Lothian under him. It would appear that Edgar, who had remained loyal to Duncan, was expelled and had to return to exile in England.

On 29 August 1095, Edgar, son of Malcolm issued a charter to Durham at Norham on Tweed on the English border. This document, whose original no longer survives, in many respects mirrors that issued by Duncan a year earlier. Edgar, who styled himself son of Malcolm, *Regis Scottorum* or 'King of Scots', had clearly assumed the position of the English-sponsored claimant to the kingship of Alba. In the charter Edgar states that his claim is based firstly on the gift of King William II and only secondly on inheritance from his father. This represents a clear attempt by Edgar to demonstrate his subordination to King William II. In this charter 'King' Edgar claims to hold 'the whole land of Lothian' and Scotland, but while the former is entirely possible, the latter seems unlikely as early as 1095. The purpose of this charter was probably to declare that 'King' Edgar held Lothian and that he intended to enforce his claim to the kingship itself in the near future. He could certainly have occupied Lothian at this time in the light of its particular sympathy towards the old English royal house. The witness list offers some support for these claims. It obviously includes his brothers Alexander and David, his young nephew William FitzDuncan and his uncle Edgar *Atheling*, who would support his full restoration in 1097. The other witnesses appear to be mainly Englishmen from Lothian, reflecting Edgar's control over that region. Perhaps the most unusual witness is not an Englishman, but Constantine, son of Macduff, who can only be the contemporary *Mormaer* of Fife. He appears to be present in England as a supporter of Edgar at this early date. This may perhaps be the origin of the later stories of MacDuff support for an exiled claimant to the Scottish throne which were subsequently transferred to the story of Malcolm and Macbeth by writers including Shakespeare.

It seems fairly clear from this Durham charter of August 1095, issued at Norham, that Edgar probably intended to invade Scotland proper either at that point or very soon afterwards. This is what Duncan had done after granting his charter to Durham in May 1094. If so, however, there must have been some problem, since no invasion actually occurred until 1097. It appears that Edgar's plans fell through, probably as a consequence of the rebellion of Robert earl of Northumbria in 1095. This resulted in the diversion of English military support from Edgar to deal with the revolt and indeed Edgar's charter was issued during the siege of Bamburgh. In

1096 the arrangements for the First Crusade distracted King William II. He was preoccupied with arrangements for taking control of Normandy from his brother Duke Robert, who was about to set off on crusade. It is possible that Edgar held Lothian, and perhaps Strathclyde, from 1095 to 1097 but was unable to advance further into Alba without outside help. If so, it is possible that he, or his brother David according to William of Malmesbury, managed to capture and imprison their turncoat brother Edmund in the process. It may indeed be questionable whether King Donald or Edmund ever had secure control over Lothian.

It was not finally until early October 1097 that Edgar *Atheling* was able to lead a military force supplied by William II to restore his nephew and namesake Edgar to the Scottish throne. Edgar, son of Malcolm III managed finally with this assistance to defeat his uncle Donald III in a 'severe battle' somewhere in Scotland, according to The Anglo-Saxon Chronicle. He also succeeded in capturing his uncle, either in this encounter or soon afterwards, something that his half-brother Duncan had failed to do in 1094. It was not long after this that the aged Donald was blinded and killed at Rescobie in Angus to remove the possibility of his ever claiming the kingship again. If he had not already been captured in Lothian earlier, then Edmund was also taken in 1097 and imprisoned for life. He was spared the fate of his uncle Donald, only because he was a full brother of Edgar. Edgar, King of Scots had been successful in eliminating his rivals where his half-brother Duncan had ultimately failed. This was probably because Edgar had more support within the kingdom itself. It was support from English-speaking Lothian that provided the springboard from which Edgar was able to conquer the rest of Scotland. He had followed the same path as his father, Malcolm III by securing assistance from Lothian and from England to seize the kingship.

King Edgar, son of Malcolm III and Margaret had been born with a claim to rule two kingdoms, Scotland and England. He had been named after an illustrious ancestor, who had ruled England during a period of peace and prosperity. The terrible tragedy of the death of both his parents and his older brother in November 1093 appeared to have thwarted all his hopes and ambitions. He found himself deprived of his birthright in Scotland and cast out into exile. He was forced to seek refuge and support from King William II, the very man who had usurped his birthright in England. It was a dramatic reversal of fortune for Edgar and his family and they struggled to cope with it. It brought them to consider any options to restore their position and Edgar and his brothers initially hitched their fortunes to King William's choice, their half-brother Duncan. Thereafter it appears that there was a dispute about the course to take. Edgar stuck to supporting Duncan II, but his brother Edmund pursued an accommodation with his uncle Donald III in the search for influence. In 1094 Duncan's murder opened up opportunities for both. Initially Edmund managed to secure a share of the kingdom through his part in the betrayal of Duncan. Ultimately, however, Edgar triumphed against Donald and Edmund by securing English aid as his father had done. He emerged triumphant to secure control of Scotland, the kingdom that had seemed completely lost to him only four years before. In 1097 Edgar was King of Scots and in possession of his paternal birthright.

What were the prospects for his maternal birthright? It must have been clear to King Edgar from the fate of his father and elder brother in 1093 and his own subsequent experiences that there was little prospect of his securing the English throne. Edgar, King of Scots simply did not have sufficient resources to pursue a claim to the English throne. He could no longer challenge the Norman rulers of England without drastic political changes which were beyond his control. He had therefore to be content to accept his current subordination to King William II and the abandonment of his claims in England in order to secure the Scottish throne.

In 1098 King Edgar, who was no doubt busy consolidating his authority over his newly restored kingdom, faced a new threat from an unexpected quarter. It had been over thirty years since the disastrous defeat suffered by King Harald of Norway at Stamford Bridge in 1066. In this year, however, King Magnus III, the grandson of Harald led a major expedition to Orkney and down through the Western Isles. This Norwegian campaign is mentioned in contemporary sources from England, Wales and Ireland. It is only much later saga tradition that mentions an agreement between King Edgar and Magnus of Norway, which supposedly conceded the Western Isles to Norway but left the mainland under the control of Edgar. This is not much of a story for the saga-writer since it does little more than confirm the practical extent of the power of these monarchs. King Magnus of Norway had control over the Western Isles because of his personal presence there but little or no control over the mainland. In contrast, King Edgar had control of the mainland because of his personal presence there but little or no control in the islands. It is not adding much to propose a formal treaty, whether real or imaginary, that confirmed this practical arrangement. The saga account does little to confirm that such an agreement was ever actually negotiated. The real meat for the saga-writer was the story of how Magnus was supposedly able to secure control of Kintyre by hauling a fully-rigged sailing vessel across the isthmus at Tarbert. It appears from contemporary records that King Magnus simply had little interest in Scotland and directed his attentions primarily towards England and Ireland until his death in 1103.

In 1100 there were significant changes in the English kingdom that opened up opportunities for King Edgar. On 2 August 1100 King William II was killed in the New Forest. This immediately freed Edgar from the personal homage to William that had been extracted from him in 1095 as the price of his restoration. He no longer held his kingdom by the 'gift' of William II but as an independent ruler. More good news for King Edgar followed when William's younger brother Henry seized the English throne, ignoring the claims of his older brother Duke Robert of Normandy. King Henry I was anxious about the relative weakness of his claim to the English throne compared to that of his older brother. He was therefore anxious to secure support from every conceivable source, including – for the first time for a Norman ruler – from his English subjects. He therefore opened negotiations to conclude a marriage alliance with the family of King Edgar of Scotland, which now represented the old English royal line. On 11 November 1100, the Norman Henry I, King of England married the Englishwoman Edith, the sister of King Edgar of Scotland, at Westminster Abbey. It was not quite what King Malcolm III had intended, when he had hoped back in the 1070s to place a descendant on the English throne, but it was far more than King Edgar could have hoped for as a lonely exile in 1093.

This Anglo-Scottish marriage alliance was very attractive to King Henry I since it provided him with a link to the English royal dynasty through Edith, who would be known to the Normans as Matilda, the great-niece of King Edward the Confessor. He could now present himself as the true successor of the old English kings as well as the successor of his brother King William II. It secured him the support of the English population against his brother Duke Robert of Normandy, which proved useful at the Battle of Tinchebrai in 1106. The marriage was also attractive to King Edgar as it made him brother-in-law of the ruling king of England. In 1068 Malcolm had married Margaret in the hope of securing such a relationship when Edgar *Atheling* recovered his inheritance. It was a dream that had ended with Edgar *Atheling*'s dismal failure to secure the English kingship. It had now come to fruition under his son Edgar. It also effectively ended Edgar's subordinate status and transformed him into a close relative of the English King. The benefits of this relationship for both men clearly overrode any potential losses.

In 1100, when Queen Edith or Matilda went south to head up the English royal Court she was accompanied by her youngest brother

David. He would spend the next fourteen years immersed in the Anglo-Norman culture of the royal Court. The influence of his sojourn in England was much greater on David than that of his father Malcolm III had been on him. In 1040 Malcolm had arrived in England as a friendless exiled prince from a foreign land to face an uncertain future. In contrast, David arrived as the younger brother of the Queen of England, to be welcomed into the heart of the royal Court and the highest circles of Anglo-Norman society. As a result of this higher status David was offered an intimate insight into the Anglo-Norman state. This offered him a model of administration and government that he would seek to introduce into Scotland when he later became ruler of that country in 1124.

In 1102 Edgar *Atheling* was finally free from duties in support of his nephew, King Edgar in Scotland and able to embark on a personal crusade to the Holy Land. In 1096, Duke Robert of Normandy, Edgar's close friend had participated in the First Crusade, which captured Antioch and Jerusalem after much fighting. In late 1100 Duke Robert had returned with stories of the military exploits of the crusaders. Edgar had missed this, the greatest event of the era because he had been preoccupied with preparations to assist his nephew to recover his throne. In 1101, according to William of Malmesbury, he set out for the Holy Land with a small company of men, including a Robert, son of Godwine, who had fought in the Scottish expedition of 1097 and been rewarded with land in Lothian by King Edgar. The party reached the Holy Land in time to participate in the siege of Ramleh in May 1102, where Robert was captured and killed by the Muslims. Edgar *Atheling* himself survived to return via Constantinople and Germany to Scotland, arriving probably at some point before 1105. In 1105 the Annals of Inisfallen report that 'a *camall* an animal of remarkable size was brought from the King of Scots to Muirchertach Ua Briain'. This camel, or some have suggested elephant, can only have been brought back from the Holy Land by Edgar *Atheling* or one of his followers and presented to King Edgar. The latter swiftly disposed of this exotic beast as a gift to the King of Ireland, although what this ruler then did with it is unknown.

In 1107 King Edgar died peacefully and the succession passed without apparent incident to his younger brother Alexander I. At some point after this, David demanded and secured a share of the family inheritance from his older brother, King Alexander, which consisted of a large area in the south of the kingdom. It appears that David held the regions of Strathclyde and Lothian under the authority of King Alexander, who retained control of the heart of Alba north of the Forth. It has been suggested that this division was, in fact, agreed at Edgar's death in 1107. This seems entirely possible but there is no way to establish conclusively whether it was a bequest by Edgar or an agreement reached later. The settlement, whenever it was reached, provided David with an introduction to the same southern areas of the kingdom that had probably supported his father in 1054 and had certainly backed his brother Edgar in 1095. It offered him the chance to foster the loyalty of this increasingly important region of the kingdom, which provided the bridge between the Gaelic north and Anglo-Norman England to the south.

King Alexander maintained the close relations already established with England and himself married an illegitimate daughter of King Henry I. In 1114 Alexander joined Henry on a major military expedition into Wales, as recorded in the Welsh Chronicles of the Princes. In the first major Scottish foreign venture since 1093, Alexander led a Scottish army into England, where he met Rannulf, Earl of Chester at Chester before they invaded North Wales together. There was apparently no actual fighting, however, and a long series of negotiations finally brought about the submission of the Welsh princes Gruffydd ap Cynan and Goronwy ab Owain on terms. This incident has been viewed as the military service of a subordinate king to his overlord but it might have been seen by Alexander as assistance to his brother-in-law.

In 1124 King Alexander died and his younger brother David succeeded to the whole kingdom. It has been claimed by a recent account, and with some justification, that King David was the king who made Scotland. He certainly transformed it into a new kind of kingdom on the Anglo-Norman model with mounted knights, castles, burghs, coinage, reformed monastic orders and many other things. He was, however, working on a solid foundation established by his predecessors. They had bequeathed him a vibrant multicultural kingdom that was able to accommodate and absorb these changes and progress into the future.

THE KINGDOM OF SCOTLAND

At the time of David I's accession to the throne in 1124, the kingdom of Scotland, as it was increasingly becoming known in England and across Europe, was a very different entity from the kingdom of Alba that first emerged in 900. The original kingdom of Alba had been a largely Gaelic-speaking realm confined to the north of the Forth–Clyde line. There was no indication at this time that it was on the brink of a southward advance that would transform it fundamentally. This advance brought into the Gaelic kingdom the formerly independent British or Welsh kingdom of Strathclyde and the northern portion of English Northumbria. The process of absorbing these new territories resulted in unexpected changes for the kingdom of Alba.

It is very difficult to be certain about the impact of the absorption of Strathclyde simply because so little is known about that kingdom in this key period. It had originated as a British kingdom based on the Clyde Valley in the post-Roman period with a Welsh language and culture, which contributed significantly to the wider culture of Wales itself. It is consistently referred to in our sources as a British or Welsh kingdom although it had lost its direct connection with Wales with the arrival of the Vikings in the Irish Sea during the ninth century. It had been subject to heavy English cultural influence throughout the eighth century. It had lost its capital at Dumbarton in 871 to the Vikings and its last fully independent king, Arthgal in the following year. It had been exposed to a mixed Norse-Irish culture introduced from Ireland into the region around the Solway in the early tenth century. It had been subordinate to the Gaelic kings of Alba from at least the death of King Arthgal onwards and its rulers had begun to adopt Gaelic names. It is not at all clear from all this what its linguistic and cultural background was by the eleventh century, but it was almost certainly becoming increasingly Gaelicised. The presence of Gaelic place names throughout the kingdom suggests that this was the case and stands in stark contrast to the position in neighbouring English Lothian where Gaelic place names are noticeable by their absence (see Map 5).

In contrast, the northern part of the former English kingdom of Northumbria, which had been occupied by the kings of Alba in stages between the early 950s and 1016, had retained its strong English culture. This is confirmed by the place name evidence which reveals an absence of Gaelic names in the south-east of Scotland in sharp contrast to the position north of the Forth–Clyde line and in the former kingdom of Strathclyde to the west. It is clear from this that the Gaelic culture of the kingdom of Alba completely failed to penetrate this region. A few personal and place names are the only signs of Gaelic influence in this area. It appears that this area was either more resistant to Gaelic culture or was not exposed to it for long enough to be influenced by it. The local English culture not only remained strong in this area but was actually reinforced following the influx of English refugees from the Norman Conquest. The sources focus on the important individuals involved, but there were many ordinary people too, including the captives taken on King Malcolm III's raids. It might be suggested that the captives who became slaves were unlikely to have much cultural influence, but Queen Margaret devoted herself to freeing such

English slaves. They would then have been free to settle in Alba as farm labourers or better. This process must have increased the English population and reinforced the English culture of this region and perhaps introduced English speech and culture into other areas as well. The monk Eadmer mentions 'a certain married woman of noble English descent named Eastrhild' who was restored to health by Anselm and who was associated with Dunfermline in Fife in a Canterbury obituary.

In the end, the English culture of Lothian would transform the kingdom of Alba rather than vice versa. There were a number of reasons for this, some of which have been mentioned in earlier chapters of this book. The relatively short period of Gaelic cultural dominance – 100 years – was perhaps not long enough to bring about any Gaelicisation. Strathclyde by contrast had been exposed to Gaelic influence for at least a century longer. In 1054, if not before, the return of the English-speaking King Malcolm III from exile provided a suitable focus for the loyalty of the English of Lothian. In 1068, the marriage of Malcolm III and Margaret and the birth of their Anglo-Scottish children solidified the allegiance of the English of Lothian to the new Anglo-Scottish dynasty. This happened at exactly the same time as their old loyalties were being undermined by the Norman Conquest of England. In the period before 1066 there was always a risk that the English of Lothian might transfer their allegiance to the kings of England. In the period after the Conquest this was much less likely. It is ironic but true that the English of Lothian probably found more support for their English culture among the kings of Scots than the Norman kings of England after 1066. In addition, the kings of Alba spent more time in Lothian from the reign of Malcolm III onwards and Edinburgh became an important royal residence. It was at Edinburgh that Queen Margaret died in 1093.

Malcolm III and his successors also sought to cultivate the loyalties of English Lothian by their support for the church of St

Cuthbert at Durham. The cult of St Cuthbert had survived the Viking destruction of the kingdom of Northumbria in 867 to expand throughout the remnants of English Northumbria. It was the most important church in the far north of England and it remained so in Lothian in spite of its occupation by the kings of Alba from the 950s onwards. The early kings of Alba had allowed the bishop of St Andrews to expand his authority into Lothian in an effort to counter the influence of St Cuthbert. In this same period, the church of Durham experienced a number of Scottish attacks, which were no doubt partly inspired by frustration at the continuing loyalty of the men of Lothian to St Cuthbert. In spite of all this, the inhabitants of Lothian remained steadfast in their faith in St Cuthbert and the kings from Malcolm III onwards recognised this fact and sought to exploit it to win over the population of Lothian.

On 11 August 1093, in spite of the imminent crisis in his relations with William II, King Malcolm III took time out from his journey south to negotiate with the English King to lay a foundation stone for the new Norman cathedral at Durham. He was apparently the only layman present at this important ceremony. At the same time he probably agreed the following covenant with the church of Durham:

This is the covenant which the convent of St Cuthbert has promised to Malcolm King of Scots and to Queen Margaret and to their sons and daughters to keep for ever. Namely that, on behalf of the king and queen, while they are alive, one poor man shall be nourished daily and likewise two poor men shall be maintained for them on Thursday in holy week at the common maundy, and a collect said at the litanies and at mass. Further, that they both, in this life and after, they and their sons and daughters shall be partakers in all things that be to the service of God in the monastery of St Cuthbert. And for the king and queen individually from the day of their death there shall be thirty full

195

offices of the dead in the convent and *Verba mea* shall be done every day and each priest shall sing thirty masses and each of the rest ten psalters and their anniversary shall be celebrated as an annual festival like that of King Athelstan.[15]

King Malcolm and Queen Margaret and the rest of the Scottish royal family also feature in the *Liber Vitae* of Durham, which lists the names of all those whose souls the monks will pray for.

In spite of Malcolm's death soon after this in November 1093, this initial connection with the church of Durham was actively pursued by his sons. In 1094 King Duncan II issued a charter granting to Durham lands and dues in East Lothian which had formerly belonged to Bishop Fothad of St Andrews. In 1095 King Edgar made a generous grant of Coldinghamshire and Berwickshire to Durham and although this grant fell through it would subsequently be replaced by several others. In 1104 the future King Alexander I would be the only layman invited to witness the ceremonial opening of the coffin of St Cuthbert. This active support for St Cuthbert and his church contrasts markedly with earlier Scottish raids and was clearly an important element in securing the loyalty of English Lothian.

The kind of men designed to be won over by this sort of initiative were Thor the Long of Ednam in Berwickshire, who issued a charter in around 1105, once preserved at Durham, as follows:

To all sons of the Holy Mother Church, Thor the Long gives greeting in the Lord. Know that Edgar, my lord, King of Scots gave to me Ednam lying waste which I occupied with his help and with my own stock, and I have built a church in honour of St Cuthbert and his monks to be possessed by them for ever. This grant I have made for the soul of my lord, King Edgar, and for the souls of his father and mother and for the salvation of his brothers and sisters, and for the redemption of Leofwine, my beloved brother, and for the safety of my own body and soul. And if anyone shall presume, by any violence or device, to take away this my grant from the aforesaid saint and the monks serving him, may God Almighty take away from him the life of the kingdom of heaven and may he undergo everlasting punishment with the devil and his angels. Amen.[16]

This Thor was typical of the English of Lothian, who continued to acknowledge the importance of St Cuthbert and the influence of his church but who were nevertheless content freely to acknowledge Edgar, King of Scots as their lord. He was happy to include prayers for his soul and for the souls of the rest of the Anglo-Scottish royal family. It was harnessing the loyalty of such men to the kings and the wider kingdom that would enhance its multicultural nature and ultimately contribute to its transformation into something new.

In 1124 the process of absorbing Strathclyde and, more particularly, Lothian had transformed the kingdom of Alba into a multicultural entity very different from the Gaelic kingdom of 900. The fusion of Gaelic Alba and English Northumbria had produced a unique new kingdom of Scotland. It was a kingdom where two different cultures, Gaelic and English, were felt to have a certain equality of status. It was no longer a Gaelic kingdom in which English was spoken but a hybrid kingdom in which Gaelic and English speakers existed side by side. This new reality was given concrete expression in the early charters of Kings Edgar and Alexander I, which were addressed to their subjects *Scoti et Angli* or 'Scots and English'.

This new complexity in the culture of the kingdom would be a significant contributory factor to the success of King David I in introducing Anglo-Normans into Scotland after 1124. The addition of another cultural tradition to an already mixed culture is obviously much less problematic than its introduction into a single cultural zone. In Scotland the Normans simply added another element to the existing mixture. They appear in the charters of King David as *Franci* or 'French' alongside the Scots and English in the charters of his predecessors. In contemporary England and Wales and later in Ireland the Normans arrived as cultural outsiders in a well-established monoculture. The fact that the introduction of the Normans into Scotland came about relatively peacefully under recognised royal sponsorship rather than through aggressive foreign military conquest undoubtedly also helped the process.

In 900 the kings of Alba followed a succession system that selected kings from among adult males of identified lineages derived from a common royal ancestor. In the case of Alba, the common ancestor was Kenneth MacAlpin and the lineages were the MacKenneths, MacDuffs and MacHeths. This system had proved very effective at producing suitable adult male kings who were able to rule the kingdom and lead its armies. This was essential in the dangerous period of the Viking attacks and during the days of aggressive expansion that followed. The initial usefulness of this system was, however, undermined as the three lineages increasingly diverged over time. In this context the kingship was originally shared among brothers and close cousins with minimal disruption. In time, however, the kingship became a bone of contention between men whose relationships with each other were increasingly distant and tenuous. In the late tenth century, the succession had become a bitter struggle for supremacy between what were now three entirely independent and rival dynasties. This brought about frequent violent disputes that worked to the detriment of the kingdom as a whole.

In response to this situation each of the lineages sought to manipulate the system by eliminating or excluding their competitors and confining the succession within their own lineage. This should not be confused with the introduction of primogeniture, which did not happen until later in the twelfth century. In 1124 this process was well underway and since 1058 the succession had in practice been restricted to members of the lineage of MacKenneth and the descendants of King Malcolm II. The other lineages had not been eliminated entirely but had been effectively excluded for nearly sixty-five years. The MacDuffs had either been restricted to the reservation of Moray in the north or induced to accept compensation in the form of the position of *mormaer* of Fife and the major role in future royal inaugurations for their loss. The MacHeths had been temporarily subdued for reasons that are obscure but may have involved either or both of the possibilities noted for the MacDuffs. In the period following King David's succession both of these ancient lineages would seek to revive their claims to the succession and cause problems for future kings of Scotland well into the thirteenth century.

The organisation of the wider society in the kingdom had undergone much less fundamental change than the royal dynasty itself. It remained at heart an agricultural society where the agricultural surplus produced by the farmers was controlled and administered on behalf of the king by various ranks of nobles. It had absorbed additional southern territories from English Northumbria which had a very similar social pattern. The impact of the introduction of large numbers of English-speakers on this society was therefore limited. It focused chiefly on a change in the titles for various ranks, which gradually shifted from Gaelic to English over a period of time. It happened as English titles for ranks were imported with the English-speaking population or from south of the border, slowly replacing the Gaelic titles previously employed. In this fashion the *mormaers* gradually became known as earls, the *toiseachs* as thanes and their estates as thanages. In addition to this straightforward change in nomenclature the new population brought its own nobles into the cultural mix. The ranks of Scottish society now included individuals whose names betrayed a variety of cultural origins in reflection of the new multicultural kingdom. The Gaelic *mormaers* were joined by Earl Gospatric of Dunbar and by his son and namesake. The English thanes and *drengs*, i.e. 'freemen' or 'minor nobles', of Lothian, such as Thor the Long, arrived to join the *toiseachs* of old Alba.

The purpose and actual functions of these various ranks of society did not really change in their essentials. They continued to mediate between the kings and their subjects, the farmers who produced the agricultural surplus to feed, clothe and shelter the entire kingdom. They had the dual role of representing local society at the centre and representing the king in the local area. They continued to contribute and lead local military contingents in war. It was the kind of society that was common across much of early medieval Western Europe and it had little difficulty later in absorbing Norman knights under King David. The most significant social change that would be introduced after 1124 was in fact the introduction of the borough of burgh from England as a centre for trade, manufacturing and marketing. This entity appears to have been completely absent from the kingdom of Alba before 1124 but would be a significant feature of King David's reign. There were smaller and less formally organised trading, manufacturing and marketing centres like that unearthed by archaeological investigation at Whithorn. They serve as predecessors of the burgh but do not fulfil quite the same role.

The Scottish royal Court probably witnessed greater change in the period before 1124 than the wider society outside it. This change has usually been attributed to the influence of Queen Margaret, who it is often assumed – largely on the basis of a single source – single-handedly transformed the Scottish Court on the English model. The Life of St Margaret was written for her daughter Edith or Matilda, wife of King Henry I, possibly by Thurgot, Prior of Durham. It was intended to provide a *speculum* or 'mirror' for the new Queen of the English. It sought to portray the role of an ideal queen in the person of Queen Margaret so that Edith or Matilda might model her own actions on those attributed to her mother. This clear purpose means that the work highlights and in some cases exaggerates the role of Queen Margaret. At the same time and for the same reason it obscures and, in many cases, minimises or omits the role of her husband, King Malcolm III. In a period when so few sources survive, the existence of this unique but biased source has badly distorted the historical view of King Malcolm and the contemporary Scottish royal Court.

The Life of St Margaret presents the picture of an active queen who ruled not only her husband and the Court but also had considerable influence over the Church and wider society. In the words of its author, 'All things which were fitting were carried out by order of the prudent queen: by her counsel the laws of the kingdom were put in order, divine religion was augmented by her industry and the people rejoined in the prosperity of affairs.' It correspondingly reduces and trivialises the role of King Malcolm, who is left with little to do but support his busy wife. In spite of the fact that Malcolm had been described by this same writer on the occasion of his marriage to Margaret as 'the most powerful Malcolm, King of the Scots', thereafter he meekly retreats into the shadow of this great woman, becoming little more than a cipher: 'he dreaded to displease the queen . . . he used to rush to comply with her wishes and prudent plans in all things.' This was the man who fought his way to the throne by killing two rivals and who ravaged northern England without mercy. There is clearly something wrong with this picture!

It was Queen Margaret, according to the Life, who ordered the building of a new church at Dunfermline, where she and Malcolm had been married, and decorated it in the Anglo-Saxon tradition with rich ornaments including a large gold crucifix. This was established as a Benedictine priory dedicated to the Holy Trinity as a daughter house of Canterbury Cathedral. She also made many rich gifts to other religious houses, including St Andrews, and to many individual hermits. There is no mention of her husband in all of this. In fact, a number of contemporary documentary sources reveal that the royal couple actually worked together to benefit the Church. A later charter of their son King David I reports that the Benedictine priory at Dunfermline was 'first founded by [his] father and mother'. The royal couple can be seen together granting lands to the culdees of Loch Leven in the *notitiae* included in the later Register of St Andrews Priory. They are also found together in the covenant drawn up and agreed with Durham Cathedral in 1093. The role of King Malcolm has clearly been ignored in order to enhance correspondingly the role and the reputation of Queen Margaret.

It was Queen Margaret again, according to the Life, who attempted to reform the 'many things in Scotland [that] were done contrary to the rule of faith and the holy custom of the universal church'. She is supposed to have done this through church councils, including one where 'she alone, for the space of three days, [struggled] against those who defended false customs.' The role of King Malcolm at this important church council was, supposedly, no more than to act as a 'vigilant interpreter' between his English-speaking wife and the Gaelic-speaking clergy. It is an uplifting story, but frankly unbelievable. It is much more likely that she supported the case for reform, either through her own clerical supporters or through the King himself rather than leading the debates. It is clear that the Life ignores, obscures or minimises the role of Malcolm in this area also.

The Life also emphasises Queen Margaret's activities in spheres where she would more naturally have taken a prominent role, including the rearing of children, fashion and interior design in the Court and in wider society, Court ceremonial and charitable works. It should be noted that she appears to have sought in most of these areas to introduce things familiar to her from her years in the English Court. This would be completely natural but it should not be forgotten that Malcolm himself had been exposed to English influence in his youth and might also have wanted to do these things. It may be that once again Malcolm's role in these changes is being omitted or played down. In the area of child-rearing, for example,

Malcolm must have participated in the military training of his sons, just as Fochertach did for his son Cadroe. This is not mentioned in The Life of St Margaret, however, because it did not reveal her personal role. There is clearly much that is left out of this account.

The Life of St Margaret is a unique source for the Scottish royal Court during the late eleventh century with a great deal to offer, but it must be used with the utmost caution. It was written for a purpose, that of providing an exemplar of an ideal queen, and therefore quite deliberately selects and edits its information to fulfil that purpose. It is content to exaggerate the part played by the Queen in events and to minimise or omit the role of others, including King Malcolm himself. It may be a *speculum* or 'mirror' but, if so, it comes from a fairground sideshow since it badly distorts the picture that it offers of the royal Court. It is fortunate that other sources exist to provide a corrective to the warped image of Malcolm in this one. If The Life of St Margaret were the only source available, it would be impossible to identify Malcolm for what he is, a major political figure in Britain and a key player in the transformation of his kingdom.

The English exile of King Malcolm III and the English background of his wife and children perhaps inevitably persuaded them to favour English Court models. A range of new or newly renamed officials begin to appear at the Scottish Court in the documentary sources before 1124. They include a chancellor Herbert, a chamberlain Edmund or Adam, a butler Aelfric, a constable Edward, son of Siward, and the Englishman, Aelfwine MacArchill, who would be listed under the old Gaelic title of *rannaire* or 'distributor' but who was probably already fulfilling the duties of a steward. The few records that survive provide little more than names and titles for these individuals. It seems likely, however, that these in themselves are significant indicators that increasingly more complex administrative tasks were already being undertaken by the royal Court. This nascent Scottish royal Court would develop even more rapidly along English lines under King David after 1124.

In the period before 1124 there is fragmentary evidence for the work of this royal administration in a number of administrative documents. The earliest surviving Scottish charter is that issued by King Duncan II, which was produced by the clerks of the church of Durham. It is from the reign of King Edgar onwards that there survive charters, writs and other documents on English models, which were probably produced within the royal Court. A royal seal was employed to authenticate these documents and an impression of the seal of King Edgar which survives was modelled on that of King Edward the Confessor. The practice of issuing such documents under a seal may have been introduced during the reign of King Malcolm III but, if so, none has survived. They were, however, probably coming into widespread use before 1124 and those of King David are addressed to a wide range of people from earls and bishops down to quite minor individuals. For example, a writ of David I commands that the fugitive *neyfs*, or slaves, of a minor noblewoman called Leofgifu should not be detained but returned to her. It was a new administrative system based on written documents that would become commonplace under King David I after 1124.

The period before 1124 also witnessed the small but important beginnings of major changes in the Church in Scotland. In 1107 King Alexander I appointed Thurgot, Prior of Durham and possibly chaplain and biographer of Queen Margaret, to the vacant bishopric of St Andrews. This appointment of an advocate of church reform to the senior bishopric was a clear sign that Alexander intended to modernise the Scottish Church. Unfortunately, Thurgot had difficulty securing consecration since the Archbishop of York, who was embroiled in a dispute with Canterbury, had not been consecrated himself. In any case, King Alexander was concerned that such ceremonies might compromise his own authority over the Scottish Church. It was not until 1 August 1109 that Thurgot was finally consecrated by the Archbishop of York, but only with the proviso that he preserved the independence of the Scottish Church. The new bishop attempted to introduce some reforms which, coincidently or not, appear to match those that Queen Margaret reportedly pursued in The Life of St Margaret, possibly written by Thurgot himself! He attempted to seek Papal assistance with his improvements but King Alexander, who was concerned that this might compromise his authority over the Scottish Church, blocked these approaches. In the end Bishop Thurgot became discouraged and withdrew to Monkwearmouth in England where he died on 31 August 1115. In 1120 King Alexander sought to negotiate the appointment of Eadmer, a Canterbury monk and biographer of Archbishop Anselm, to the bishopric of St Andrews. He had clearly not abandoned his intention to modernise the Scottish Church. Unfortunately, Eadmer insisted he should be consecrated by the Archbishop of Canterbury. This potential compromise to his authority over the Scottish Church proved unacceptable to King Alexander and Eadmer duly returned to Canterbury within the year. It would be King David who would finally manage to secure suitable bishops to direct the modernisation of the Church in Scotland.

As already noted, King Malcolm III and Queen Margaret were responsible for the building of a new priory at Dunfermline, staffed by reformed Benedictine monks brought in from Canterbury. There is documentary support for this foundation in a letter of Lanfranc, Archbishop of Canterbury, which mentions the dispatch of Goldwine and two other monks at Queen Margaret's request at some point between 1070 and 1089. The priory was also, according to a later charter of King David, provided with extensive lands by Malcolm and Margaret and, according to The Life of St Margaret, it was richly adorned inside in the Anglo-Saxon tradition and contained a large gold crucifix studded with jewels. The small advance party of monks was later joined by more sent from Canterbury by Archbishop Anselm at King Edgar's request and Anselm subsequently sought King Alexander's protection for these monks. According to David's charter of 1128, the priory was subsequently augmented with more lands and buildings by the sons of Malcolm and Margaret. In 1120 it was administered by Prior Peter, who was the man sent to Canterbury to negotiate the appointment of Eadmer as Bishop of St Andrews.

The foundation of the Benedictine Priory at Dunfermline by Malcolm and Margaret set the pattern for future royal foundations. In 1113 Prince David founded a Tironensian priory at Selkirk in the region of southern Scotland which he controlled under his brother King Alexander. Not to be outdone, in 1115 King Alexander himself followed this up by recruiting six canons and a prior, Robert, to provide staff for his new foundation, an Augustinian priory to be sited at Scone. The process of introducing reformed church orders into Scotland under royal patronage was now well underway. This work would be continued on a grand scale by King David on his accession to the throne in 1124 and he would be assisted in this by many of his leading nobles.

In 1124 King David I inherited a multicultural kingdom which included a majority Gaelic population alongside a significant minority English population. He followed his father and his brothers in seeking to foster the loyalty of the new English-speaking community of Lothian while holding on to the loyalty of the traditional Gaelic-speaking community of Alba itself. It was a difficult balance to maintain but he would be assisted by his genetic inheritance from his parents, his knowledge of both languages and his own highly mixed cultural background. He would seek to exploit English weakness, like his ancestors, to resume the southward expansion of the kingdom in order to restore Cumberland and secure more of Northumbria. He spent a great deal of his time in the southern part of the kingdom close to the English border, where risks and opportunities were highest. He continued with the introduction of English or Anglo-Norman cultural elements to the royal Court, royal administration, local administration and the Church. He vastly expanded the construction of reformed monasteries and speeded up the modernisation of the Church more generally. He introduced significant numbers of Anglo-Normans to add to the already rich cultural mix within the kingdom. He introduced towns, populated with English and French, as centres for manufacturing and exchange and minted the first Scottish coins. In all of this, with the exception of the towns, he was following a trail blazed to some extent by his predecessors.

In 1124 the kingdom of Scotland was already a very different political entity from the kingdom of Alba and it would be transformed almost beyond recognition in the next thirty years by King David. This was a process that built directly on all the work done by King Malcolm III during his long reign. If Malcolm had not managed to bridge the cultural gap between his Gaelic-speaking and English-speaking subjects it is unlikely that medieval Scotland, as we know it, would have emerged. In the worst case, the kingdom might have fractured into its Gaelic and English component parts. In other scenarios, Gaelic language and culture might have overwhelmed English, as it had already overwhelmed Welsh in Strathclyde. It is doubtful if King David would have found it so easy to introduce his Anglo-Normans or his towns, if the kingdom had been a Gaelic monoculture on the Irish model. The Anglo-Scottish lineage of MacKenneth might have become too closely identified with the English population and lost power to its rival Gaelic lineages. The English population of Lothian might have become a Trojan horse for English penetration into southern Scotland. Instead of any of these alternatives, the successful reconciliation of the Gaelic and English populations achieved principally by King Malcolm III opened the door to further change and to the transformation of the kingdom into its new form.

Family Trees

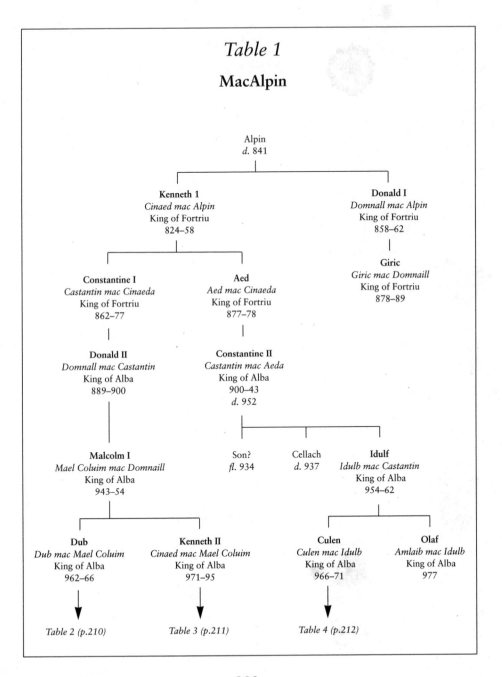

Table 1

MacAlpin

Alpin
d. 841

Kenneth 1
Cinaed mac Alpin
King of Fortriu
824–58

Donald I
Domnall mac Alpin
King of Fortriu
858–62

Giric
Giric mac Domnaill
King of Fortriu
878–89

Constantine I
Castantin mac Cinaeda
King of Fortriu
862–77

Aed
Aed mac Cinaeda
King of Fortriu
877–78

Donald II
Domnall mac Castantin
King of Alba
889–900

Constantine II
Castantin mac Aeda
King of Alba
900–43
d. 952

Malcolm I
Mael Coluim mac Domnaill
King of Alba
943–54

Son?
fl. 934

Cellach
d. 937

Idulf
Idulb mac Castantin
King of Alba
954–62

Dub
Dub mac Mael Coluim
King of Alba
962–66

Kenneth II
Cinaed mac Mael Coluim
King of Alba
971–95

Culen
Culen mac Idulb
King of Alba
966–71

Olaf
Amlaib mac Idulb
King of Alba
977

Table 2 (p.210)

Table 3 (p.211)

Table 4 (p.212)

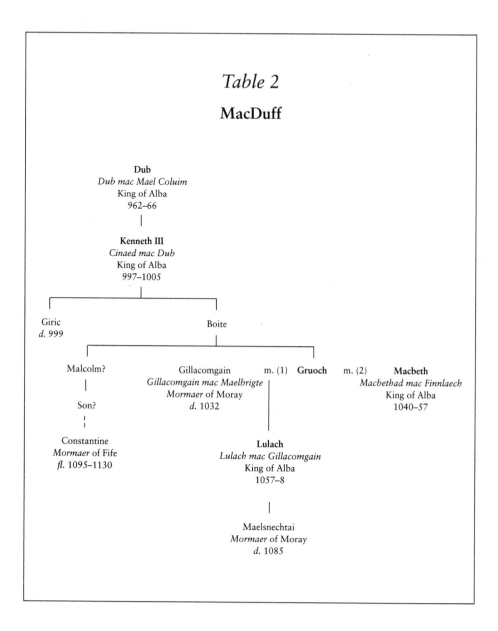

Table 2

MacDuff

Dub
Dub mac Mael Coluim
King of Alba
962–66

Kenneth III
Cinaed mac Dub
King of Alba
997–1005

Giric
d. 999

Boite

Malcolm?

Gillacomgain   m. (1)   **Gruoch**   m. (2)   **Macbeth**
Gillacomgain mac Maelbrigte   *Macbethad mac Finnlaech*
Mormaer of Moray   King of Alba
d. 1032   1040–57

Son?

Constantine
Mormaer of Fife
fl. 1095–1130

Lulach
Lulach mac Gillacomgain
King of Alba
1057–8

Maelsnechtai
Mormaer of Moray
d. 1085

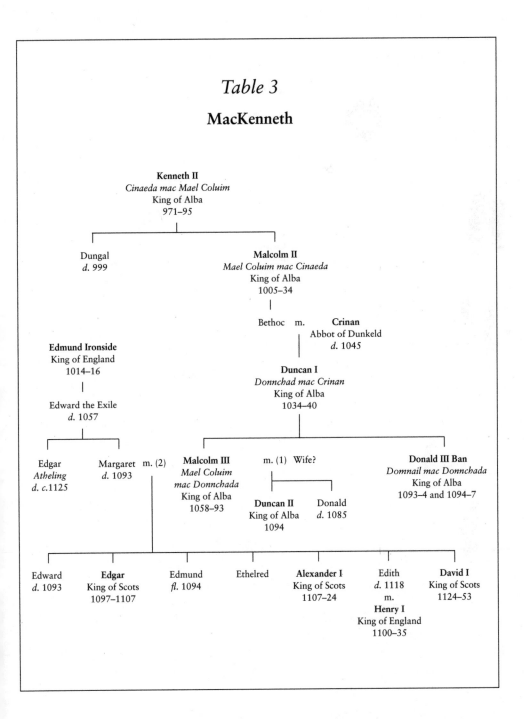

Table 3

MacKenneth

Kenneth II
Cinaeda mac Mael Coluim
King of Alba
971–95

Dungal
d. 999

Malcolm II
Mael Coluim mac Cinaeda
King of Alba
1005–34

Bethoc   m.   **Crinan**
Abbot of Dunkeld
d. 1045

Edmund Ironside
King of England
1014–16

Edward the Exile
d. 1057

Duncan I
Donnchad mac Crinan
King of Alba
1034–40

Edgar
Atheling
*d. c.*1125

Margaret   m. (2)
d. 1093

Malcolm III
Mael Coluim
mac Donnchada
King of Alba
1058–93

m. (1)   Wife?

Donald III Ban
Domnail mac Donnchada
King of Alba
1093–4 and 1094–7

Duncan II
King of Alba
1094

Donald
d. 1085

Edward
d. 1093

Edgar
King of Scots
1097–1107

Edmund
fl. 1094

Ethelred

Alexander I
King of Scots
1107–24

Edith
d. 1118
m.
Henry I
King of England
1100–35

David I
King of Scots
1124–53

Table 4

MacHeth

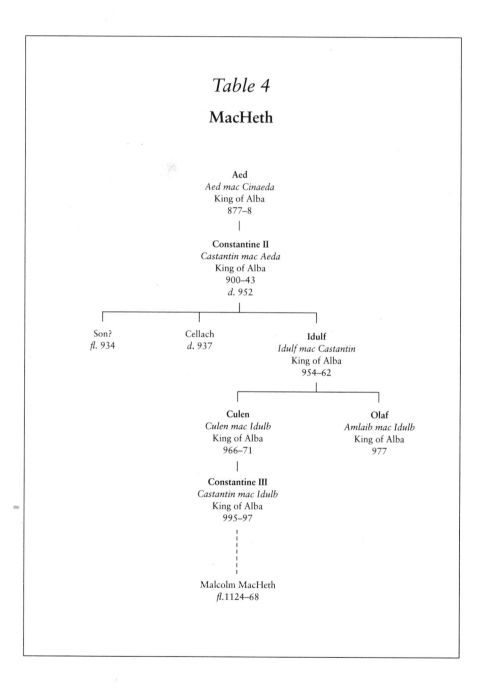

Aed
Aed mac Cinaeda
King of Alba
877–8

Constantine II
Castantin mac Aeda
King of Alba
900–43
d. 952

Son?
fl. 934

Cellach
d. 937

Idulf
Idulf mac Castantin
King of Alba
954–62

Culen
Culen mac Idulb
King of Alba
966–71

Olaf
Amlaib mac Idulb
King of Alba
977

Constantine III
Castantin mac Idulb
King of Alba
995–97

Malcolm MacHeth
*fl.*1124–68

Table 5

Strathclyde

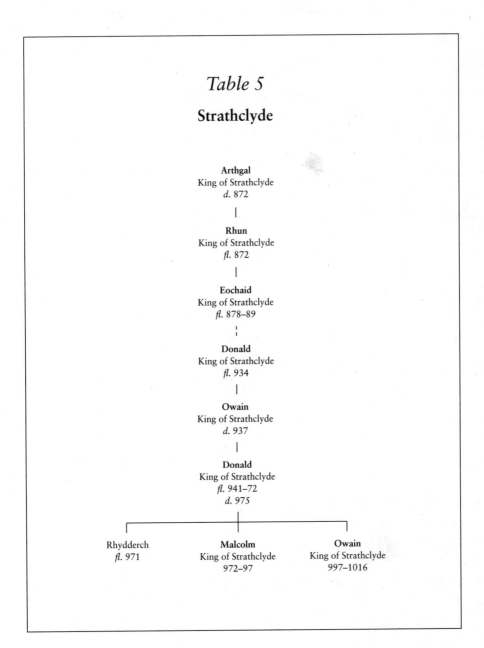

Arthgal
King of Strathclyde
d. 872

|

Rhun
King of Strathclyde
fl. 872

|

Eochaid
King of Strathclyde
fl. 878–89

Donald
King of Strathclyde
fl. 934

|

Owain
King of Strathclyde
d. 937

|

Donald
King of Strathclyde
fl. 941–72
d. 975

Rhydderch
fl. 971

Malcolm
King of Strathclyde
972–97

Owain
King of Strathclyde
997–1016

Table 6

Northumbria

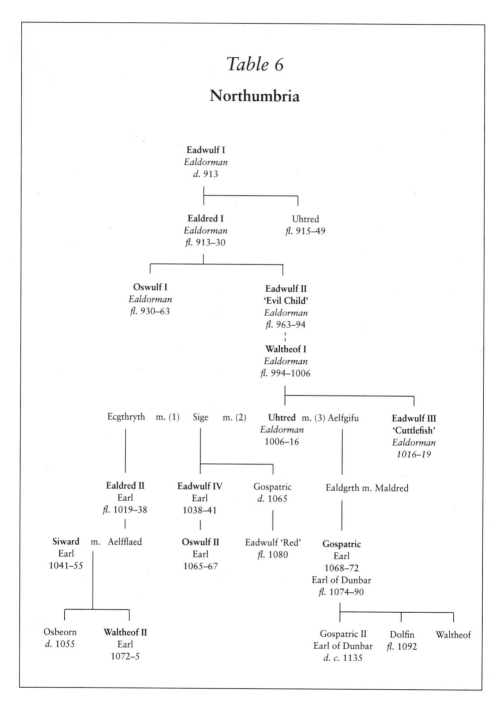

Eadwulf I
Ealdorman
d. 913

Ealdred I
Ealdorman
fl. 913–30

Uhtred
fl. 915–49

Oswulf I
Ealdorman
fl. 930–63

Eadwulf II
'Evil Child'
Ealdorman
fl. 963–94

Waltheof I
Ealdorman
fl. 994–1006

Ecgthryth   m. (1)   Sige   m. (2)   **Uhtred** m. (3) Aelfgifu
Ealdorman
1006–16

Eadwulf III
'Cuttlefish'
Ealdorman
1016–19

Ealdred II
Earl
fl. 1019–38

Eadwulf IV
Earl
1038–41

Gospatric
d. 1065

Ealdgrth m. Maldred

Siward   m.   Aelfflaed
Earl
1041–55

Oswulf II
Earl
1065–67

Eadwulf 'Red'
fl. 1080

Gospatric
Earl
1068–72
Earl of Dunbar
fl. 1074–90

Osbeorn
d. 1055

Waltheof II
Earl
1072–5

Gospatric II
Earl of Dunbar
d. c. 1135

Dolfin
fl. 1092

Waltheof

MAP 1: ALBA 800–1125

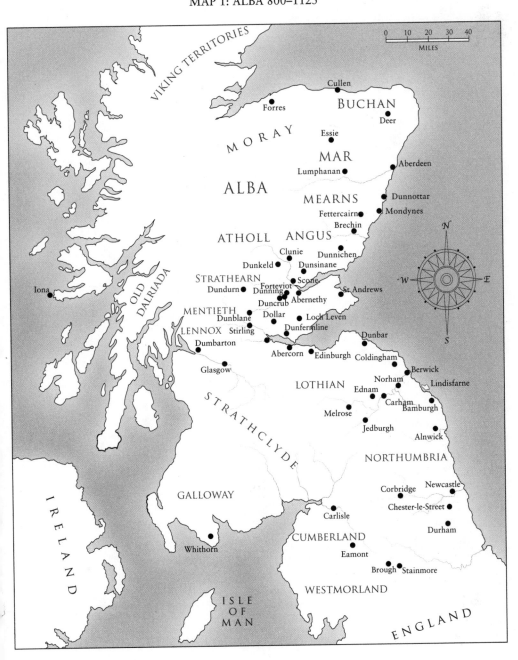

VIKING TERRITORIES

MILES
0 10 20 30 40

Cullen

Forres

BUCHAN

Deer

Essie

M O R A Y

MAR

Lumphanan

Aberdeen

ALBA

MEARNS

Dunnottar

Fettercairn

Mondynes

Brechin

ATHOLL

ANGUS

Clunie

Dunnichen

Dunkeld

Dunsinane

STRATHEARN

Scone

Dundurn

Forteviot

Dunning

St Andrews

Duncrub

Abernethy

MENTIETH

Dollar

Dunblane

Loch Leven

LENNOX

Stirling

Dunfermline

Dumbarton

Dunbar

Abercorn

Edinburgh

Coldingham

Glasgow

Berwick

Norham

Lindisfarne

LOTHIAN

Ednam

Carham

Bamburgh

Melrose

S T R A T H C L Y D E

Jedburgh

Alnwick

NORTHUMBRIA

Corbridge

Newcastle

GALLOWAY

Chester-le-Street

Carlisle

Durham

I R E L A N D

CUMBERLAND

Whithorn

Eamont

Brough Stainmore

WESTMORLAND

ISLE
OF
MAN

E N G L A N D

Iona

OLD
DALRIADA

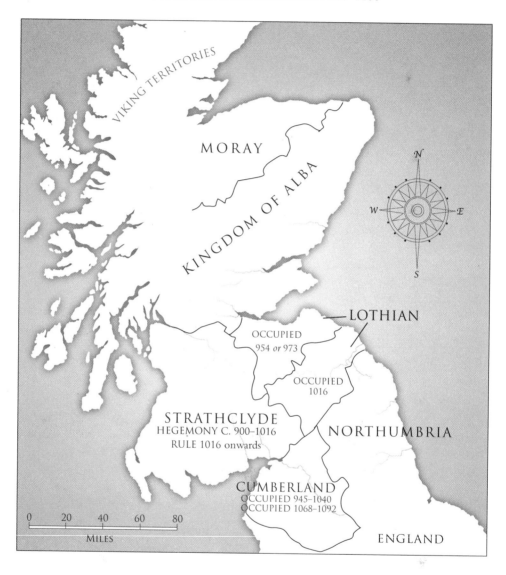

VIKING TERRITORIES

MORAY

KINGDOM OF ALBA

LOTHIAN

OCCUPIED
954 *or* 973

OCCUPIED
1016

STRATHCLYDE
HEGEMONY C. 900–1016
RULE 1016 onwards

NORTHUMBRIA

CUMBERLAND
OCCUPIED 945–1040
OCCUPIED 1068–1092

ENGLAND

N
W — E
S

0   20   40   60   80
MILES

MAP 3: PROVINCES AND THANAGES

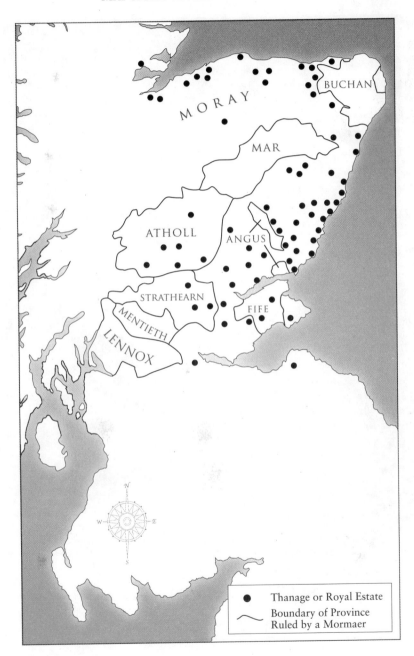

MAP 4: EARLY DIOCESES AND CATHEDRALS

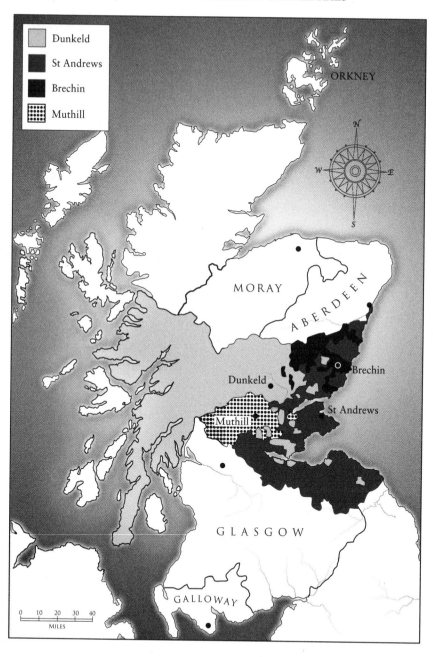

Dunkeld

St Andrews

Brechin

Muthill

ORKNEY

MORAY

ABERDEEN

Brechin

Dunkeld

St Andrews

Muthill

GLASGOW

GALLOWAY

0 10 20 30 40
MILES

MAP 5: LINGUISTIC AND CULTURAL MARKERS

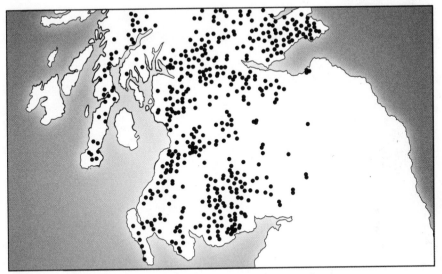

5a: Gaelic place-names in southern Scotland

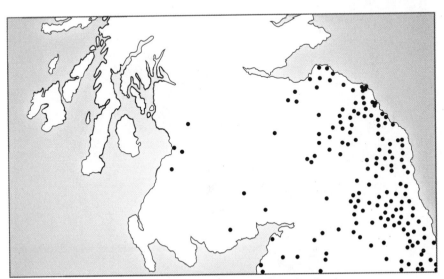

5b: English place-names in southern Scotland

Notes

CHAPTER 1

1. Anderson, A.O., *Early Sources of Scottish History A.D. 500–1286*, Stamford, 1990, pp. 273–4, n. 4
2. *Ibid.*, pp. 263–5
3. *The Triumph Tree*, tr. T.O. Clancy, Edinburgh, 1998, p. 144

CHAPTER 2

4. Jackson, K., *The Gaelic Notes in the Book of Deer*, Cambridge, 1972, pp. 33–4
5. Clancy, *Triumph Tree*, p. 183

CHAPTER 3

6. *The Annals of Ulster to A.D. 1131*, ed. S. MacAirt and G. MacNiocaill, Dublin, 1983, pp. 368–9
7. Hill, P., *The Age of Athelstan*, Stroud, 2004, p. 200
8. *Armes Prydain*, ed. I. Williams, Dublin, 1972, pp. 2–3
9. *The Anglo-Saxon Chronicle*, ed. D. Whitelock, D.C. Douglas and S.I. Tucker, Westport, 1986, pp. 69–70
10. Anderson, *Early Sources of Scottish History*, pp. 431–43

CHAPTER 4

11. *The Chronicle of John of Worcester: Volume II*, ed. R.R. Darlington and P. McGurk, Oxford, 1995, pp. 422–5

CHAPTER 5

12. Morris, C.J., *Marriage and Murder in Eleventh-Century Northumbria: A Study of* De Obsessione Dunelmi, York, 1992, pp. 1–2
13. *English Historical Documents: Volume I*, ed. D. Whitelock, Oxford, 1979, p. 339, No. 18

CHAPTER 6

14. *John of Fordun's Chronicle of the Scottish Nation: Volume 2*, ed. W.F. Skene, Lampeter, 1993, pp. 289–90

CHAPTER 7

15. Barrow, G.W.S. 'The Kings of Scotland and Durham', in *Anglo-Norman Durham*, ed. D. Rollason, M. Harvey and M. Prestwich, Woodbridge, 1998
16. Donaldson, G., *Scottish Historical Documents*, Edinburgh, 1974, p. 18

Select Bibliography

PRIMARY SOURCES

The Anglo-Saxon Chronicle, ed. D. Whitelock, with D.C. Douglas and
 S.I. Tucker, rev. edn, Westport, 1986
The Annals of Inisfallen, ed. S. MacAirt, Dublin, 1951–77
The Annals of Tigernach, tr. W. Stokes, Lampeter, 1993
The Annals of Ulster (to A.D. 1131), ed. S. MacAirt and G. MacNiocall,
 Dublin, 1983
Armes Prydain, ed. I. Williams, Dublin, 1972
Brut Y Tywysogyon (Chronicles of the Princes) Peniarth MS. 20 Version,
 ed. T. Jones, Cardiff, 1952
The Charters of David I, ed. G.W.S. Barrow, Woodbridge, 1999
The Chronicle of John of Worcester, Vol. II, ed. R.R. Darlington and
 P.J. McGurk, Oxford, 1995
Early Scottish Charters Prior to A.D. 1153, ed. A.C. Lawrie, Glasgow,
 1905
Early Sources of Scottish History A.D. 500–1286, ed. A.O. Anderson,
 2 vols, Stamford, 1990
The Ecclesiastical History of Orderic Vitalis, ed. M. Chibnall, 6 vols,
 Oxford, 1969–80
English Historical Documents: Vol. I, c. 500–1042, ed. D. Whitelock,
 London, 1979
English Historical Documents: Vol. II, 1042–1189, ed. D.C. Douglas and
 G.W. Greenaway, Oxford, 1981
Florence of Worcester's Chronicle, tr. J. Stevenson, Lampeter, 1989
Fragmentary Annals of Ireland, ed. J. Radner, Dublin, 1978

Select Bibliography

The Gaelic Notes in the Book of Deer, ed. K. Jackson, Cambridge, 1972

John of Fordun's Chronicle of the Scottish Nation, ed. W.F. Skene, 2 vols, Lampeter, 1993

Liber Vitae Ecclesiae Dunhelmensis, ed. J. Stevenson, London, 1841

'The Life of St Margaret' in Huneycutt, L.L., *Matilda of Scotland*, Woodbridge, 2003

Orkneyinga Saga, tr. H. Palsson and M. Magnusson, London, 1978

Prophecy of Berchan, ed. B.T. Hudson, Westport, 1996

Regesta Regum Scottorum: Malcolm IV, ed. G.W.S. Barrow, Edinburgh, 1960

Scottish Annals from English Chroniclers A.D. 500–1286, ed. A.O. Anderson, London, 1908

'The Scottish Chronicle' in *Caledonian Craftsmanship*, ed. D. Howlett, Dublin, 2000

Scottish Historical Documents, ed. G. Donaldson, Edinburgh, 1974

Simeon of Durham: A History of the Church of Durham, tr. J. Stevenson, Lampeter, 1988

Simeon of Durham: A History of the Kings of England, tr. J. Stevenson, Lampeter, 1987

The Triumph Tree, tr. T.O. Clancy, Edinburgh, 1998

William of Malmesbury – A History of the Norman Kings, tr. J. Stevenson, Lampeter, 1987

William of Malmesbury – The Kings Before the Norman Conquest, tr. J. Stevenson, Lampeter, 1989

SECONDARY SOURCES

Aitchison, N., *Macbeth: Man and Myth*, Stroud, 1999

——, *The Picts and the Scots at War*, Stroud, 2003

Anderson, M.O., *Kings and Kingship in Early Scotland*, Edinburgh, 1980

Barrow, G.W.S., *The Anglo-Norman Era in Scottish History*, Oxford, 1980

——, *The Kingdom of the Scots*, Edinburgh, 2003

——, *Kingship and Unity*, Edinburgh, 2003

Byrne, F.J., *Irish Kings and High Kings*, London, 1973

Cowan, I.B. and Easson, D.E., *Medieval Religious Houses*, 2nd edn., London, 1976

Driscoll, S., *Alba*, Edinburgh, 2002

Duncan, A.A.M., *The Kingship of the Scots*, Edinburgh, 2002

——, *The Making of the Kingdom*, Edinburgh, 1975

Foster, S.M., *Picts, Gaels and Scots*, London, 2004

Grant, A. and Stringer, K.J. (eds), *Medieval Scotland*, Edinburgh, 1993

Higham, N.J., *The Kingdom of Northumbria 350–1100*, Stroud, 1993

Hill, P., *The Age of Athelstan*, Stroud, 2004

Hudson, B.T., *Kings of Celtic Scotland*, Westport, 1996

Kapelle, W.E., *The Norman Conquest of the North*, London, 1979

MacQuarrie, A., *Medieval Scotland*, Stroud, 2005

——, *The Saints of Scotland*, Edinburgh, 1997

——, *Scotland and the Crusades*, Edinburgh, 1985

Marshall, R.K., *Scottish Queens*, East Linton, 2003

McDonald, R.A., *Outlaws of Medieval Scotland*, East Linton, 2003

McNeill, P.G.B., and MacQueen, H.L. (eds), *Atlas of Scottish History to 1707*, Edinburgh, 1996

Morris, C., *Marriage and Murder in Eleventh-Century Northumbria*, York, 1992

O'Corrain, D., *Ireland Before the Normans*, Dublin, 1972

Oram, R., *The Canmores*, Stroud, 2002

——, *David I*, Stroud, 2004

——, *Kings and Queens of Scotland*, Stroud, 2001

Rollason, D., *Northumbria 500–1100*, Cambridge, 2005

Rollason, D., Harvey, M. and Prestwich, M. (eds), *Anglo-Norman Durham*, Woodbridge, 1998

Smyth, A.P., *Scandinavian Kings of the British Isles*, Oxford, 1988

——, *Scandinavian York and Dublin*, Dublin, 1987

——, *Warlords and Holy Men*, Edinburgh, 1984

Wainwright, F.T., *Scandinavian England*, Chichester, 1975

Williams, A., *The English and the Norman Conquest*, Woodbridge, 1995

Williams, A., Smyth, A.P. and Kirby, D.P., *A Biographical Dictionary of Dark Age Britain*, London, 1991

Wilson, A. J., *St Margaret, Queen of Scotland*, Edinburgh, 1993

Index

Index